BACK TO THE LAND IN
SILICON VALLEY

OTHER BOOKS BY
MARLENE ANNE BUMGARNER

The Book of Whole Grains

Organic Cooking for (not-so-organic) Mothers

The New Book of Whole Grains

Working with School Age Children

BACK TO THE LAND IN
SILICON VALLEY

MARLENE ANNE BUMGARNER

This memoir is dedicated to Jamie,
who has been after me to write it since she was five years old.

ACKNOWLEDGMENTS

I have to start with a big thank you to Steven Radecki of Paper Angel Press, who not only agreed to publish my book, but also helped me fine tune it and make it more personal and immediate. And to his book designer, Niki Lenhart, for her infinite patience as I made request after request for changes. The final result speaks for itself.

The Morgan Hill Historical Society, especially Ellie Weston, was a valuable source of facts.

My first reader was Teri Spevak. She read the rough cuts, the myriads of stories, and my first attempt to bring them together in one place. Teri promised to be brutally honest — and she was. She helped bring my characters to life and give the stories a logical sequence. My childhood friend Barbara Kaiser read the result, and copy-edited it within an inch of its life (and responded cheerfully to my late-night texts asking for help with several nuances of Microsoft Word).

A special thank you to Paul De Angelis. He edited my first book in 1976 and, after reviewing an early draft of this one, introduced me to Jeanne Martinet, whose thoughtful editing put me on a path to publication. My wonderful daughter Jamie then read every page of the manuscript, and identified errors that no one but a family member could have spotted.

I received incredibly helpful feedback from my many critique group friends and beta readers, especially Laura, Elecia, Kim, Alliee, and Nina. Your comments were my roadmap as I progressed along the bumpy road from draft to manuscript. Each of you brought your personal strengths to the process, and identified the sections of the book where those strengths matched my weaknesses. Thank you so much for the time you spent reading and writing comments.

Last, but far from least, I want to thank the friends who shared my adventures living on the land, Quincy, Bob, Jan, and Nina. Thank you for helping me to tell my story and to include you in it. Thank you for giving your permission to use ancient photos in the book, and thank you for answering my many questions as I struggled to remember the details and sequence of those years. Thank you for your patience and — most of all — thanks for the memories.

CONTENTS

PROLOGUE

"**G**RANDMA, WHY ARE YOUR GLOVES WAY UP THERE where you can't reach them?" my seven-year-old granddaughter, Stella, piped up.

I dropped down on my heels and gently asked her to move so I wouldn't hit her with the pruners. I reached up again, reaching high over my workbench, stretching as high as I could.

When had a simple activity like retrieving a tool from the pegboard become so challenging?

I held my breath, lifted the pruner off its hook, and caught one handle to soften its fall. It landed on the bench with a satisfying clunk.

I turned toward Stella. Her upturned face still held a questioning look. "The gloves? Why are they up there with your tools?"

"Oh those," I said, trying to stay on task. "I don't use that pair anymore."

"But why —?"

"They're worn out. Let's go back to the garden, Lovey, before it starts to rain. Here. We both have perfectly good gardening gloves in this basket, and there are my secateurs. You can cut the frost damage off the morning glory while I trim the broken branches on the persimmon tree."

I looked at the gathering clouds, inhaled the rich scent of wet earth. "We have just enough time to finish before the rain starts again."

I thought I had distracted her, but I underestimated this child's persistence where mysteries are concerned.

1

She began interrogating me again.

"But why keep those old gloves if you don't use them, Grandma? Why not throw them away, or give them to Goodwill? Why put them way at the top of the pegboard where you can't reach them?"

"I *can* reach them," I said, standing on my toes again and demonstrating.

When I held them up, two of the glove's fingers hung sadly, torn most of the way through. I pulled the gloves on to my hands, the hairs on the back of my neck standing to attention from the way the suede felt, rough on my palm. The stiff leather crunched slightly as I flexed my hands open and shut. A brown scar ran across one palm of one of the gloves. The acrid scent of the old leather tickled my nose.

"These aren't ordinary gardening gloves, Stella. They're meant for heavy work. I keep them up there to help me remember," I said softly.

"Remember what?"

"Oh, honey, so many things. When I was young and lived on the land."

"Tell, me, please, Grandma. Did you use them when you were raising rabbits and goats?"

It was at that moment I realized it was time. Time to tell the stories. Nearly a decade of my life — a period that changed how I perceived the world and my place in it — had drifted into the recesses of my memory as I had raised my family, pursued a career, aged. My land partners were aging, too. Dorrie passed first, and then John. Quincy couldn't remember the details of our time together anymore, and I hadn't seen Nina in years. Bob and Jan are so busy with their family they don't have time to reminisce. I'm seventy-two years old. If I don't share my memories soon, they will be gone. I perched on a barrel filled with wild birdseed and pulled the precious child onto my lap. Her turquoise ponytail hung below my knees.

"Did I ever tell you about the first time Grandma tried to build a fence?"

*   *   *

2

My husband John and I moved off the grid in 1973 to create a safe space for our daughter. We wanted to escape the divisiveness and violence of the Vietnam War era — the televised scenes of battle, protests, and students bludgeoned in the streets. We were both disillusioned and demoralized by the media's portrayal of the war, the deaths of our national heroes, the years of political conflict. All the time we were making our way through college and graduate school, unrest had been roiling across the land. Now that we had a child, we wanted to shield her from the discord. I was 26; John was 33. Time to settle down.

Over the next several years, we and a group of friends created a life in the country that nourished our souls. We grew vegetables and flowers. Milked goats and birthed kids. Built fences. Mucked out rabbit cages, chicken coops, goat pens. Built compost piles. Lit our homes with oil lamps and heated water on propane stoves. In time I gave birth to a second child: a son.

During this time, we all worked together. Ate together. Sang together. Learned together. We had a good life. After living close to the natural cycles of the earth year after year, good and not good, we grew stronger and more resilient, learned to manage our occasional conflicts with tolerance and love. One by one, our friends left the land for other adventures. As much as I loved our life in the country, I couldn't carry on without them. Eventually, I left too, to pursue my dreams of teaching and writing, and to help our children learn how to live gently on the land.

Once again, our nation is being pulled apart. School shootings, public Twitter fights, innocent children jailed at the border, young men and women sent into harm's way, talk of a border wall. Years of efforts to reduce our human damage to the earth reversed by the stroke of a pen. And now a global pandemic, police brutality, and riots. Sometimes it feels overwhelming, especially for those of us still living in Silicon Valley. The rapid growth of technology spawned during this era has affected our world, the state of the earth, and how our children grow up.

It must be tempting for families to turn away from the noise, to hide in their homes, to keep their children close. I found it so back in the 1970s. I know that retreating to the land isn't the only solution.

However, it is one way to heal our pain and come to appreciate the natural cycles of life. Standing in my garage that day with Stella, feeling the old work gloves on my hands and a rush of memories in my heart, I understood that, truly *grokked[1]* it.

It is time to share my story with the next generation. I want them to understand the joy (and the pain) of living close to the earth, and the deep knowledge of themselves that it can bring. Families don't have to go back to the land to learn how to care for the earth. But if they do, they may begin to see the world differently.

That evening, I began to write.

---

1 Grok /ˈɡrɑːk/ is a word coined by American writer Robert A. Heinlein for his 1961 science fiction novel *Stranger in a Strange Land*. It means to understand (something) intuitively or by empathy.

ONE

MOVING TO THE LAND

1973

- Stanley Cohen of Stanford University and Herbert Boyer of UC San Francisco create the first recombinant DNA organism, effectively inventing "biotechnology"
- Vinton Cerf of Stanford University coins the term "Internet"
- Hewlett Packard releases HP-45 printing desktop calculator
- The Arpanet has 2,000 email users

1974

- Ed Roberts invents the first personal computer, the Altair 8800.
- The barcode, invented by George Laurer at IBM, debuts.
- Sam Hurst invents the touch-screen user interface.

1

AN ADVENTURE CALLS

I T WAS NOVEMBER 1973, and my mother-in-law wasn't speaking to me. My husband, John, and I were living with our 11-month-old daughter, Doña, and our German Shepherd pup, Elsa, on Mount Hamilton, an hour's drive up a winding road from San Jose, California. We had courted on Mount Hamilton in 1966, announced our engagement at Thanksgiving dinner in the Lick Observatory diner, filled that night with astronomers and friends. We had worked in the technology sector for several years and attended college and grad school at night. Now we were back, living in a tiny apartment at my in-laws' home while we looked for a house.

That afternoon, Bea had entered the kitchen just as Doña began rubbing mashed banana into her hair. I sat beside the high chair, deep in my studies. I felt grateful for these few moments of peace afforded by Doña's sensory exploration. Blonde hair falling out of the scarf she'd tied around her head, Bea muttered a few choice words about my parenting and the state of the kitchen floor. She carried Doña away for a bath. I put away my book and reached for a sponge, feeling like Cinderella.

"How would you like to move to the country?" John asked that night as he took off his coat and hung it on a kitchen chair, placing his new HP-45 calculator on the table for me to admire.

Turning from the stove, I stared at him. *Had he been reading my mind?*

"You know I would." Ever since reading *Little House on the Prairie* as a teenager, I had dreamed of living on the frontier. After the banana episode, pioneer life sounded better than ever. In some ways I enjoyed this interlude on Mount Hamilton, 25 miles from the city of San Jose, nestled into the foothills of the Diablo mountain range. It was isolated and beautiful. The idea of leaving it to live in busy Silicon Valley was not appealing.

John worked as a computer programmer at Electromagnetic Systems Laboratory, ESL, in Sunnyvale, an over two-hour drive away. It was 9:00 p.m. by the time we had this conversation. He looked tired from his commute, and I felt exhausted from picking up Doña's toys, washing the kitchen floor, cleaning her high chair and all the cabinets and other furniture that she had touched that day with her inquisitive, sticky hands. I served his meal, then collapsed beside him.

"A guy I work with at ESL — remember Quincy? He came over for dinner one night when we lived in D.C." He stopped to chew his meatloaf.

I did remember Quincy, with some embarrassment. Newborn Doña had been colicky that night. Quincy had paced the floor with her while I prepared our dinner.

"Yeah, I remember him."

"Well, he roamed the halls this afternoon, asking everyone he saw if they'd like to go halves on ten acres of land. A high school friend of his wife, Dorrie, told them her dad planned to sell a remote plot of land cheap to pay some debts."

"Where's the land?"

"It's 34 miles south of San Jose, in the hills west of Morgan Hill, above Chesbro Reservoir."

John dove back into his meal. When he came up for air, he pushed his long brown hair behind his ears, scratched his beard, and stretched his long legs.

"Quincy hasn't seen the land yet, but he's interested. It's only about a 40-minute commute to ESL. It doesn't have any electricity or telephone, but it does have a shared well and a road."

John wiped his plate clean with a piece of French bread. I reached for his now-empty plate.

"Thanks, love. You know I appreciate you cooking for me so late." Before I could grab his plate, he pulled me into his lap. We smooched. Between his long commute and our lack of privacy, caresses were a rarity these days. He laced his hands together across my waist so I couldn't escape. Before he arrived, I had changed out of my spit-up-soaked house-cleaning clothes into a Liberty print granny dress I'd bought in Cornwall, and I draped the skirt over his legs in what I thought to be an attractive pose. My dangly earrings tinkled and tangled in my long red hair as I wriggled to get comfortable. I pulled them free.

"When can we see this property?"

"Dorrie wants to visit the land this weekend. They're going to drive there on Saturday and meet the owner. Should we tag along? It might be just what we're looking for."

"Seems a bit crazy," I replied, unlacing his hands, clambering to my feet and putting his plate in the dishwasher, "partnering with a couple we don't really know."

I watched him gulp the pink grapefruit juice I'd poured into a tall glass. He looked weary, and his eyes were shuttered.

"No crazier than taking a baby to Africa," he quipped, grinning tiredly. The previous summer we had flown from our home in Washington D.C. to England to join a friend and members of the British Astronomical Association on a ship that sailed to the path of a solar eclipse off the coast of West Africa. It had been an amazing adventure that included a visit to drought-damaged Mauritania, followed by our return to Washington D.C., and a cross-country trek back to California in our VW bus. Doña had been fussed over by everyone she met, and adapted well to the time and scenery changes. She was a natural traveler.

"I can't disagree with you there. It wouldn't be the craziest thing we've ever done."

"I've been thinking about what you said," I began later when John suggested a postprandial walk. The telescope domes, a schoolhouse, diner and a dozen or so houses stretched along the ridge of the mountain. The loop road that connected them, flanked with trees and brush, allowed a view of the sky, the valley lights, and the telescope domes. We often walked the loop before bed.

"I do want to live in the country, "I said, putting on my boots," but it would be nice to have a house."

"Yes, it would, but what are the chances we'll find one?"

In three months of looking, we hadn't found even a rental we could afford within driving distance of John's office. Property values had skyrocketed in the four years we'd been away from the Bay Area. The 3-bedroom home in Mountain View we had purchased for $12,500 in 1967 — and sold for $14,000 in 1970 — was now worth $36,000. The money we had saved from the sale of our last house fell short of a down payment. In 1973 the area north of San Jose, already being called Silicon Valley, was growing fast. The countryside had shrunk. What were once apricot and prune orchards in Sunnyvale, Mountain View, and Cupertino, and before that, the home of native tribal people, had become suburbs and acres of industrial development. VALLCO Business and Industrial Park, soon to be expanded into a huge shopping center, was built right over the top of where my aunt and uncle had once raised chickens and rabbits.

But we couldn't stay on Mount Hamilton. John's mother and I had differing views on child rearing. I liked to give our baby lots of physical and emotional freedom; Bea believed in structure and rules. She also thought I'd been breastfeeding Doña too long, and wanted to wean her to a cup. For the last six months, she and I had worked side by side in her classroom three days a week. We prepared and ate our meals together — often in stiff, uncomfortable silence — and we sat in front of the TV each night waiting for John to come home. I deferred to Bea in the classroom, but when it came to my child, I set the boundaries. Bea's tight-lipped silences told me — often — when we didn't agree.

Bea was doing us a favor, I knew that. While we'd been out of California, a change in educational legislation meant that after September 1974 my Bachelor's degree would no longer qualify me to earn an elementary teaching credential. In order to secure a credential before the deadline, I attended classes at San Jose State University. John's mother served as both the principal and only teacher at the one-room Mount Hamilton School. She supervised my student teaching and helped me with my homework. San Jose State required two semesters of student teaching, in different settings. In six weeks, when the Fall semester ended, I would need a placement at another school. I only had one more semester and a summer session in which to complete my coursework and practice teaching before the deadline.

John loved his job at ESL, but felt increasingly exhausted by his twice daily commute through the fields and orchards, and frustrated that his wife and his mother weren't getting along. I was cranky and tearful much of the time. The stress had affected my breast milk supply.

I checked on Doña. Pop — which is what we called John's father — was in the living room, cradling his sleeping grandchild in his arms.

"Go for your walk," he said. "We'll take care of her until you get back. We want to watch *M*A*S*H* anyway." I cringed. *M*A*S*H* was a dark comedy set during the Korean War. It romanticized war and included scenes of operating rooms with visible blood and wounded soldiers writhing in pain. I felt relieved that Doña was asleep.

John and our puppy, Elsa, were waiting for me on the front porch. John led me along the dark driveway to the road. I linked my arm in his and felt his body relax. He stopped and looked up for a moment before continuing on. The total darkness that made Mount Hamilton a good site for an observatory also meant we could see the Milky Way and other celestial formations that were far less visible in the city.

John had introduced me to the sky on our first date in 1966. We had met at the junior college where we both attended classes and worked in the Data Processing department. After dinner and a Kirk Douglas movie, John had driven to a popular make-out spot and

11

actually shown me the stars. At 18 I was accustomed to boys my age having only one thing on their mind … and it wasn't constellations. After I got over my surprise, I found this 25-year-old man, recently out of the Air Force, far more interesting than boys my age. We talked until midnight and he told me he hoped to work for NASA one day. His full name was John Owen Bumgarner, he told me. It was the tradition in his family to call the first boy John, but they all had different middle names. I liked his name. It suited him. No one ever called him Johnny or Jack.

When I asked him to show me Orion's belt and the Pleiades, he had apologized for the June sky as if it were his fault. "Neither the Orion Nebula nor the Pleiades star cluster is visible at this time of year," he'd explained, pointing out Ursa Major and Minor instead.

By the time John delivered me with a chaste kiss to my parents' front door, I knew I wanted to spend more time with this interesting person.

We were married a year later at a little Methodist church in San Carlos. That year we worked at Sylvania Electronic Defense Labs and attended classes at San Jose State. It was difficult to get all of our classes due to the returning Vietnam vets, who were given registration priority. We moved to San Diego to finish our Bachelor's degrees, then after a summer traveling in Great Britain, we drove to New Mexico State University in Las Cruces for graduate studies. I dreamed of being the next Margaret Mead, but we soon discovered that the Anthropology program we'd heard so much about resided at the *other* university, the one in Albuquerque. When I learned there were no graduate level courses in Anthropology at NMSU, I settled for six units of Educational Psychology and a secretarial job.

John studied Astronomy. NMSU had just started a doctoral program in that field. His financial contribution came from the GI Bill. Two years later, when things didn't work out for him, he went to work for ESL, and I stayed in New Mexico to sell our house. A year later we moved to Washington D.C. where John supported image processing software for ESL at a federal agency. I gave birth to Doña while we were there.

As we walked that night on Mount Hamilton, I thought about the house we'd left behind in New Mexico. It had five spacious rooms, a deck where John had installed his Questar telescope, and a large yard, which I had filled with vegetables and flowers. It would have been a wonderful place to raise a child. I still missed the life we had planned there — and hadn't completely forgiven John for abandoning his doctoral program and forcing us to move.

I had given up an Anthropology fellowship so John could go to NMSU, then left my Ed Psych degree unfinished to travel east. I still mourned those uprootings. Perhaps a new start would help. Now I was concerned more about family than academic achievement. I wanted so badly to create a cozy home for our daughter. John seemed to believe we could build one on this piece of property.

By the end of our walk, I wanted to believe it, too.

The next day dawned sunny and bright. While I fed the thirsty plants in Bea's kitchen window box, I imagined our little girl in the country with a watering can, or feeding chickens and helping me weed a bountiful vegetable garden. The thought was seductive. As I drove Doña the 50 miles north from Mount Hamilton to my parents' home, where she stayed while I attended classes, I felt hopeful. Along the way I sang *This Land is Your Land, This Land is Our Land* to Doña, and allowed myself to dream of a future in the country.

"I think we should go with them on Saturday," John declared that night just as I began to close my eyes. "I talked more with Quincy today. He's very energetic. I think he would make a good neighbor."

I propped myself on my elbow. "Ok, let's consider this," I told him. "I've been doing some thinking. If there's no house, where will we live until we can build some kind of structure?"

"I thought we'd put up a really large tent." In the darkness, I couldn't tell if he was joking. I hoped so.

"That's not feasible, John. Could we get a travel trailer or something? I still have to do my student teaching, and we can't live in a tent with a baby when it's raining."

"Let me see if my parents will loan us theirs."

"How will we get water to the trailer? Can we run pipes uphill from the well?"

"I'm not sure. We may have to put in a water tank above us to get pressure."

"What about electricity?"

"We can fuel most things with propane."

"What's involved in dividing the land into two parcels?

"I haven't a clue."

In the end, we decided that we didn't know enough to decide, and agreed to meet Quincy and Dorrie on Saturday. It wouldn't hurt to look.

2

A HIKE AND DINNER
WITH THE ADAMSES

S ATURDAY MORNING, John and I drove south to Morgan Hill. It took nearly two hours. The freeways that cut across San Jose today hadn't been built yet. The first ten miles, down Mount Hamilton Road to Grant Ranch, had many hair-pin turns, making conversation difficult, but the eastern foothills, with their lush hills, rushing streams, and coyote bush kept my attention. In spring, these hills were covered in wildflowers, yellow buttercups, California poppies, and monkey flowers, orange columbine and lavender larkspur and clarksia. Today the hills wore their autumn colors. Long brown grass, orange leaves and thick stands of shrubby oaks lined the road.

This route had been cleared in 1875 to accommodate horse-drawn wagons transporting material to build Lick Observatory. John enjoyed pointing out where drovers stopped along the way to change horses.

Once we made it to Quimby Road, we began talking about the advantages of moving to an undeveloped piece of land. Getting away from the 70s political turmoil. The chance to build a homestead from scratch. Living simply. Room for a large garden. Animals for Doña to care for. Peace and quiet.

"We have to keep our minds open, John," I said at last. "Please, let's not make any decisions today."

His eyes on the road, John agreed. "You're right. I'm excited about the possibilities, but I agree. No decisions today." I squeezed his shoulder.

"Thanks."

John and I had a history of spontaneous decisions. Five years earlier, while we were sitting on the roof of our Pinto watching a lunar eclipse, John decided to transfer from studying physics at San Jose State to astronomy at San Diego State. I was having trouble getting into classes in my major due to the returning veterans, so I assented. A month later, we sold our house and drove south with three cats: no jobs, no home, and no college acceptance.

Fortunately, because San Diego was booming, we both landed good jobs and found a sweet little house to rent. This time, though, I wanted us to take more time to think before deciding.

We had left Mount Hamilton early that chilly morning. As the sun rose over the foothills, it warmed the air. By the time we reached Highway 101 — just a two-lane road in those days — our car windows were open and the cool breeze buffeted our cheeks. In spite of our best efforts to stay calm, we were both excited as we approached the property. Once again, we reminded ourselves: we didn't need to decide that day.

We met Dorrie and Quincy on the edge of town, followed them west along a winding wooded road to Chesbro Lake Drive. With a grand name like that I had expected a paved road, but the asphalt ended a few car-lengths in, and we were soon on a sharp uphill slope covered in slippery gravel. By the time we got to Hawkins Lane, we were driving on dirt and swerving to avoid ruts and potholes. Our surefooted VW bus had a low clearance, and we bottomed out a couple of times as John negotiated the bumpy road.

16

We parked at a gate with a tilted and faded For Sale sign and two large pumpkins marking the rutted dirt road heading up the hill. We walked along the eastern boundary of the parcel as well as we could determine it from the plot map Dorrie's friend had provided. Fortunately, it had been a dry November, and hadn't rained for several weeks. The soil was dry and firm, easy to walk on.

As we walked, Dorrie and I took turns carrying Doña in our well-travelled yellow corduroy Snugli baby carrier. The men carried the rolled-up plans and a clipboard each, and stopped periodically to confer or write on their notepads. It was clear by the easy banter that they had much in common. Even though John was six years older than Quincy, they had a good rapport. The Adams' two dogs, King and Crosby, romped happily beside us. Our spirits were high. To look at us, we might have been out for a day hike in a regional park.

The land was heavily wooded. Several horse paths and fire trails allowed access to most of the ten acres, so we meandered a bit, exploring as much of the land as we could. At first, we walked along a narrow dirt road, but after we reached the top of the hill we went cross-country. The thick blanket of fallen leaves lay rotting and melting into the soil, and we laughed as we slipped and slid down the slope. I noted where we were — the rotting leaves would make great compost. As I sat on a pile of leaves at one point, I breathed in the rich loamy fragrance of mulch all around. It seemed unlikely, but after an hour we ended up, as we intended, back at the gate. We had explored most of the parcel.

Both over six-feet tall and fit, John and Quincy were a matched set that day. Quincy had fastened his medium-length red hair into a kind of bun at the back of his neck; John's long brown locks hung around his face. They had started the day in jeans and plaid Pendleton shirts, but, as the unseasonably warm day progressed, they shed their plaids for t-shirts. John borrowed my hair tie to fasten his locks into a ponytail.

Dorrie wore practical denim pants and a long-sleeved shirt. Her short brown hair looked comfortable, and she walked briskly, confidently. I wore shorts and a tank top. I soon learned that wasn't such a great idea. Between wild berry vines, poison oak and the always-present possibility of snakes, long pants and long sleeves would have been far more suitable. John had persuaded me to wear hiking boots, so at least I wouldn't sprain an ankle.

Dorrie narrated animatedly as we walked. "Look … those two trees would be perfect for a hammock," and "This moist spot where the road has been cut into the side of the hill might hide a spring." and "That level area would be a good place to put a milking shed. We could fence in the side of that rise for the goat pen."

Her enthusiasm was contagious. Dorrie seemed smart and warm and friendly. As we talked, I learned she had grown up on a farm in San Luis Obispo. Her parents were both teachers. She had five younger sisters and brothers — all of whom worked on the farm after school and on weekends. She and Quincy had met at the nearby California Polytechnic College (Cal Poly), where they were both members of a Methodist student group. They had been married three years, and were anxious to stop paying rent and buy a house. Although older than Dorrie, I felt far less prepared to embark on a rural life. I had grown up in San Francisco apartments and suburban houses. *Would she believe I could do this?* I felt as if I were interviewing for a job.

With no particular tasks to accomplish on our walk, and actually not being too sure what to look for, I eventually fell behind the others, taking in the beauty of the oaks, manzañitas, sage, and tall grasses. I stopped occasionally and stood still, breathing in the sweet-smelling air and enjoying the silence. This little ten-acre parcel was surrounded by hundreds of acres of undeveloped chaparral. As we walked, we heard no human voices but our own. It took my breath away.

As we came to a wide swale, I remembered a pastime of my childhood. "This would be a great slope to slide down on a sheet of cardboard." I called to the others.

"I was imagining an archery course," answered John, wistfully.

"This grass will need to be mowed at least twice a year to reduce the fire danger," Quincy warned. "The lower clearing looks like the best bet for you guys and, if you decide to build there, you could put your septic tank lines down this hill."

Dorrie turned to John. "The swale would make a great place to put a garden, and you could have an archery course too."

Dorrie and Quincy planned to live in a school bus until they could afford to purchase a house in the valley. Since we wanted to build, and they just wanted to save money, they had quickly waived any claim to the lower half of the parcel, which had a large area already cleared of trees.

Eventually, the seller, William Carter, showed up in a beat-up old Ford pickup truck. He confirmed that shared water rights were indeed part of "the deal," as well as access to Chesbro Reservoir, the large body of water we had passed on the way up. That was good. Otherwise we would have had to sink our own well. A tall, wiry man of about sixty, with a craggy face and thick grey hair, Carter bragged about his influence with local government officials as we walked. "Just call Sig Sanchez," he said, naming a county supervisor. "He'll take care of any problems you have getting planning approval. Tell him you're a friend of mine, and he'll fix you up." He swaggered a little as he said this, his back bent forward, unruly hair falling over his eyes, reminding me of a villain in a children's story.

Mr. Carter pointed out the well housing and pump on his side of the property line, and the large storage building on the other side. Because of its semi-circular shape and sheet metal construction he called it a Quonset hut and so, forever, did we. He said we could keep tools and equipment there, and access his electricity if we needed to. We then followed him back down Hawkins Lane and Chesbro Lake Drive to a narrow path that led to the beach. On the way he pointed out an empty mobile home on his side of the property line.

"I usually rent that out," he said, "but I'm thinking of moving in myself." My heart sank. I wasn't looking forward to having this rather creepy man as a next-door neighbor.

"This is a great place to cool off after working all day," Carter remarked when we reached the beach. "And your daughter will love it when she gets older. Just always remember to shut this gate because the beach is not open to the public." We didn't know it then, but shutting gates would soon become a regular part of our lives.

Before he left, Bill Carter went over the plans with us again, and verified the boundaries of the parcel. Among other things — such as the names of our nearest neighbors and the location of the communal garbage dump — he told us that he had "taken care of" the rattlesnake problem several years earlier, by poisoning all the rodents.

"You'll never see a snake on this piece of land," he said proudly, I suppose thinking to reassure us.

We exchanged horrified looks. The idea of poisoned rodents did not reassure us. What had that done to the native fauna on the property? What would it do to our cats and dogs? To the owls and the hawks?

But no one said anything.

After Carter left, we ate lunch beneath a large oak tree with low horizontal branches that Doña would soon be able to climb. Meanwhile, she devoured her sandwich and began to explore the outer boundary of the blanket I had laid on the grass. Her light brown hair framed her chubby face, and we laughed as she tasted a piece of clover and made a sour face. As she explored, the four of us discussed the logistics of getting a trailer and other vehicles up the road, and when it might be feasible to do so.

"I'd like to move our school bus up here next month if Carter will let us," said Dorrie, looking inquiringly at Quincy.

He nodded his head.

I asked if she had any concerns about Carter. "Janet's dad? No — I've known him for years. He's a bit weird, but he's ok."

Thus reassured, I put my concerns aside. Pleasantly tired from the efforts of the morning and sleepy from lunch, we rested in the shade. I pulled Doña into my lap. She settled sleepily into my arms, and I let my thoughts wander.

This wasn't the first time John and I had considered living in the country. In the 1960s, he had read Robert Heinlein's serialized blueprint for surviving a nuclear attack and taken it to heart. *Farnham's Freehold* depicted a group of friends who survived the atomic bomb by retreating to a fallout shelter under Hugh Farnham's home, then living a pioneer life. John had been heavily influenced by the story, which he read about the time of the Cuban missile crisis, when for a few days we all thought we might die. He talked longingly of building a "freehold" for our little family.

When we were undergraduates, we had almost moved to a commune east of San Diego. John had planned to dig an underground turf-covered bomb shelter there. It didn't work out. Since then he had been following the work of Buckminster Fuller. Inspired by Bucky's ergonomic and efficient designs, John had been developing plans for a two-story geodesic house. His copies of *Handmade Houses, The Owner-Built Home*, and *Operating Manual for Spaceship Earth* were dog-eared with use. I liked his new direction. I especially liked the idea that our new home would be above ground and not covered with dirt.

While we drove cross-country the previous summer, John and I had visited three communes: *Twin Oaks* in Louisa, Virginia, *The Farm* in Summertown, Tennessee, and a *Lama Foundation* settlement near San Cristobal, New Mexico. A high school friend of John's, Annie, had lived there since 1966. We named our daughter Doña Ana — Lady Anne — after New Mexico and Annie.

Annie introduced us to Helen and Scott Nearing's new manifesto, *Living the Good Life: How to Live Sanely and Simply in a Troubled World*. The Nearings preached the benefits of homesteading communally, and we wanted to see if we could embrace this lifestyle.

We appreciated and enjoyed the bonds that people developed on these communes, and the gentle leisurely pace of life. But we were uncomfortable with the group decision-making that we saw practiced there. We wanted to plan our own destiny. To do that, we needed our own piece of land. Having neighbors nearby seemed important, especially for sharing the work of major projects, such as putting in gardens and building fences and other large structures. But we wanted our independence.

Living on the land seemed as natural to us as any other life choice in the 70s. Young people and old were moving to the land in droves. One issue of *The Whole Earth Catalog*, a fixture on most of our friends' coffee tables, featured Scott and Helen Nearing's book. Their ideas of subsistence farming and healthy living fueled the dreams of thousands of people. Even couples who had recently signed mortgages began selling their homes and moving to the land.

I had also been influenced by the written word, although not of the survivalist variety. Starting with *Little House in the Big Woods*, which I found at a church rummage sale in junior high, I had read all the books written by Laura Ingalls Wilder. In them, she depicted the travels of her pioneer family as they crossed the prairies in covered wagons and built farms from scratch. I had re-read the books while pregnant with Doña. Autobiographical but fictionalized, Wilder's stories fueled my fantasies of living in the country, raising our family simply, away from the clamor and conflicts of modern life. It was a seductive chimera.

Our spot under the big oak tree was pleasant. While Dorrie and Quincy tramped back up the hill to scout out where they might park their school bus, John and I lounged beside Doña, now asleep. Soon birds began calling to one another, the tall grass rustled in the breeze, and what might have been goats bleated in the distance.

"This could work for us, honey," John said, gently caressing our daughter as she lay between us. I rolled onto my back and looked up at the trees and the sky. I also felt that I could grow to love this land.

Flushed with optimism and bursting with ideas, we drove to the Adams' home in the Santa Cruz Mountains. The sun was setting as we drove up their private road. On the brick entryway sat a dozen terra cotta pots filled with herbs, flowers, and winter vegetables. Dorrie explained that this was a portable garden — it could move with her to the property. I suddenly decided to start some seedlings in Bea's kitchen window.

We spread our plans and notes on a large wooden table while I pulled Doña into my lap to nurse. As Dorrie took out wine, and Quincy roasted garlic and toasted French bread, I looked around in admiration. We might have been in a rural European home. Above the large gas stove, a variety of pots and pans hung from hooks on a metal rack. Open rafters were strung with braids of onions and garlic, drying herbs, and large bunches of lavender. Beside the handsome stone fireplace in the adjacent living room stood a pile of freshly split firewood, a basket of kindling, and two large cushions on which the resident dogs relaxed. The Adams' home smelled like a cross between a candle shop and a barn. I wanted to live there.

While Doña, sated, crawled over our feet in pursuit of the Adams' cats, we ate and drank and sketched our ideas onto the plot map. We imagined a water tank feeding a communal vegetable garden, various animal pens, and a pond. John suggested building a communal barn where we could store animal feed and house animals during the rainy season. He and I could live in it while we obtained a permit to build a dome house.

We discussed renting a bulldozer to smooth the road for our arrival, possible moving dates, and inviting friends for a work party. We hadn't seen any deer, but Dorrie assured us they were there, and would eat anything we planted if we didn't build very high fences. "They're a real menace at my dad's farm," she told us.

One bottle emptied, we opened another, and began to talk about money. John's and my funds were in a Certificate of Deposit, but we would be able to access them at the end of December. Carter was selling an undivided ten-acre parcel and would carry a note.

The Adamses agreed to front the down payment he required, and we would pay them back when our CD matured. The men both planned to keep their jobs at ESL; Dorrie and I would continue to attend college. Each couple would pay half the monthly payment — less than the cost of an apartment in Sunnyvale — and split the cost of feed for the animals. That left a little money each month to save for the costs of a land division. Dorrie and her family would provide the animals and in exchange for learning to care for them, John and I would help feed them and share in all the other chores around the farm. Once we each had five acres in our own names, John and I could begin construction.

"How long before we can build the barn?" I remember asking, totally forgetting our decision to "take time to think this over." Clearly the Adams' were ready to sign a contract.

"By next year this time we will be breaking ground," John assured me.

Dorrie and Quincy exchanged looks. I wondered what they were thinking, but didn't want to break the spell and ask. It may have been the wine we drank on Saturday night, or perhaps the euphoria of our dreams being fueled by our first exciting visit to the land. The peaceful ambience of Quincy and Dorrie's home didn't hurt either. I imagined our geodesic dome interior looking just like their kitchen. Whatever it was, by Sunday morning we all believed we could make this happen.

3

EXPLORING MORGAN HILL

D ORRIE AND QUINCY DROVE THEIR 1961 SCHOOL BUS to the property in December 1973. Even though Quincy had removed the original engine and replaced it with an International Harvester straight-six, we agreed that it would be unwise to drive the bus up the steep road to the top of our property during the rainy season. Instead, they parked it at one side of the clearing where John and I planned to establish our own homestead. John and I would stay on Mount Hamilton until I finished final exams in late January. Meanwhile, we set up an army surplus tent on the remaining side of the clearing, and outfitted it with camping stove, lamps, sleeping bags, etc.

During December and January, John and I drove to the property every weekend to clear poison oak and other invasive shrubs from the edges of the clearing, help Dorrie and Quincy build animal pens, and prepare meals together. We bought a large metal garden shed from Sears and assembled it on a concrete block foundation. We began to move our tools and boxes from Mount Hamilton into the shed, and to gear up our search for a small travel trailer or all-weather tent to live in.

Meanwhile John and Quincy each bought a classic four-wheel drive vehicle. Quincy acquired a 1942 Jeep. It looked like all the Jeeps I had ever seen in WWII movies. He named the vehicle "Nuts" because it didn't have doors, and one day a large branch got caught in the open cockpit while he was driving and … well, you get the picture. My husband fell in love with a rusty 1939 Dodge flatbed truck. He found it sitting on the side of Mount Hamilton Road with a "For Sale" sign on it. After negotiating an affordable price, he drove it to Morgan Hill — over 50 miles — at 15 miles an hour, using only back roads. It had no front windshield, but John enrolled in a welding class at the local high school and soon had fashioned an authentic-looking windscreen. He named his acquisition "Sarge" and bragged that it would "climb a tree" if he asked.

Nuts and Sarge were versatile vehicles. They could negotiate the unpaved and ungraded pathways and roads on our land, carry large objects or many objects, tow other vehicles, and haul water in 50-gallon fiberglass tanks that the men constructed on the bed of each truck. They were important members of our homestead.

Sometimes during those early weekends, we hiked to the top of our property, just because we could. Dorrie and Quincy dreamed about where they would put the school bus, animal sheds, and a barn. John and I enjoyed the peacefulness of the setting, and the glorious view from the top of the hill. Other days we went further afield, visiting the Polish family down Chesbro Lake Drive or walking to the edge of the reservoir and going for a swim. One day we decided to drive into the nearby town of Morgan Hill

Morgan Hill in 1974 was small — only 6,500 people were reported in the 1970 census, compared to 45,037 in 2017. It hadn't yet been impacted by the technology boom in places like Sunnyvale, Mountain View, and San Jose. No freeways or overpasses yet. Highway 101 was still a narrow two-lane road that widened only slightly through the main part of town. There, its shoulder served as a parking lot for a string of commercial properties. Running at right angles to the highway, Main Street housed the Post Office, two banks, a general store, dry cleaners, and a pharmacy in its three blocks. Several small eating and drinking establishments dotted the highway both north and south of Main Street.

That day we decided to explore some of the businesses along the highway. As Quincy parked his Chevy pickup on the shoulder, I wondered how the proprietors of these local stores would feel about long-haired young people walking through their door.

We were all aware that a group of hippies had been forced out of residential camps in the Santa Cruz mountains a year earlier, and John and I had encountered some unpleasantness from locals when we drove through Georgia and Arkansas in our VW bus in 1971. The film *Easy Rider* had come out in 1969, pitting bikers, hippies, and farmers against one another in a creative plot that reflected the tensions of the time. While we didn't identify ourselves as hippies — we didn't use hallucinogenic drugs, for a start, and both men had paying jobs — we did meet the generally accepted definition of hippies as being of unconventional appearance — having long hair and rejecting mainstream values. Our experience in the South had sensitized me to how we might look and seem to others. I knew we wouldn't be popular with everyone.

John and I exchanged thoughtful glances as we climbed out of the bed of the Adams' truck and crossed the yard into Gunter Brothers' feed store. Seeing a forklift heading our way, John hoisted Doña onto his shoulders. As we walked, I expected some kind of reaction from the workers in the yard. But they were busy unloading a truck piled high with sacks of feed and ignored us. Quincy and John were dressed in their usual Pendleton shirts over white t-shirts and faded blue jeans. Today they were sporting ponytails fastened with matching thick black rubber bands. John had grown his beard out over the last few months; I wore a long skirt and my usual dangly earrings, and my red hair reached nearly to my waist. Dorrie was dressed like a guy, in a blue work shirt and loose blue jeans. She had tucked her close-cropped hair into a straw hat. We looked pretty normal for Santa Cruz or Berkeley. But so far, we had seen no one else in Morgan Hill who looked like us. We had arrived at the entrance of the feed store. A dour-looking old man in overalls and a worn baseball hat stood at the front counter. I held my breath.

With perfect timing, Doña turned on the charm from her perch on John's shoulders, and while Quincy explained to the old gentleman that we owned property up by Chesbro Reservoir and needed supplies, the overalled man made goo-goo eyes at Doña. He grinned broadly when Dorrie and I chimed in together, asking where we would find chicken, rabbit, and goat feed. He introduced himself as Merv (Mervin Gunter, it later turned out, one of the owners) and inquired about our farm and our animals. He walked around the store with us, pointing out various items he thought we might find useful, such as feeders, salt licks, hay hooks, goat harnesses, and halters. Dorrie handed a list to Quincy.

While the men collected and paid for our supplies, Dorrie and I explored the further reaches of the store. I stopped to examine the wide variety of equipment and supplies available for sale, most of which I'd never seen before. There were bins of goat, rabbit, pig, chicken, dog, cat, and cattle pellets. They all looked the same to me. Also, several varieties of pasture seed, vitamins and minerals, equine and canine de-wormer paste, and pine pellet horse bedding, which Dorrie said her dad used for his cat litter boxes. Buckets of loose vegetable seeds: watermelon, kale, collards, spinach, lima beans, and soybeans — and that was just the front row.

Dorrie held up a bright green, cube-shaped can of Bag Balm. "You should get some of this," she said.

"You're joking!" I laughed.

"I'm not. It's a really useful item to have on hand. It's meant for sore cow and goat nipples and chapped udders, but my dad uses it on his hands in the winter after milking or working in the barn."

Ok, I could see how that might be useful, but most items along the back wall bewildered me. What was a clevis? A baffle? A barn door single box rail splice bracket?

Back up front, waiting for Dorrie to pay for the Bag Balm, I read some of the notices on the wall. Most of the handwritten cards advertised lambs and kids and calves for sale. Someone advertised a flock of guinea fowl — whatever those were. Other cards listed various services: hoof trimming, horseshoeing, butchering. I looked around, inhaling the smell of alfalfa hay mixed with grain, molasses, veterinary pharmaceuticals, and old wood. I had been a bit overwhelmed by it when we first came in, but I could sense the fragrance growing on me.

I could learn to love this stuff, I decided. I just need to take it one step at a time.

Emerging from the shop, we found John and Quincy chatting with Merv. The truck had been loaded and covered with a tarp. We all piled in, Doña on Dorrie's lap in the middle of the bench seat, me on John's lap by the passenger door. Merv grinned broadly at us and waved as we drove away. He'd been friendly, but I couldn't help wondering what he was thinking.

We were also greeted warmly at Squeri Bros. Hardware. Joe and Jane Squeri (I never did see another brother) sold an unbelievable variety of items. The guys roamed happily around the large warehouse, making special note of tools, latches, metal and PVC pipefittings, and spigots. Nails, screws, nuts, and bolts were in large bins with scales nearby. As they had for decades, customers weighed their purchases themselves, and wrote the weights on the little paper bags provided.

Dorrie carried on a running commentary as she led me around, pointing out objects we might need in the future. "We'll want these gate hinges and latches for the new goat pen. That's the kind of wire fencing we'll use for the garden and the permanent animal pens." Stopping to pick up some metal objects, she added, "You use these clips to fasten the wire to those metal poles over there."

We saw chicken feeders and waterers, shovels and rakes and hoes. Baffles and clevises again, and this time they were accompanied on the wall by shackles.

"We put one of those baffles inside our wood stove," Dorrie explained when I asked what they were used for. "It keeps the top from getting too hot. But it doesn't have anything to do with clevises or shackles. Those are used to attach ropes or chains to something you want to tow." She continued the tour.

When Dorrie noticed my eyes glazing over, she suggested I think of this place as "a fabric store for a farm." That made me smile. I relaxed a bit, and took notes in the little notebook I'd brought for that purpose.

After leaving Squeri Bros., Quincy drove to the Standard gas station, which had a sewer dump station and an auto repair shop. Thinking about the hippies who'd been chased out of their encampment in the Santa Cruz Mountains the year before, we had decided not to build an outhouse. Instead, we would be bringing portable chemical toilets down here to empty. We watched an RV driver use the dump station. The process wasn't difficult; it just involved taking a long flexible tube that the driver kept inside a hollow rear bumper, and attaching it to a threaded hole on the concrete bib of the dump station. I noticed a plastic fitting on the end of the hose that had threads and screwed into the valve. The man opened a valve on his camper and the contents of his mobile septic tank flowed into the underground sewer.

We walked over to the repair shop, Doña on Quincy's shoulders this time, and found a mechanic working under a car suspended on a lift. Seeing Quincy, he wiped his hands and came over to greet us.

"Let me know if you need help the first time you use the dump station," he said, after Quincy introduced John and me. "But most people using it know all the ins and outs of attaching the hoses and cleaning the station, so you probably won't need me. Just watch them and ask questions." He turned back to his work.

I felt relieved knowing that at least these three business owners would accept us into their shops without issue. We could obtain most of the supplies we would need in our own community.

Done with our tour for the day, we took Jane Squeri's parting suggestion and headed for Al Statti's Corner Drug, back toward Main Street. There, we relaxed and, sitting at the counter on tall stools that probably dated back to the 1950s, we treated ourselves to the first of many thick and delicious old-fashioned milk shakes, vanilla, strawberry, and chocolate — $.50 each.

4

THE
GREAT TRAILER INSTALLATION
PROJECT

FEBRUARY 1974

T HE DAY WE OFFICIALLY MOVED TO THE LAND, I awakened before dawn, washed, dressed, and crept upstairs to make coffee. I should have been organizing the details of the day, but instead I was thinking about my mother.

I'd been so excited when we signed the contract to purchase the property that I had driven the 50 miles to my parents' home in Belmont, wanting to tell them the news in person. I felt sure they would be just as happy as me that we had finally found a place to live, and pleased to know that their granddaughter would grow up in the country.

In 1941, my mother had left her widowed mother to join the British Army. When she and Dad returned after the war to a bombed-out neighborhood, she persuaded him to leave both their families behind and move to America. She, of all people, would understand why I wanted to take this step — and what a wonderful opportunity it would be for us. She had always been an adventurer and it seemed to me that this would be the adventure of a lifetime.

Mom and I were drinking tea at the kitchen table. When I announced that we had found a piece of property, and would be moving to it at the end of the semester, she didn't said anything at first. Then I explained that we wouldn't have electricity or running water for a while. She banged her cup into the saucer and stood up.

"I can't believe you want to do this," she wailed. "It feels like a slap in the face."

"We came all the way from England so you could have a better life." She said more quietly, her voice guttural with emotion. "I grew up with outdoor toilets, a water pump in the garden, and a single light bulb hanging from a cord." She paused, rubbed her knuckles, disfigured by arthritis. "Even after the war, we were still on rations and rebuilding bombed out houses. We brought you here so you wouldn't have to live that way."

Pacing around the kitchen, she began to talk in a controlled, persuasive, "mother" voice. "Wanting to live in the country, I understand. You'd like a garden and chickens and all that. But why throw away what we brought you here to enjoy? Why live without electricity, without running water? Especially with a baby!" She looked down at Doña, playing on the floor between us.

She took a deep breath and, when she spoke again, her voice sounded angry. "How will you keep her warm? Safe from wild animals? Wash her diapers?" She seemed to be losing control. "This is a crazy idea. You young people today have absolutely no appreciation for what you have!"

This was definitely not the response I had expected. I sat, stunned into silence, while Mom continued to pace back and forth, her dark hair framing her troubled face, her hands gesticulating helplessly.

From the floor, Doña looked up at each of us in turn. She started to pout, and looked like she was about to cry. I stood up and put my arm around my mother, gestured for her to sit down, picked up Doña and put her in Mom's lap.

"Mama, calm down. It's not as bad as you make it sound. We won't be without electricity forever. Just until we get permits. Besides, it'll be good for us to learn how to live more simply. Like you did. It will be an adventure." I trembled with emotion as I spoke. Inside, I felt like a teenager pleading for permission to go to the prom.

From behind his newspaper in the next room, ensconced as usual in his reclining chair, my father had called his disapproval. "Taking our granddaughter into the wilderness ..." he grumbled. "It's gormless! Why can't you live with *us* while you finish school, give us some time to get to know our granddaughter?"

Hah! Like *that* was going to happen.

Smiling, hoping to lighten the mood, I quipped, "What if I bring Doña's diapers here to wash? You'll get to see her then." Silence.

It went on like that, going nowhere. No matter what I said, they didn't appreciate my aversion to media coverage of the war, our hopes for the community we hoped to build, or why living with them wasn't an option. They thought our decision meant I didn't appreciate the enormity of the gift they had given me by coming to America, and blamed John for persuading me to go along with his "cockamamie" plans.

I suspected their objection grew partly out of jealousy. They had never warmed to John or his family, had refused to visit while we lived on Mount Hamilton. And now the Bumgarners had agreed to loan us their trailer to live in — the ultimate insult. I felt terrible. I hoped Mom and Dad would come around in time, but they definitely wouldn't be with us for the move.

The coffee aroma had awakened John, and he joined me in the kitchen, jolting me out of my reverie. Soon we were packing our vehicles and the Chevy pick-up with the possessions we had in our basement room and the boxes we'd stored in their garage. Pop hitched their travel trailer to his truck while Bea watched Doña and packed a basket of food for our midday meal. My mother-in-law sang as she worked, probably as happy to have us leave her home as I was to be leaving it.

We returned to the kitchen, ate a hurried breakfast, and were soon driving down the mountain road in convoy. John led in our 1963 VW bus with our young German Shepherd, Elsa, her head and half her body out the window. Pop and Bea followed him in the pick-up with their travel trailer hitched behind. Doña and I brought up the rear in our white Pinto Runabout, Doña in her brand-new face-forward General Motors car seat.

As we pulled out of the driveway, I felt elated, pushing my parents' objections out of my mind. This was a day to celebrate — we were moving to the land!

The drive down Mount Hamilton and on back roads to San Jose and then down 101 to Morgan Hill took longer than two hours this time. John and Pop kept stopping to discuss the route, adjust the hitch or rearrange the tarp over the pick-up bed. I sang to Doña until she went back to asleep, then fiddled with the radio for a while. I could get no reception in the hills and suspected I wouldn't until we reached San Jose. Giving up, I tried to relax into the long drive. It was early February, not quite spring, but the hills were turning green, and there were a few flowers dotting the countryside. The sun shone, setting the stage for a lovely day.

After what was beginning to feel like a major cross-country trek, our convoy finally stopped at the bottom of Chesbro Lake Drive on the back side of Morgan Hill's iconic landmark — a tall cone-shaped hill named El Toro. The men climbed out of their vehicles to discuss the final ascent, and I took Doña out of her car seat to change her diaper. John and Pop were head-to-head over a USGS geodetic map. It might have been Mount Everest we were climbing, for all the elevations and angles and possibilities they discussed before they climbed once more into their respective drivers' seats. John was loving this. I could tell by the way his steps bounced as he sprung into the VW bus and put it in gear. He would be the trailblazer, and we would follow him.

Back in December, we had hired a heavy equipment operator to grade the mile-long Chesbro Lake Drive and our private access road, Hawkins Lane. We did that so Quincy and Dorrie could drive their school bus up to the property. Since then, heavy rains had left both roads pretty soggy, and there were deep ruts at most of the curves. Pop, accustomed to towing his trailer on paved roads, now had to deal with loose rocks, ruts, and slippery mud. John would try to find the best route around the obstacles, and Pop would follow his trail.

Doña and I, trapped at the back, were getting bored. I sang some more — every song I could think of — then I started on nursery rhymes. At last, Pop reached the uphill hairpin curve that ended just above the clearing where we planned to put the trailer. He would have to get around that corner, pull into the driveway and continue down into the clearing. Then he would need to turn the truck and trailer around so he could drive back up the driveway and maneuver the trailer down the driveway into the clearing again, backwards this time and up to the pad John had prepared under a large oak tree. It would be a very long process.

We agreed to take a break. I parked the Pinto on the side of the road, lifted Doña out of the car, and walked the rest of the way. From the top of the driveway, I surveyed our new home. In front of me lay a sunken clearing surrounded by trees and lush spring grass. In the foreground, flowers and weeds had been trampled, releasing a pungent bitter herb fragrance. Directly across from where I stood, at the far right end of the clearing, a large oak tree spread low horizontal branches above a grassy knoll. On one side of the knoll, a flat pad had been bulldozed and smoothed in preparation for the trailer.

To my far left, nestled in a sheltered corner of the clearing, sat Dorrie and Quincy's school bus, its door side facing away from me. I knew from our weekend visits that they had added an awning over the door and windows, and some outdoor furniture, making their campsite look homey and welcoming. Trees and bushes screened them from the road and the breeze that came through the clearing each afternoon.

Anxious to stop paying rent on their house in the Santa Cruz mountains, Dorrie and Quincy had moved to the land shortly after Thanksgiving. We were just beginning what would turn out to be the wettest winter in a decade. The road to the top of the property was impassable, and it would be months before Quincy would be able to drive the bus up there. Meanwhile, they would stay in the clearing with us.

While the men strategized, Dorrie showed me what she and Quincy had done in her new kitchen. It was not nearly so large as the one she'd had in the Santa Cruz mountains house, but it smelled just as good, like an Italian delicatessen. Quincy had removed all the seats in the bus, leaving Dorrie a large space to work with. Herbs hung from hooks fastened to a long narrow board he had somehow attached to the bus ceiling. They were flanked by braids of garlic and onion; a ceramic vase on the stained wood counter held fragrant lavender. A shelf held jars of beans, pasta, rice, and oats. Cupboards under the sink and stove held pots, pans and ceramic plates, cups, and bowls. On the stove sat a cast iron pot in which bubbled a fragrant, deep red soup. Across from the cooking area stood a large table with long benches on either side. Dorrie demonstrated how the table could be removed when it wasn't serving as a dining room, study hall, or office. The benches could then be made into a double bed. At the far end of the kitchen, a heavy tapestry drapery hid from view the queen-size bed where Quincy, Dorrie, and both of their dogs slept.

I gratefully sipped the hot tea Dorrie handed me. "What a great space you guys have made for yourselves," I exclaimed.

I meant it. Dorrie had given me all kinds of ideas of how to make our own metal house feel cozy.

On my way back down the steps of the school bus, I noticed that they had replaced the driver's seat with a chemical toilet.

"We're going to hang a curtain around that for visitors," Dorrie said quickly, "but we haven't gotten there yet."

Outside, I was greeted by some of Dorrie's family members and friends who were camping for the weekend. They were there to help clear more poison oak and weeds from our acreage, flatten out some of the hills, and build a fenced enclosure for the dairy goats they had brought from the family farm. Their vehicles and tents dotted the hills above and below us, and a distinctive sweet fragrance followed them wherever they clustered.

There were at least four guys with beards, several young women with identical long brown hair, and Dorrie's parents, Mummy and Pooby. They greeted us warmly, but quickly went back to work.

Pop had brought a supply of strong wide boards. John and Quincy built ramps to flatten out the angle the truck would have to navigate. Pooby and two of his sons left their fence-building to look on. From time to time, they made suggestions, and occasionally were actually helpful.

Once again, it was slow going. I would soon learn that everything we did on the land took longer than I expected. As the trailer wheels moved over one set of boards, someone would take the wood from the back of the trailer and move it to the front. Driving over this plank road Pop inched his way up the hill and down into the saddle beside the school bus.

The next task was to turn the trailer around. But everyone was hungry, so John called a lunch break.

Having no role in the Great Trailer Installation project, Dorrie, Bea, and I had been sitting under the oak tree on a mat of blankets, talking and playing with Doña. Dorrie's sister Sarah had joined us and strung colorful beads into a necklace for Doña. Bea watched the men intently. As she watched the trailer making its painfully slow ascent, she clenched and unclenched her hands, occasionally running them through her unruly hair and pushing it back behind her ears. I knew John and his dad had pressured her into loaning us their new vacation trailer, but I hadn't considered what that would mean to her. It had clearly been painful for her to watch Pop inching up the road and around the corner. She must have been imagining the worst.

I asked her to help unfold the port-a-crib and we tossed in some toys. I lifted Doña in, suggesting she might like to play with Pooh Bear and look at some books. Sarah sat beside the playpen, engaging Doña with her books and toys. The bright yellow plastic stood out against the lush grass and early spring flowers.

We unfolded a table in the shade and brought sandwiches, lemonade, beer, and wine out of ice chests carried in the various vehicles. John and I hadn't thought to bring a container of water, so we drank what we had. The men grazed the length of the table, gathered food and drink, and sat down heavily beside the crib, one after another engaging our daughter in silly songs, lilting conversation, or affectionate noises. I loved that. I had been so lonely since we'd returned to California. The conversation was animated at first, then quieted as we ate. Elsa, who had been playing rambunctiously with the Adams' dogs ever since we arrived, collapsed at our feet and fell into a deep sleep. Before long, lulled by the food, drink, and warm sunshine, several people fell asleep too.

They were awakened by the sound of a vehicle gripping the ruts of the hairpin curve and squealing up the last rise. The driver braked hard at the downward slope, skidded down the driveway and turned just in time to keep from hitting Pop's trailer. It was Quincy's brother, Buzz. A younger version of Quincy with longer hair and tighter jeans, he climbed out of the car, rummaged in an ice chest for a beer and flopped on a blanket as if nothing had happened. My heart still pounded from my fear that he would hit the trailer. But Buzz didn't notice.

"Geez, guys, it's two o'clock! I thought you'd have this metal house in place by now and we could start thinking about a barbecue. Why the heck is it over there?"

Everyone began to talk at once, explaining the problem. I zoned out when the discussion began to take on the appearance of General Patton planning his landing at Casablanca. John sketched in the dirt. Two other men were waving their arms, suggesting different strategies to get the trailer turned around. Finally, they stopped talking and Pop climbed into his truck. Dorrie, Bea, Sarah, and I stood on the sidelines as Pop skillfully turned the trailer, incrementally, 180 degrees, then backed carefully up the hill toward the tree. He made it part way, but then the steep slope caused the front of the trailer to push down on the hitch until it dug into the ground. His truck appeared to be beached.

The men brought out the boards again, and they took turns putting planks in front of the wheels of the truck to level out the slope, taking them out from behind, then putting them back in front. Eventually Pop pulled the trailer up the driveway far enough to straighten it out. Then he began to back down and slowly began to climb the uphill rise toward the saddle. When he got about halfway to the top of the knoll, his wheels began to spin. Quincy and John hooked up two pulleys with a rope threaded between them, anchoring one end to the big oak. Pop got back into the truck, and John pulled on the rope as the trailer moved inch by inch toward its final destination. I heard Pooby explaining to one of his sons that they were using a "come-along."

I wished Dad were here. He would have loved being part of all this if he hadn't been so opposed to the whole concept of what we were doing.

Meanwhile, I changed Doña into warmer clothes and started dinner preparations inside our VW bus. No need for shade now, so Bea and I moved the table into the clearing. She laid out pans of lasagna and garlic bread made the night before, then a bowl of salad and a pile of paper plates. Dorrie clambered out of the school bus with a large tureen of soup, followed by Mummy carrying a stack of bowls. Sarah flourished a plate of chocolate cookies. I suddenly found myself craving my mother's potato salad.

The workers were ready to call it a day. They filled their plates and grabbed drinks, then stood on either side of the truck, eating and drinking standing up and calling encouragement to John as he continued to pull on the rope. His hands were giving out; Quincy took a turn. John washed his hands and put some pain-relieving crème on them from Dorrie's first aid kit, then put his gloves on again and took the rope back.

The light began to fade. An owl called from a tree across the road, and a nighthawk swooped down to see what we were doing. As Dorrie and Mummy and her sisters began clearing plates and bowls and taking them over to the bus, I unfolded two patio chairs and set them where we had a good view. I offered one to Bea and pulled Doña into my arms to nurse. As the light faded into darkness, and Doña drifted into dreamland, the flickering light of hand-held propane lamps illuminated the trailer inching backwards to its final destination under the big oak tree.

5

EARLY DAYS ON THE LAND

J OHN'S PARENTS SLEPT IN THEIR TRAILER that first night and we slept nearby in our VW bus. Early Sunday morning I awakened to muffled voices coming from the trailer, then the welcome sounds of breakfast preparation. The door banged against the latch as Bea fastened it open, and I heard the hissing of frying food, the chinking of dishes, and Bea humming softly. The sweet aroma of coffee drew me out of bed and to the trailer. Barefoot, my feet tingling from walking on cold, damp grass, I gratefully held out my mug to Bea, who filled it to the top.

Soon John, Pop, and I were perched just outside the trailer door, sitting on our haunches while we sipped our steaming coffee. John and Pop, both tall, nevertheless hunkered down quite easily and were, as always, thoroughly at ease with one another. Doña sat beside us on the grass, pulling up tiny flowers and putting them in a pile. Looking around, I slowly absorbed the reality that we were finally here — we wouldn't be driving back to Mount Hamilton that night. I felt as if I had been released from indenture. Tomorrow and the next day and the next I would wake up here and I would be home.

Dorrie and Quincy's work crew still slept in tents and vehicles around the property and hadn't yet begun appearing. Soon it would feel like a busy campground and we would get drawn into the activities, but for the moment we could enjoy the peace and quiet. I noticed Doña watching a lone seagull fly overhead. Looking for a beach? We were fifty miles inland. Perhaps the bird thought Chesbro Reservoir was the ocean. Its repeated cry, *"keow, keow,"* seemed to ask a mournful question: where is everyone?

When Bea appeared in the doorway balancing three plates heaped with scrambled eggs and sausages, we leaped up to help her. The fragrance of the food made my mouth water. Pop fetched folding chairs and we were soon seated in a cluster, eating enthusiastically. I fed Doña from my plate while John and Pop discussed what they needed to do to get our campsite set up.

"I need a work table," John announced. "I can use a sheet of plywood and two sawhorses. That will be my first project. And a second shed — where we can store kitchen supplies and animal food."

Pop looked thoughtful. "Be sure to use 4 x 4's for the legs of the table, and 1-inch plywood so it doesn't bow." Bea had joined us with her own plate, but after eating a few bites of egg, she set it on the ground and looked around.

"I wish I were your age, Marlene." She gazed at the tiny purple flowers emerging through the thick grass that covered the knoll. "To wake up to this every morning … It's so unspoiled and beautiful." She took a deep breath and sighed. "This will be such an adventure for you. I'm jealous."

I searched for an appropriate response. Bea's words were unexpected — especially after our difficult months together. Until that moment, I had assumed Bea's cheerfulness reflected her relief that we were moving out of her house. However, it made sense. John's parents always accepted our life decisions without negative comment. Even when we went backpacking on our honeymoon, or suddenly moved to San Diego, then to New Mexico, then to Washington, D.C., they never questioned us. So different from my own parents. But jealous? As I struggled to form a reply, Pop spoke up.

"I'm pretty happy too." He looked pointedly at John. "I plan to spend lots of weekends up here, helping my son build things and fixing things that break." We all laughed. Pop's responsibilities at Lick Observatory included keeping the boilers running, providing heat to the homes that dotted the road to the 36" telescope dome, and keeping the optical equipment clean and operational. A licensed electrician, he had shown himself on many occasions to be a skilled handyman. His occasional presence on our land would be most welcome. *But so would have been my father's,* I thought sadly, with his carpenter's knowledge of wood and construction techniques.

Bea returned to the trailer and began to remove the curtains and cushion covers. After we finished eating, Doña and I helped her prepare them for travel. I folded the fabric into squares and handed each one to Doña, who proudly put them in the box beside her. Later I would use my hand-operated Singer sewing machine to make replacements. While we heated water for dishes, Bea helped me measure the windows and cushions.

Watching Bea cooking and organizing, laying her hands gently on the folded covers, I could see how much she truly loved the trailer. She and Pop had talked about buying the rig for several years, and had finally done so the previous winter. It had been a very large purchase for them. On Mount Hamilton, Bea used the trailer as an art studio, but they were also planning a long summer trip. The deciding factor for Bea seemed to be that John and I began talking about constructing plywood walls inside the Quonset hut and moving there. She later told me that the thought of her granddaughter sleeping in a shelter like the ones used during World War II for storing munitions and housing refugees had upset her. No insulation, no plumbing — just thin corrugated metal between Doña and the elements.

A few weeks before we were about to move out, she sat down beside me as I studied. "We've decided you may borrow our trailer," she announced. "But only until June. And you need to be really careful with it." John gave her a big hug when he heard the news that night, and assured her that by June we would have title to the land. With that, we could apply for a permit to install a larger trailer. Removing the curtains and cushion covers and replacing them with our own had been one of her conditions.

As we washed and dried the breakfast dishes, Bea told me that Sears had advertised a sale on indoor-outdoor carpet squares.

"Why don't you buy some to put down on the floor?" she suggested, pointedly looking down at her imitation wood-grained floor.

I agreed, and reassured her that before we moved in, we would replace all the upholstery coverings and cover the floor as she wished. "John wants to build a shelf under the window next to the bed, wide enough for books and a lamp, I told her. "He says he can make it so you can remove it easily if you want to."

She nodded her agreement, her lips tightly closed. I hoped she wouldn't regret her decision. I gave her an awkward hug and promised her one more time that we would take very good care of her trailer.

Dishes washed, covers and curtains packed, measurements taken, Bea took a long, wistful look at the trailer and its surroundings, then climbed into the truck beside Pop. Dorrie and Quincy's friends and family, in various stages of undress, emerged from their tents and vans to wave and call their goodbyes. I picked up Doña and walked partway down the path that ran between our clearing and the Quonset hut, waving to them as they drove down the road. Then the older couple left, back to their life and their responsibilities, leaving us to our adventure.

As soon as Pop and Bea's truck cleared the gate, I crossed over to the trailer to figure out where I could store things, and what supplies we would need to buy. It was a classy trailer — a 15-foot white 1973 Aristocrat Mainliner with a well-appointed kitchen and separate toilet and shower. Without a piped-in water supply, those last two facilities were useless to us. I would buy an adjustable tension rod and install it across the shower compartment so we could hang clothes there. We would need to buy a chemical toilet with a removable base that we could take to the RV dumping station in town. The toilet in the trailer was fixed in place.

The following day we drove to an RV supply depot in San Jose and bought a green Port-a-Potty. Being only 15 inches high, it fit in the bottom of the clothes closet. John built removable shelving above the original toilet so I could stack toiletries, diapers, etc., there. We also purchased window screens to keep out the many varieties of flying insects being nurtured by the wet spring weather.

I soon learned that, in order to manage bedtime and breakfast routines in such a small space, I needed to follow a strict routine each evening. Before retiring, I prepared our breakfast grains in a thermos, washed the dishes and cleared the counters, and laid out clothes for the morning where I could reach them from our bed. It would be cold when I awakened, and I wanted to be able to dress before emerging completely from my cozy comforter. Then I leaned the port-a-crib, folded up, against the sink.

I would then nurse Doña to sleep, and either fall asleep with her or lie beside her and read. John would unfold the port-a-crib when he joined me and move Doña into it.

The first few mornings of waking in our comfy bed were delicious. The sun shone through the cracks in the curtains, waking us gently. I would nurse Doña, then roll her toward John's sleeping form so I could get out of the raised bed without her falling off. I had to fold the crib before I climbed all the way out of bed because otherwise there was nowhere for me to stand. At 6 feet, 2 inches, John could not have managed this maneuver.

We had spent many weeks on Mount Hamilton trying to teach Doña to sleep in her own bed, and she had been doing so contentedly for several months. But with the complications of folding the crib, and unfolding it several times a day in such a limited space, we soon gave up. Instead, we kept the crib in the tent for use during the day, and Doña returned to sleeping in the bed with us. It seemed easier, and everyone got more sleep. It's hard to reverse a decision like that, however. Co-family sleeping became a part of our family life for the next ten years.

Other than the bedtime routine, the trailer didn't feel cramped to me because the windows were low and large. When we pulled the curtains aside or opened the door, all outdoors came inside for us to enjoy. Unfortunately, John's head barely cleared the ceiling, and he spent much of his time bent over to avoid walking into one of the cabinets that jutted out from the walls. Grumpily, one morning he insisted that I store his clothes in the cupboards high above the bed, where he could more easily reach them. I argued that they should go in the closet with my clothes. That way we could use the higher cupboards for things that needed to stay out of Doña's reach, like glass food containers and medicines. We never agreed on that, so I finally did as he asked. His height made working in the kitchen awkward, too, and he soon talked his way out of cooking or washing dishes inside the trailer.

We both loved the peacefulness of our new home. Most mornings only the tinkle of the goats' bells, and the sounds of Quincy making coffee, broke the early morning silence. Later, songbirds would announce the rising of the sun, followed by Rudy the Rooster crowing his own morning announcement. John made it his habit to sit outside the trailer door to drink his morning coffee, basking in the morning sunshine and enjoying the silence. After breakfast, if I brought the dishpan outside and set it on a chair, he would wash dishes.

6

SETTLING IN

AT FIRST, LIVING ON THE LAND FELT LIKE CAMPING. We had driven our VW bus from Washington, D.C. to California the previous summer, and the tiny trailer felt very much the same. We lit the trailer with kerosene lamps and slept on the foldout bed that, by day, served as a couch. Our clothing selections were limited to what fit in the tiny closet. And our entire kitchen could be reached while standing in front of the sink. But this wasn't camping — it was our home, and we would be living in it for five months. It took a while, but we gradually came up with a routine that worked. Soon we integrated work and school, animals and gardening into our life, and it began to feel rich and full.

Thanks to Pop's masterful maneuvering of the trailer, we were nestled under and inside the big oak tree, and it felt very cozy. I thanked Bea and Pop in my head every morning for loaning us their travel trailer for the winter. We might be sleeping in a tent come June, but for now we were warm and dry. We moved to the land during semester break, so I could spend large blocks of time working the soil in what would become our communal vegetable garden. I built outdoor shelving and furniture to make our camp more comfortable, potted herbs and repotted houseplants. I started several flats of vegetable seeds, and John built a plastic greenhouse atop our German-shepherd-sized doghouse for me to put the plants in. I loved this interval in my life. No homework. No commuting. No stress.

Doña grew each day in her independence and ability to walk up and down the uneven slopes of the property and I loved watching her. Sometimes I just sat and watched her play. She didn't need toys. She collected sticks and leaves and flowers and put them into cupcake liners and egg cartons that I provided. Then she took them out again and laid them in lines, or circles, on the dirt. She could play like that for hours. Sometimes she harassed the chickens as they foraged in the long grass. She liked the squawks they made when she ran toward them, waving her little arms in the air, but they soon learned not to fear her.

In the afternoons, while Doña slept, I wrote in my journal or worked on one of the several articles I hoped to publish. I had begun submitting my work to free parenting magazines when we lived in D.C. — the ones that doctors stockpile in their waiting rooms, or that come with the diaper service each week: *Baby Talk, American Baby, Mother's Manual.* I'd had some success, but they didn't pay much — only $15 or $20 per article. John had bought me a subscription to *Writer's Digest.* I started submitting articles to mainstream magazines listed in the WD Markets feature — *Parents, Women's Day, Good Housekeeping* — and hoping for the best. I had recently sent a feature article to *Mother's Manual* about our trip to Africa for the solar eclipse; I hoped to earn at least $100 for that effort.

As much as I loved to write, my main focus that year had to be to earn a teaching credential. Doña had become comfortable with Dorrie, so one morning I left the two of them on the property and drove the 40 miles to San Jose State to register for spring classes and pay my fees. California residents paid no tuition in 1974, and I had already paid the initial registration fee of $300. I still had to come up with $65 in miscellaneous "fees" for the spring semester, and buy my texts. We were basically broke, so I was going to use our American Express card, the only credit card we had. I couldn't apply for a loan without collateral and, until Bill Carter recorded our purchase of his land and we got the title, we didn't have any collateral. In the bookstore, I found my textbooks and selected two sizes of spiral–bound notebooks — one for taking notes in class and the other to use as a journal. American Express expected full payment of the balance by the end of the month. I hoped there would be enough left from John's paycheck to cover the whole amount. Budgeting was new to me. We had always had two incomes before, and now we only had one.

On the first day of classes, I carried 15-month-old Doña across campus in her yellow Snugli carrier. I wasn't ready yet to leave her with a caregiver, and I only had two classes that day — both in the Education department.

Since childhood, the first day of school has always been a big deal for me. Even though a change in California law had forced me to return to college sooner than I planned, I felt the familiar bubbly anticipation as I walked to class, listened to the professors' introductions, and reviewed the syllabi. Babies and small children were a fairly common sight on that commuter campus, and I had cleared bringing Doña to class with both of my instructors for the first week of instruction. She sat contentedly on the floor beside me, playing happily with her new farm set while I took notes in my new notebook.

Walking back to my car after class, I saw two other women wearing their babies as I did, and we waved at one another, wordlessly acknowledging our sisterhood. On the drive home, I put a Hap Palmer cassette of children's songs in the player and entertained Doña by singing *Funky Penguin* along with Hap, using funny voices. She giggled and made her arms flap like a chicken while she wiggled her little bottom in the car seat.

On the first day of student teaching, the alarm rang before sundown. After pushing the button on the top to stop the noise, I opened the curtains surrounding our bed and turned on the light. Bringing the outside inside made the arrival of morning much easier for me, and the light helped me wake up. John shielded his eyes with his hands and mimicked being attacked by light rays. He would have stayed in bed until 9:00 or 10:00 a.m. if left to his natural body rhythm.

But he had agreed to this schedule for the final semester of my student teaching, and he kept his word.

Doña now slept with us regularly, and still nursed in the morning, which I easily accomplished before becoming fully awake. Once we had all emerged from the covers, I folded the bed into a couch and set up the table. John would usually go outside while I maneuvered the foam pads into place, retrieved the metal center post from wherever it had landed the night before, and put the table back together. Then I could put Doña into a seat that hooked onto the table and prepare breakfast for John and me. Entertained by a few Cheerios or slices of banana, she enjoyed watching me work. Sometimes we sang together.

Following a routine he had started on our very first camping trip in 1966, John took a morning walk. Meanwhile I packed lunches, fed Doña breakfast, and got myself ready for the day. Once I drove down the road, John would feed the chickens and take Doña to child care, then drive the 34 miles north to ESL, where he showered, ate a bagel, and began his work day. John enjoyed his work with the new digital image compression technology, which would eventually become the basis for JPEG, the photo files we use today. He and Quincy now worked in the same department at ESL.

We had anguished over what to do with Doña while I attended class or student teaching and John worked. Before learning about the new legislation that required me to finish my teacher training by the end of the year, I had planned to stay home until Doña started school. Until then, we had never left Doña alone with anyone but her grandparents. John's parents had integrated her into their everyday lives once we moved into their home. We ate together and sat together in the living room each evening; Bea and I working on lesson plans and Pop watching TV. During that semester, my mother had happily welcomed Doña on the three days a week I attended classes at San Jose State. Doña grew to love her "Ganma" and always seemed happy when I arrived to retrieve her. That arrangement required me to drive nearly two hours north from Mount Hamilton to Belmont and then backtrack another half hour south to San Jose State. It wasn't feasible to drive that far north while I taught in Morgan Hill and attended classes in San Jose. We had to find a better solution.

Doña had been eleven months old when we bought the land. We didn't know anyone who could advise us on child care centers or licensed family child care homes, so, at first, we scanned newspaper advertisements and posters stapled to telephone poles. Most preschools I called wouldn't take children until they were potty-trained, and the few that did were full. We obtained a list of licensed homes and centers from the county, but there had been no rating system or mechanism for talking to parents whose children attended them (no Yelp yet). I cried a lot, just thinking about leaving my baby with a stranger, but good sense told me I needed a teaching credential to earn money to build our permanent home on the land, so I persisted in my search. I asked other college students, parents with babies at the grocery store, people I met at the public library.

By February we had decided on a gentle grandmotherly woman who lived between Morgan Hill and San Jose and who took care of her two-year-old grandson and two other children about the same age. Doña would be the youngest, but Mrs. Fierro scooped her up expertly when I arrived timorously on her doorstep the first morning. Seeing my worried expression, she told me she would tuck Doña into bed beside her sleeping grandson while she made breakfast — and I wasn't to worry. The next day Doña reached her arms out for Mrs. Fierro, and the next day and the next. Each morning I drove to school feeling more confident that my precious child would be ok. When I picked her up after my school day had ended, she seemed happily engaged in play but pleased to see me.

One afternoon after I came home from San Jose State, Dorrie drove me down to the well in their pickup and helped me fill four five-gallon water containers from the pump. I felt like a school girl, studying Farm Skills 101. After lifting the containers into the truck bed, we drove up the road, then marched like Jack and Jill up the knoll to the trailer — me with Doña in the Snugli, hanging off my chest like a monkey. I put Doña on the ground and hoisted the containers as Dorrie demonstrated. I slowly angled the spigot up to the water intake of the trailer, which came up to my shoulder.

When I lifted the third water container to the intake, I felt a sharp pain in that shoulder. "Owwww — This might not have been a good idea," I moaned.

I was clearly not so fit as Dorrie, nor so strong. Using the ancient rhyme, "a pint's a pound the world around," we calculated that a five-gallon container of water weighed 40 pounds. I'd probably never lifted anything heavier than Doña in my life.

I set one of the five-gallon containers of water on the kitchen counter with the spigot hanging off the edge, and we used it like a faucet. This approach motivated John and me to become extremely frugal water users, because neither of us wanted to replace the empty water bottle with a forty-pound full one. We would wait to use the storage tank in the trailer until we had a water tank on the hill, and a hose we could just stick into the intake hole.

Dorrie continued to orient me to the chores that needed doing around the property. After the new semester started, she would need daily help feeding the animals. I appreciated her tutoring. Feeding the chickens and the goats was easy. But then I watched her carry a bale of alfalfa hay from Quincy's pickup to the goat pen, using two big hooks. I tried to lift the bale the same way she had, but couldn't lift it off the ground.

"It'll get easier," she assured me. "You'll get stronger just doing the normal work around here."

I hoped she was right.

That weekend, John and I discovered the Morgan Hill Flea Market. To celebrate finishing my first week of classes, we had driven into town to get bagels. The line of traffic we encountered at the Main Street traffic light at 7:00 a.m. turned out to be vendors waiting to enter the market grounds just across the railroad tracks. We peeked through the fence surrounding the market and decided to stick around until it opened.

Thus began a regular Saturday routine. Most weeks from then on, when the gates opened at 8:00 a.m., we were among the waiting shoppers, squeezing through the opening and heading for coffee, juice, fresh biscuits, or pancakes. The food smells wafted over the parking lot. We were salivating before we passed through the gate. Later in the day, the food vendors would turn on the popcorn machine and make hot dogs.

We rarely shopped with a specific item in mind. The vendors and customers were such a fascinating polyglot of people and wares that we enjoyed wandering from table to table just to see what was on offer.

After making it past the food booths, John and I usually split up. He headed for the tool area, Doña on his back in the new Gerry frame carrier he had purchased. Freed from baby care, I would slowly make my way through housewares, children's clothing, toys, and books. The sounds of the market became our navigation tools. Just inside the gate, a radio station playing Mexican music blared from the food vendors' speakers facing the parking lot. As families purchased food and settled on the picnic benches the sounds of conversation, laughter, and sometimes children's tears created a tapestry of sound that served as a transition zone. Further in, vendors selling cassette tapes competed with one another for the sound waves. Some vendors walked out from their booths, loudly hawking their wares when they saw us coming. The energy felt stimulating and fun. I loved the market.

Some vendors were regulars, and we soon got to know the types of goods they sold. Others were homeowners clearing out their garages, or families moving away. That's where the really good bargains were. The first week we left with a pink plastic baby bath ($.50), a Sunbeam electric egg cooker that looked like a space ship ($1.00), and a yellow ceramic milk pitcher, perfect for holding wooden spoons, which it did for many years ($.75). John found some odd little metal pieces that he thought might be parts for a windmill.

After that, we drove to the market for the food, for the thrill of the search, and for the people. I liked to watch people, especially families with children. John enjoyed talking to strangers. Just about anywhere we ventured — concert, movie line, campground — he would find someone to talk to.

When I finished wandering around the farmer's market, I would usually find him back in the food area, coffee cup in hand, talking to someone he had just met. He carried a notebook in his pocket for writing notes about work. When he met someone new, he would bring it out and record the name and phone number of his newest acquaintance. Then he would explain that we didn't have a telephone, but that we were easy to find, and tell him or her how to get to our place. Some of our life-long friends started as people he wrote down in his little book.

7

MUD!

THE WEEK AFTER WE MOVED TO THE LAND, the rain started again. It rained steadily through February, turning the sky grey, and patches of Hawkins Lane, where our property lay, into a squishy kind of quicksand. Even along Chesbro Lake Drive, the mile-long stretch of private road leading up the hill to our road, two or three unpaved patches lay buried deep in mud. Quincy, driving his pickup with the bed empty, mired out on the bad curve close to our camp a couple of times. The first time it happened, John put a shoulder to the cab and helped him drive out of the muck. The second time, Quincy threw two bales of alfalfa hay in the back of the truck, which gave him about 300 pounds ballast, and then he could drive himself out. We all had so much to learn.

One of the items John had written on his clipboard when we walked the boundaries back in November had been "Buy new tires." Now it was the height of the rainy season, and I could see that our worn street tires wouldn't provide enough traction to handle serious mud. I'd lost traction a couple of times before we moved to the land, when the temperatures on Mount Hamilton Road dropped below freezing and the wet surface turned to ice. I knew it was only a matter of time before I had an encounter with mud.

The VW bus was first in line for tires; you could hardly see the tread in some spots. Because the bus's engine was in the back, the vehicle tended to be pretty sure-footed, even with old tires, and, so far, John had made it all the way home each night. I'd been watching for tire sales but, as the Middle East oil crisis started to impact our lives in the form of gasoline shortages and hours-long lines at the pump, buying tires had fallen to the bottom of my list.

On Mondays, I left the college in mid-afternoon to allow myself time to pick up Doña and prepare for my weekly night class. Several of the sixth-graders at Morgan Hill Elementary School had limited English skills. My high-school Spanish was rusty, so I had enrolled in a conversational Spanish class to help facilitate our communication. As I drove home from San Jose State with Doña that Monday, I practiced the vocabulary words from the previous class, and planned to review tonight's lesson while she napped.

The rain fell steadily in Morgan Hill, making the road more slippery than it had been that morning. Once I entered Chesbro Lake Drive, I maneuvered my Pinto Runabout around the mud puddles and uphill curves carefully, making a mental note to buy a Sunday paper and search again for tire sales. As my tires slipped on one muddy patch after another, however, I thought, *"Forget the tire sales — just bite the bullet and buy new tires."*

On the last uphill curve on Hawkins Lane, just below our encampment, the Pinto fishtailed and the back end slid into the piled-up dirt on the right side of the road. I tried to drive forward to free the wheels, but I could hear one tire slipping in the mud, and the engine whirred uselessly. Trying to remember what I knew about traction — very little — I tried backing up and turning the wheel, but it just seemed to make things worse.

When I realized I was well and truly stuck, I felt my chest grow tight. I'd never been totally stuck in mud before and I found it frightening to be stuck and alone. Since John and I had been together,

I'd always been near enough to a phone to call him when I had car trouble or a flat tire. Nearly every house had a land line in those days, and there were public phone boxes on corners of well-traveled streets. No portable phones yet, but Ma Bell had pretty much saturated the nation with telephones without them.

Without John around to help, and no way to reach him, I realized that I had absolutely no idea what to do. No one would be coming up this road for hours and, in any case, I didn't really want anyone to see how badly I'd screwed up. It was only a short walk to the trailer from here, but I couldn't risk leaving my car unattended in case someone else came up the road.

As I pondered my situation, my face grew warm. I felt the hair on the back of my neck stand up, and my palms grew moist. My stomach churned and suddenly I felt embarrassed. I had done something terribly stupid. After Quincy's experience on that turn, I should have known better than to attempt it. It would have been smarter to park my car down by the Quonset hut.

Shivers ran through my body like they always had when my father caught me grinding the gears, failing to signal, coming home late. Whenever I did something irresponsible, I heard the voice of my dad berating me, even when he wasn't there. One time before I got married, I got stopped for speeding and I started sobbing before the officer even asked for my license. I suppose I expected Dad to come down the highway and start yelling, shouting that I didn't have the brains I was born with. And now I was doing it again, waiting for him to show up and remind me of my incompetence. My heart beat like a rabbit, high in my chest: *thump-thump, thump-thump.*

Come on, Marlene, think of something.

I stayed in the car for a while, eyes closed and breathing slowly, trying to get my body to calm down. Dad wasn't here, and he wouldn't be driving up the road. That was the good news. The bad news was that Help wouldn't be driving up the road either. I needed to figure out what to do all by myself. Doña still slept in her GM car seat. The rain had stopped, so I clambered out of the car to assess the situation. I struggled to stand upright in my stroppy city shoes as they slipped in the muck. Since I had no blankets to keep Doña warm in the February chill, I put my coat over her sleeping form. I didn't have a shovel, either, but I clearly needed something to dig the mud away from my tires. As I looked around for a branch or a stick, I heard a car engine. A vehicle had turned on to Hawkins Lane from Chesbro Lake Drive.

Oh no — I had forgotten Dorrie would be coming home early, too. She had offered to feed Doña dinner. If Dorrie had driven through the gate at the bottom of our hill, she would soon be here. I should warn her; she wouldn't see my car until she arrived at the curve. She might plow right into the Pinto.

Since Doña still slept in the car, and it had started raining again, I decided to leave her be. Grabbing a piece of notebook paper and a pen from my backpack, I headed down the path on foot to put a note on the gate. Too late. On the road below, I saw Dorrie's green BMW heading toward the final curve. Running back up the hill, I shouted and waved my arms, but she couldn't hear me. By the time I got to the curve, Dorrie 's car had slipped in the mud too. She had tried to drive around the Pinto on the left and skidded into the left-hand bank; two useless cars, both stuck in the mud.

I stood in the middle of the muddy road, feeling helpless, and watched Dorrie climb out of her car. I felt so foolish. I wished she hadn't come home to find me in this predicament. Surely she'd be upset with me for being so inept and blocking the road. But when she emerged from the Beemer, wearing far more appropriate footwear than I, Dorrie had a big grin on her face.

Before I could wail "I'm soooooo sorry," she laughed. "Don't look so devastated. We can fix this."

"We can? Just us?"

"Sure. It happens all the time at my dad's place in the winter. We're big strong women. No problem. This is just part of living in the country."

"Which I think you forgot to mention."

"Well, yeah. Probably. Never mind."

While I watched in admiration, Dorrie lifted a pair of rubber boots and a small folding shovel out of her trunk, along with two already rather mud-stained burlap sacks. A stuck-in-the-mud kit. She smiled reassuringly.

"Here, put these boots on. And throw those silly pumps in the trunk. They'll need a wash."

"So will my Pinto," I observed. My previously white car had been spattered with mud everywhere, especially the hatchback. I wouldn't be able to see out the rear window.

While I looked mournfully at my formerly pretty little car, Dorrie dug away some of the piled-up dirt from behind her own car and demonstrated how to put the burlap sacks under the back wheels, pulling on them to get out the folds and wrinkles. She slowly backed her car over the sacks, turning the steering wheel to get a better angle. The burlap soaked up the mud, and her tires were able to get the traction needed to move out of the muck. Just like what we had done with wooden planks to get Pop's trailer up the soft dirt bank to where it sat now under the big oak tree.

I laughed in recognition. No mystery — just physics.

Dorrie then instructed me to move the sacks in *front* of the wheels and push her car while she slowly inched forward. To my amazement, it worked. The wheels no longer spun, but bunched up the burlap sack as they rolled over them and onto a more solid patch of ground. I retrieved the sacks and took them over to my car.

"Is the Pinto front or rear wheel drive?" Dorrie asked, after moving the BMW to a dry spot and walking back.

"Not a clue." I guess I should have known that, but it had never come up.

"Ok, we'll just assume it's rear wheel drive. Most cars are. So, the sacks should go under the rear wheels like with my car."

We repeated the steps with the Pinto, me at the steering wheel and Dorrie digging away the dirt, moving the sacks and pushing the car until I broke free of the muddy patch. I went back to help her put the sacks and the shovel in her car and we both drove up the road. I would have liked to put my feet up, but that wasn't going to happen. Instead, I handed Dorrie her boots and walked barefoot back to the car. Doña had been awake for the last few scenes of our drama, and she wanted out of the car seat. I unfastened her and set her down on the ground and retrieved my notes from the back seat.

"Can you still feed Doña her supper and put her to bed" I asked, picking my girl up again before she began playing in the mud. "John will take over when he comes home."

"Sure. Bring her over whenever you're ready."

Dorrie tromped off toward the goat pen and I sighed with relief. I would still have time to get ready for class.

Back in our little trailer, I put a large kettle of water on the stove. After Doña nursed, I took some of the hot water to wash my bare legs and feet, then my arms, neck and face. Somehow, I had managed to get mud on every exposed part of my body. I exchanged my dirty skirt for a clean one, brushed my hair, and sat down to read.

Over a pot of tea, I read my Spanish notes from the previous week and practiced a few sentences on Doña, playing beside me. She looked up and smiled as if she actually understood me. Just then Dorrie appeared at the door to make good on her promise. I gratefully kissed Doña good night and went back to my books.

After a fifteen-minute drive to the high school I walked in from the parking lot, and entered another world. I enjoyed the ordinariness of the conversational class. Unlike the Spanish 1A class I had taken years earlier, this teacher emphasized words and phrases that students and parents were actually likely to use, and she taught the Latin American accent rather than the Castilian one we were taught in high school. In minutes, she had challenged us to order an evening meal from menus she provided, in Spanish only. For the next three hours, I found myself engrossed in solving each exercise she presented.

By 9:30 p.m., I felt relaxed and hummed a Mexican folk song as a group of us walked to the parking lot. I even joked with another student when he asked about my muddy car.

"Yeah, I had a bit of a run in with a mud puddle this afternoon." Laughing, I climbed into my car, visualizing the warm feather comforter that awaited me.

But the day wasn't over yet.

I drove slowly up Chesbro Lake Drive, nervous because of the late hour. It had stopped raining, but I still didn't want to get stranded and have to walk up the road in the dark. I planned to stop short of the bad curve, but I hoped to make it at least to our gate at the base of Hawkins

Lane. Before I'd gone even half a mile, I encountered a Chevy El Camino parked right across the road. I didn't want to stop in case I couldn't start up again on the slippery surface, and it looked like I could go around on the far side. I steered my car in that direction. Bad idea. I found myself stuck in the same muddy patch that had trapped the El Camino. That part of the road was as sloshy and mushy as a pigpen in the rain. My feet, wearing boots this time, made loud sucking noises as I climbed out of the car and into the mud.

I couldn't believe I'd gotten stuck twice in the same day. Although annoyed, I didn't feel as overwhelmed as I had during the earlier incident. Dorrie had said this was normal. I would act as if it were normal. My newfound confidence began to slip away, though as I evaluated my options. I hadn't had time to get gunny sacks or a shovel, and the only thing I could think of to do short of walking up the road in the dark was to ask someone for help. It was 10:00 pm by this time — a bit late to be knocking on doors.

I did know one man who might not mind: Hugh Graves owned a large ranch at the bottom of the hill. He had driven up to our property to welcome us the week before. He seemed like a decent guy, and I felt I could approach him. I suspected that the wimpy truck belonged to one of his sons, but even if it didn't, he might be willing to help. I grabbed a flashlight from the glove box and hurried down the road to his house.

Hugh was great. It turned out the truck did indeed belong to one of his sons, and he already knew it was blocking the road.

"Honestly, Mrs. Bumgarner, I didn't expect anyone to come up the road this late. I figured we could wait until first light to deal with it. My boy had to go into town tonight, and I wanted him to be part of the rescue effort. But, given the circumstances …"

He cheerfully drove me home, handily making it around both cars and up Hawkins Lane to our camp. After we explained the situation to John, he jumped into the Jeep with Hugh and they drove farther along Chesbro Lake Drive to ask Walt and Fran Peters if their teenage son, Wally, could help. Shortly afterward, I heard three cheerful voices rising above the sound of the engine as if this was all just a great lark.

They got the El Camino out fairly quickly. With two men pushing, John was able to get enough traction to drive the Pinto through the puddle and onto drier ground. Hugh delivered Wally to his parents and went back home while John filled the puddle with drier soil. I was asleep when he finally came through the trailer door.

What a day, I thought, burrowing back under the comforter. Is this really what "normal" looks like?

The next day, while I was student teaching, John smoothed the remaining muddy patches of Chesbro Lake Drive with a shovel, and added some sand to Hawkins Lane where it went around the sharp curve. At noon, he drove me to San Jose State, then on the way home, after picking up Doña from Mrs. Fierro's, we stopped at an auto parts store to buy towing cables, gunny sacks, and two folding shovels. It was dark again by the time we started up Hawkins Lane, so we left the Pinto at the bottom of the hill and drove the more sure-footed VW bus. It had been another very long, very muddy day.

POSTSCRIPT

On Hugh's way back down the hill that night, waving to John as he skidded around the corner, he hit a mother possum. As Hugh's taillights disappeared into the long driveway below, John was sitting in the mud beside the Pinto, putting baby possums in his pockets and carefully watching the mama possum for signs of life.

When he arrived back at the trailer, John had tiny possums crawling all over him. They were naked and about three or four inches long, with very long tails and cute pink noses. He had walked from the Quonset hut in the moonlight, fretting about what to do with the orphans. Regretfully, I climbed out of the comforter, found an eye dropper, and helped him feed the babies milk and applesauce.

I put them to bed in a tissue-lined shoebox, thinking as I did so of the two baby birds he had rescued just before we were married. Although the birds grew feathers and flew away, I didn't have much hope the possums would survive. But I had to do something to comfort John.

His mother once told me that shortly after John returned home from the Air Force he'd gone on a day-long hike on Mount Hamilton and come home late, having missed dinner. In his arms he carried a spotted fawn whose mother had been shot and abandoned. John had found the baby deer curled up next to the carcass.

"It was filthy and filled with ticks," his mother complained. "He laid it on my good couch. I told him to call the ranger and I made him put it in the garage on an old mattress."

True to form, John sat weeping over the possums when I finished making the shoebox bed. He knew they were too young — we wouldn't be able to keep them alive on our own — and there were no wildlife rescue centers in our area yet. (Years later, a parent at Doña's school opened an animal rehabilitation center, and for several years John helped injured eagles learn to fly.)

Eventually I convinced him to go to bed. In the morning we took the babies back down the hill in case Mama had recovered, but she still lay in the middle of the road. John put her under a bush and let the babies climb on her. We said a little prayer, and sadly left them to their fate.

8

MAMA, HORSE!
OR GOOD FENCES MAKE
GOOD NEIGHBORS

"Mama, horse! Look! Horse, Mama!"

"No, love, it's a goat."

"Mama — No. Look! Horse!"

Doña pressed her nose to the window of our tiny trailer, gesticulating excitedly. The Adams' pens did not always contain their goats and capturing wandering nannies had become a daily adventure for all of us.

The morning before, I had awakened to find Dorrie's Toggenburg goat standing on her hind feet, trying to reach plants housed in the plastic greenhouse John had built on the roof of the doghouse. I had managed to chase her away before she succeeded. Some of her targets were houseplants I'd had for years, and others were seedlings that would soon populate our communal vegetable garden.

But Doña had it right. Today it *was* a horse munching my Purple Velvet. Calling back to John to watch our daughter, I grabbed a broom, jumped out the door of the trailer, and tried to shoo it away. The broom had worked for the goat, but not so well with the horse — since I was barefoot and terrified of the huge black animal. Quincy heard me shouting, and emerged from the school bus he and Dorrie called home, laughing at my ineffective sweeping. Crossing the clearing between us in long strides, he grasped the horse's bridle firmly like a knight of old, and confidently led the horse up the driveway and down the road toward Bill Carter's place, his long red locks adding to his Ivanhoe image.

Bill Carter had moved into the trailer adjacent to our shared well. Before we moved to the property, he'd let his two horses graze freely, and we hadn't yet convinced him to stop. He would rather let them scavenge than contain them and feed them a proper diet.

The horses knew how to get a good meal. Just a few days earlier, they had broken Quincy and Dorrie's fence and found their way into the barrels of goat feed. I listened to the clip clopping of hooves as man and horse made their way down the hill, past the Quonset hut and the well. I heaved a sigh of relief when I heard the metallic clang of a gate as Quincy returned the horse to its enclosure. Disaster avoided once again, I gazed across our camp.

Morning sunlight filtered through the oak, madrone and cedar trees covering our communal property, turning the branches orange and red. Most of the trees were deciduous, and their leaves had not yet fully grown back, allowing me to see the bones of the trees in full color. Even the manzanita and low-lying shrubs, toyon, rock rose, and sage appeared to have been painted with an artist's brush. John and I had lived on the land several weeks by now, but I still felt in awe of the beauty that surrounded us.

Dorrie and Quincy had painted their school bus pale pink. On that Saturday spring morning, the windows glinted garishly like a Warhol painting. Dorrie must have been snuggling with their dogs, King and Crosby. She waved through a window near the back of the bus, and I heard Crosby's tail go *thump, thump, thump* as he pushed her hand away, trying to look out too. The scene before me — the

colorful vehicle with its occupants waving through the window —
could have been a Beatles' record album cover.

The smell of lemons made me look down, and I saw that I stood
in a patch of miner's lettuce, *Claytonia perfoliata.* I had crushed some
of the plants on my way to the greenhouse, releasing their pungent
fragrance. I plucked some leaves, chewing them with pleasure as I
picked my way carefully back through the weeds to the trailer. I offered
some to Doña, playing with the busy box John had fastened to the wall
at the foot of our bed, and John, still wrapped up in our comforter.
Turning once more toward the outdoors, I stood, bare feet on the
threshold, studying our surroundings.

Our five acres lay in an unincorporated part of California known
as Llagas-Uvas, originally home to the Ohlone and other
Costanoan-speaking people and then, later, a part of a Spanish land
grant. Eighty miles south of San Francisco, it sat on the eastern side of
the Santa Cruz Mountains, just west of the town of Morgan Hill.
Nestled as we were in a bowl-shaped clearing surrounded by grass and
trees, I found it easy to believe that we were living in the wilderness. In
fact, we could be in the center of Morgan Hill in just 15 minutes.

The lower half of our property lay along the ridge of a hill, long and
odd-shaped. A tree-lined dirt road dubbed Hawkins Lane wound steeply
uphill from Chesbro Lake Drive, through a creaky metal gate, past the
Carter place, then through a gap in the old barbed wire fence that marked
the perimeter of Carter's remaining land and the edge of ours. The road
continued up the hill, around a steep left turn, past our homestead and a
spring dug out of the side of the hill, to Dorrie and Quincy's future
building site at the top of the hill. The opposite edge of our land ran along
the center of a canyon, a grassy swale that guided water runoff from the
top building site down the hill to a rusted and immovable metal gate that
would have opened up onto Chesbro Lake Drive, if it had worked.

We couldn't see Carter's trailer from our camp or the road, but
we passed it each time we drove to or from town. Beyond us, further
up Hawkins Lane, no one. We were on our own on a ten-acre parcel
surrounded by hundreds of acres of uninhabited open land.

In the weeks that we had been there, a carpet of light green grass
had covered the scar made by the installation of Bea and Pop's trailer.

Even the driveway had healed. Tiny bunches of fragrant baby blue eyes, pale blue and white, framed the red soil trail, now packed down into two distinct tire tracks. Grass grew between the tracks and on either side of them. At the base of the grand old oak beside our trailer, tiny white, purple, and yellow flowers formed a fairy circle of color. Across the clearing, the Adams' bus — which had been in place since just after Christmas — looked like it grew directly out of the soil, its tires hidden in the tall grass. Quincy's new lean-to faced away from us, but I could tell by the fragrance wafting in the air that he had started cooking breakfast.

The Adams' goats were milling around on the hillside, hoping for breakfast, and I could hear morning sounds from the animal pens across the valley. Our neighbors, Fran and Walt Peters, lived a half mile further along Chesbro Lake Drive. The more distant noises were probably the Peters feeding their horses and chickens.

A swell of emotion washed over me as I surveyed the scene. I felt safe and at peace. No longer just a campsite, this piece of land had become our home, just as we'd imagined it would. Feeling Doña peeking out from between my legs, I lifted her into my arms and held her tightly against my chest. I kissed her milky cheek and inhaled her baby sweetness. Life was good.

Soon after the goat/horse episode, Doña and I returned home one evening to find both horses grazing along the side of the road just inside our gate. Delighted, Doña gleefully called out, "Horses, Mama!" With a sinking feeling, I pulled into the driveway next to our little trailer and saw in the headlights that my herbs and bedding plants — the ones I had nurtured carefully from seed and that were nearly ready to transplant into the garden — had been chewed down to nubs. What remained of the vinyl greenhouse, now in tatters, blew loosely in the evening breeze. Blood rushed to my face as I stared at the plastic and what remained of my plants. Hot tears stung my eyes.

Before I took Doña out of her car seat I ran to the top of the rise and screamed "Go!" at the horses. Trying to make myself big, I planted my feet far apart, waved my arms in the air and stomped my feet. I yelled again, but this time my voice shook, "Go home, you stupid horses!!! Go away!!"

Both horses looked up for a moment, then calmly returned to grazing. Clearly I wasn't going to win this battle. The horses were, quite literally, out of the barn, and they had no plans to go back in. I wiped my eyes and went back to the car to get Doña.

By this time, Quincy had returned the horses to Bill Carter many times. Each time he pleaded with the craggy old man to contain them so that we could get on with the development of our homes and gardens. I could see now that nothing had changed, and it wasn't likely to any time soon. Carter had our money. He may have been our closest neighbor, but we were pretty much powerless to make him keep his horses in their own space.

I mulled over the situation while I fixed Doña's dinner — crackers and hummus, raw green beans, and a wedge of orange. My hands still shook. My rage at Carter and the horses had overwhelmed me. I didn't like feeling so violently about something. As I cut open the juicy orange, I decided that I should do something about it. So far, I'd been the sleeping partner in this venture. I saw myself — and I suspect everyone else did too — as the baby nurturer and chief cook and gardener. Before moving to the land, we had spent most weekends camping on the land in our VW bus since our reconnaissance in November. Dorrie, Quincy, and John made all the major decisions and did most of the physical work. I kept myself busy caring for Doña, drawing sketches of our future communal vegetable garden, baking bread, and making hearty soups in a giant pot.

Dorrie had lived on a farm all her life and had skills and knowledge the rest of us needed to acquire. I had been quite happy to let her lead us as we began to plan and build out the footprint of our homestead. With the men's assistance, she had field-fenced a small goat corral, and installed a chicken coop — which had arrived on Dorrie's father's flatbed truck one weekend fully-built and complete with young chickens. We now had two goats, six chickens and a rooster, and two renegade horses that liked our camp better than their owner's. Dorrie's family planned to bring additional goats and chickens, rabbits, turkeys, and ducks as a kind of housewarming gift. John and I had agreed to share the animal duties and their bounty. Dorrie would teach us what we needed to know to care for the rest of the livestock when they arrived. But she couldn't do everything.

As I nursed Doña and prepared her for bed, I decided we needed a fence to serve as a barrier around our trailer, the doghouse, the storage shed, and our nascent vegetable garden. The timing worked for me to start on one now. Dorrie and Quincy had stayed in town to watch a movie, and John wouldn't be home from work for hours. No one to try to change my mind. But could I actually do this? I decided I had to try. I needed to stop these horses from eating our plants. I would build a fence. I knew I would need help unrolling the welded fencing — the 300-foot rolls were insanely heavy — but decided to start digging the post holes before someone — including myself — told me I couldn't do it.

I had watched the others construct field fences, and knew the process they had used to set the poles: dig holes with a post-hole digger, then hammer metal T-posts into the holes with a post driver, a heavy steel cylinder with a handle on each side and a welded cap on one end.

Since it had been raining lately, but not in the last couple of days, the soil had become soft, but not muddy. Except for the setting sun, the conditions were perfect. I had been afraid of the dark since childhood, but I decided I would feel better digging holes for a fence than trying to do my college work. Once Doña fell asleep, I placed pillows next to her to keep her from rolling off the high bed, grabbed a flashlight and our pressurized Aladdin oil lamp, and went outside to collect what I would need.

It was fully dark now, but I knew where the tools were and where a stack of T-posts lay on the ground. I could still feel vestiges of the adrenaline rush I had experienced when I first saw the damage to my herbs and bedding plants. Hands shaking, I unearthed John's tape measure from a stack of tools on the worktable, put the lamp on top of the doghouse, and went to work.

I knew the posts needed to be in a straight line, but I had no idea how far they should be apart. Wielding my flashlight, I zipped my jacket against the chilly night air and picked my way through the soft soil and the high grass to the goat enclosure, inhaling the rich scents of moist earth and vegetation. Using John's tape, I measured the distance between the poles. I hooked the end of the tape over the fence wire next to one post and pulled it out as I edged over to the next one. I measured two other spans. The distance between them varied between eight and ten feet. I decided then that it wasn't critical. Turning back toward our trailer, I could hear the horses milling around on the hill above me. They were probably watching from their lofty perch and laughing. The light from the lamp comforted me. I crossed the clearing quickly.

John had stacked some two-by-fours under the trailer. I took two of them and lay them end-to-end as measuring sticks. That looked right, and measured about eight feet. Using the two-by-fours seemed easier than using the retractable tape measure. I drew a six-inch circle in the soil at each end of my wooden line, raked back the grass and miners' lettuce with a claw weeder, moved the wood out of the way, and began ramming the post-hole digger into the ground inside the first circle.

It looked easy when John and Quincy did it, but they were taller than me, and stronger. The two blades of the post-hole digger barely creased the soil. Whatever had possessed me to think I could do this? I began to waver in my resolve. Was I making a mistake? Then I remembered the tattered greenhouse. I had to do this.

I retrieved a concrete block from where John had stacked them, dragged it back to where I wanted the post, and settled it endwise into the soil. The grass I crushed in the process released a pungent scent, not unpleasant. Balancing on the block, I stood at a better angle. The post-hole digger bounced several times before I got a decent purchase in the soil. It took me nearly twenty tries to get a hole deep enough to place a post into it with the little stabilizer fins below the soil. One post, and my hands already hurt. I could feel a blister starting on one thumb. After sucking on it for a minute, I went back to the bench for John's work gloves.

They were too big, of course, but with their protection I managed to get the next hole deep enough in only ten or fifteen tries. I put the two-by-fours back on the ground, clawed back another patch of grass, drew another circle, started a third hole.

Once I had three holes dug, I tried again to set a metal T-post into the loose dirt at the bottom of the hole. But the post kept falling over when I reached for the post driver. I finally laid the post on the ground and put the 20-pound driver over the top of it while it lay there. Then I stood the post up and gently coerced it into the soil by lifting the post driver up just a few inches each time, not going above the top of the post. After the tip of the post went in an inch, I increased the height of the driver so I could pound it down with more force. *Thwonk! Thwunk!* The sound of the metal driver connecting with the metal post echoed off the nearby hills. As I continued to lift the post driver and jam it down on the post, I felt strong and competent. I was on a roll, and enjoying myself. As I took off my jacket and laid it on the ground, I imagined standing on the frame of a partially built geodesic dome, reaching into a carpenter's apron for a handful of nails … House in the country, here we come!

By the time John drove up the road and around the corner, I had placed six posts and rammed them in until they stood up straight. I, however, couldn't stand up straight to greet him, and my arms had gone numb.

"I saw the horses," John said as he climbed out of the VW bus. He left the headlights on and walked over to me, hands on his hips.

"What the hell have you done to yourself?"

I stood in front of the last post I'd planted, the post driver still on it, my throbbing arms held out in front of me, his oversized gloves hanging off my blistered hands. I held back tears — and grinned broadly.

Proudly, I called to him, "I'm building a fence to keep those fucking horses out of my garden!"

The next day, John and I completed building a secure fence around our trailer that also enclosed the doghouse, my garden, and a play area for Doña. John suggested that we build a stile instead of an ordinary gate at the entrance, modeling it after stiles we had seen in farmers' fields in England. Horses couldn't pass through it … or miscreant goats either. But we could walk through with our hands full. When we finally finished the stile and the fence, I buried my blistered hands and arms in a dishpan filled with cold water. I felt exhilarated when I dug those first few holes, unwise though it may have been, and I wanted to feel that way again. I felt proud to have instigated its construction, and to have taken my turn at pounding in fence posts and stretching the wire with a fence puller. In my mind, it was my fence.

*   *   *

My hands and arms soon healed, and I grew stronger as the weeks and months passed. John came home from work one night shortly after we finished the fence with a pair of leather work gloves for me — my first pair. For weeks afterward, whenever I put them on, I remembered my fury at the horses, and the satisfaction I felt when I hammered in that first fence pole.

9

LEARNING TO BE A FARMER

WE HAD NO SHORTAGE OF PROJECTS to work on that took strength and persistence: unloading bales of alfalfa hay, enlarging and double digging the garden, carrying five-gallon containers of water from the well to my car and from the car to the trailer. I discovered that two five-gallon containers fit perfectly behind the front bucket seats of the Pinto, although I found it challenging to pull them back out again full and carry them to the trailer. I liked to do it when no one was around with an offer of help, because then I could just keep at it, twisting the container this way and that until I got it over the metal lip of the car doorway, through the fence, and up into the trailer.

On weekends, our population swelled with Dorrie's family and John and Quincy's colleagues who enjoyed camping on our land in exchange for labor. There were usually other people around who could help if I got into trouble with a project. After a few weeks, I asked for less help, and felt more able to be a contributing member of our homestead.

I began accompanying Dorrie as she did the "chicken chores." I would dump kitchen scraps into the coop to occupy the chickens while Dorrie collected eggs, changed the water, put mash and pellets in the feeders. On weekends, I helped her rake out the soiled bedding and add new hay, then cart the manure-rich hay over to the garden to be used as compost or mulch. Chicken manure, I learned, is too strong to use directly on the garden. It needed to "mature" for several months in a compost pile before being applied. Soon I found myself feeding the chickens, collecting eggs, and turning compost.

One afternoon, I watched Dorrie milk Dreyfus, her mature Toggenburg goat with a taste for houseplants. Dreyfus calmly munched on alfalfa pellets while Dorrie brushed her underside and udders, then washed her teats with a disinfectant before beginning to milk. Dreyfus had jumped onto the milking stand as soon as Dorrie led her out of the pen; I wondered how one would get a goat on the stand if she wasn't already trained to do so, but left that question for later.

I had read about milking goats in Jerry Belanger's book, *The Homesteader's Handbook to Raising Small Livestock*, but watching Dorrie actually do it made the process much clearer. After cleaning and disinfecting the udder, she pinched off the upper end of Dreyfus' teats with her thumb and forefinger, then expertly emptied the udder with a repetitive motion, each finger in turn drawing the milk from a teat. She directed the milk flow into a large stainless steel pail that looked just like the one carried by milkmaids in Doña's nursery rhyme books. When Dorrie had stripped all the milk from Dreyfus' udder, she poured the milk through a filter into a second, lidded pail to keep it clean until she could pour it into quart containers and put it into the old propane refrigerator we used for storage. Once she did that, she handed me the pail and tossed a third of a bale of alfalfa hay into the pen. Then she raked the old hay into a pile in a corner to be moved to the garden later. She made it all look easy, but I knew that came from years of practice.

Dreyfus had been bred before coming from Dorrie's parents' farm, and had been confirmed to be pregnant.

"I'm going to dry her off soon to allow her body to prepare for the birth of her kids," Dorrie told me one day as she milked. "We'll cut her grain ration in half and only milk her once a day. In a week, we'll stop milking her all together. We'll need to go back to buying our raw milk from a dairy until they're born." Dorrie had introduced me to raw milk when she lived in Los Gatos. Although still nursing, Doña enjoyed having fresh goat milk in her breakfast cereal, and I didn't want to introduce her to pasteurized homogenized grocery store cow's milk any sooner than I had to. She showed no sign of food allergies, and I wanted to keep it that way.

"Kids? How many do you expect?"

"Most does have twins."

After the birth, she explained, Dreyfus would produce much more milk than she was doing now, and we'd have extra for yogurt, cheese, and butter if we wanted. And if she birthed a doe, we would breed her the following year and then we'd have fresh goat milk year round.

By the end of February, a month after John and I joined Dorrie and Quincy on the land, our life had settled into a comfortable routine. John and Quincy drove, usually separately, to their office at ESL in Mountain View, about forty minutes each way. Their different commute schedules reflected their personalities and work habits. Quincy liked to leave the property at first light, returning home in time to do evening chores — and return wandering horses to Carter — before cooking dinner. On the other hand, unless he had an early meeting, John tended to start slowly, puttering about with Doña for a while after I left for school, feeding and dressing her, reading to her, sometimes putting her in the Gerry pack and working on his own projects around the property. He would leave work an hour or two after Quincy, taking Doña to her caregiver, Mrs. Fierro, on the way.

John had always liked to write his computer programs and documentation at night, when the office was quiet, and he rarely came home before 9:00 p.m. Without a telephone, I didn't know exactly when he'd arrive. I had to learn to live with some measure of ambiguity. John talked glowingly of the day when we would all have computers in our homes, and public access to the infant Internet would allow us to communicate online. It couldn't come soon enough for me.

Being wary of the dark, if I came home after sundown, I had to force myself to stay calm while I unloaded the car and carried Doña into the trailer. I always heaved a sigh of relief once I'd fed our rapidly growing German Shepherd, Elsa, and shut the trailer door. Each week I found it a little easier.

Dorrie and I both drove to San Jose each day, about thirty minutes each way. In her second year of nursing school, she attended classes in the morning. In the afternoons and evenings, she had clinical practice, often getting home, like John, long after dark. I left the property at 6:30 a.m. and drove to my student teaching assignment at Morgan Hill School. After lunch, I went to San Jose State to attend classes, getting back to Morgan Hill to retrieve Doña by 5:00 p.m. Sometimes Dorrie and I carpooled, but most of the time our schedules were just enough different that it wasn't feasible.

All of this commuting took place in the midst of the Middle East gas crisis, which had been triggered in 1973 by the Yom Kippur War. Gas lines were long, gas stations were limited in the amount of fuel they could purchase, and regularly ran out the third week of each month, causing us to drive around looking for a station that still had gas. Prices were escalating, too. By the time we moved to the property in Morgan Hill, regular gas cost $.55 a gallon, double what we had paid a year earlier. Each of us spent a certain amount of time every week looking for gas and sitting in hours-long lines once we found it.

I usually fed Doña as soon as she and I arrived home, then we played together and I read and sang to her, bathed her and nursed her to sleep. Water being precious, I depended Mrs. Fierro to give her a proper daily bath. In a short time, her new routine of lying on a towel and being gently massaged with a warm washcloth became Doña's signal that it was bedtime. After she went to sleep, I organized John's and my dinner, ate, and left John's meal in the oven while I studied or did my homework.

One of our purchases in preparation for our move to the land had been the Aladdin oil lamp I had used to work on the fence posts. It gave a bright white light, and made studying at night possible, even pleasant. Sitting in the trailer in the rays of the Aladdin, I could forget that the world outside the trailer had turned pitch black.

After dinner, I usually heated a kettle of water, made a cup of tea, and poured the rest of the hot water into a dishpan with whatever dishes had accumulated since that morning. After they had soaked, I would boil more water for rinsing, add a little cool water to the dishpan, and wash and rinse the dishes. We used far less water than we had in the city, but I didn't feel deprived. We were clean, our dishes were clean, and, if we wanted hot water, we could produce it. I did miss hot showers, though.

I had searched through my parents' garage and located my old manual typewriter from high school. I typed letters and school papers using that. I soon learned to appreciate the time alone after Doña went to sleep and before John came home. When I finished my homework, I wrote in my journal and read poetry or novels, pursuits I hadn't had time for when we were in graduate school. Once I became accustomed to the very dark darkness that came from the absence of street lights, I began to enjoy the stillness and the silence — and even the darkness — of our home.

John and Quincy became known at ESL as the guys whose Vibram-soled boots dropped breadcrumbs of dried mud in the halls, and their colleagues continued to stand in line for the privilege of spending weekends working on our land. In the following months, we put up hundreds of feet of field fencing, enclosing a large communal vegetable garden, a chicken coop, four rabbit hutches, and two goat pens. Quincy even helped me overcome my fear of horses, helping me up onto the back of one and leading it down to Carter's place with me on its bare back. I protested all the way that I would fall off, but I did finally figure out that the horse posed no threat. Day by day, we were on our way to becoming a food-producing farm, and I was on my way to becoming a farmer.

10

MARCH MADNESS

ON A RAIN-FREE SATURDAY IN MARCH, Bill Carter stopped by with a comely woman in his pickup. They got out and, holding hands, came down to the clearing where we were doing our weekend chores. He had a rifle in his hand, and his companion wore a fur coat. I found both of these facts strange and unsettling. Hunting season hadn't started yet — even I knew that — and her fur coat would pick up no end of debris if she wandered around in the brush. I was double-digging the garden and adding compost; I kept my head down, not wanting to be drawn into conversation. Increasingly, Bill Carter gave me the creeps. He swaggered over to John and Quincy, who were unloading supplies from the feed store. Quincy, always friendly, looked up and smiled. John, like me, kept working, piling hay bales beside the goat pen.

"This here is my friend, Meg," Carter began. "I'm going to show her some land up the hill."

"Didn't know you still owned land up there," Quincy said.

"I don't, but Hugh Graves does, and he might want to sell some. Anyway, I thought I'd see about getting me a buck while we're up there." He looked at Meg, his face contorted into a lopsided smirk. "So, if you hear shots, you're not to worry, you hear? And don't call the sheriff, neither. I'd have to split the meat with him."

Quincy spoke quietly.

"You know it's illegal to shoot deer out of season, even on private property."

"Suppose it is? I have an arrangement with Sig Sanchez."

Sig had been the County Supervisor for several terms. Carter had alluded to him before, just before we signed the contract to buy the land. A neighbor down the road had told us about new slope density guidelines requiring that building sites on the hillsides above Chesbro Reservoir be 20 acres or more. When we asked Bob about it, he assured us we'd be able to get our ten acres divided into two parcels and obtain building permits for each one.

"If you have any trouble, just go to Sig Sanchez and tell him Bill Carter sold you the land. He'll square it with the Building Department."

We believed him. For all we knew, that's how things worked around here. We had signed the contract and were making monthly payments on the land.

Carter and Meg returned to the truck and headed up the hill, toward Dorrie and Quincy's future homesteading site. We could hear the truck's raspy engine for a long time, stopping, backing up, starting again on the rutted dirt road. Eventually they drove out of our hearing, probably down the other side of the hill. We put them out of our minds and went back to work.

As dusk fell, we heard them making their way back down, laughing and singing. They sounded drunk, and the closer they got, it became clear that they were. They were on foot, and Meg had removed her fur coat. They came running down the last section of the upper road, racing to the bottom and giggling like children.

"Fuckin' truck got stuck up there. We need a tow."

In the country, neighbors help neighbors, even when they are being foolish and obnoxious. Quincy led Carter to John's truck, Sarge, while John fetched the towing cables and a shovel from the utility shed.

While the men began their ascent of the Adams' hill, Dorrie invited Meg into the school bus for tea, bringing out some biscuits she had made the day before.

"How sweet you've made it in here," Meg gushed.

Even tipsy, Meg seemed friendly, and I relaxed a bit as we chatted. She told us that she and Bill Carter were old friends, and she had recently returned to Morgan Hill after a long absence. She had been looking for a place to live and planning to make some investments.

We were just finishing our tea when we heard the low *chugga chugga* of Sarge's engine.

Meg ran out to greet the men, calling to Bill in a high-pitched sing-song voice, "Welcome back, Loverboy! Wait for me!"

Meg climbed on Sarge and the four of them disappeared down the hill. By the time the guys returned, Dorrie and I had returned to our tasks and pretty much forgotten about the intrusion.

Three months later, we received a certified letter from a bank in San Jose. The writer informed us that the new owner of our mortgage was Margharita Langwell, and instructed us how and where to make our monthly payment. Bill Carter had sold the note on our land to Meg.

$$*\qquad*\qquad*$$

By mid-March, I struggled with my student teaching assignment. My master teacher, a no-nonsense woman, was strict and sometimes caustic, both to her students and to me. Often reeling from her criticism myself, I felt sorry for the children who drew her ire. The school district was on double sessions that year. Her class met from 7:00 a.m. until 12:30 p.m. A second class of children sat in the same desks in the afternoon, taught by a different teacher. Our students came in each morning yawning; many of the youngsters worked in the fields with their parents until dusk. Others took care of younger siblings while their parents worked, sometimes being responsible for family meal preparation as well. Most of these students read below grade level. Consequently, they performed poorly in any subject that required reading. It was nearly impossible for these children, who ranged in age from 11 to 14, to complete the homework expected of 6th graders.

My master teacher had been teaching under these circumstances for years, and seemed to be burned out. She made few concessions to children's limitations, and taught as if everyone could go to the library after school, work at a clean table or desk, and have access to pens, pencils, scissors, and glue. Her assignments would be fun for many children. We were studying Greece, and she encouraged them to make dioramas and write stories about their characters. But children living in migrant housing rarely had a workspace or school supplies.

I drove four boys to the public library one day after school to do some research, and ran aground of the district rules about field trips. Next, I ordered free reading materials from farm equipment companies, and borrowed some high-interest low-reading-level books about race cars for my reading group — the six oldest boys in the class, who had never attended school regularly and were disengaged. We had a good time together once we moved to the school library and started looking for books about Greece, but it didn't take me long to realize that I wouldn't be able to solve the problem in a semester. Trying to do so had made me ill.

I had been plagued with stomachaches for weeks. I'd been drinking milk and eating yoghurt to calm the upset, but now I had sharp pains in my abdomen. I knew I needed to see a doctor. I didn't have a regular physician; hadn't seen anyone but an ob/gyn in years. A friend recommended a woman doctor in Gilroy and I made an appointment.

"You have ulcers," the doctor announced. "What's going on with you?"

I mumbled that it was complicated. *How could I explain my life?*

"Ok, I'll write a prescription for an antacid and pain reliever combination," she said sternly "But only for six months. You can use that time to figure out whatever is going on in your life and fix it. Don't come back for a refill."

I felt like the doctor had scolded me. I took the prescription and crept out of her office., thinking that my father would have had a few choice words for me too. The medicine helped with the pain, but it made me constipated. In six months, student teaching would be behind me, and I could go back to drinking milk whenever I needed to soothe my stomach.

My respect began to grow for my mother-in-law, who prepared lesson plans for six grade levels every week at Mt. Hamilton School. I drew on her methods and examples as I prepared my own lessons, including individualized contracts and peer tutoring. In a few weeks, I would be expected to teach the whole class, and I hoped I could show my master teacher a more sympathetic way to present the material and engage the students in learning it.

*   *   *

The stray cat we adopted in Virginia, who John had named Newton, went missing in March. During a morning walk, John heard sad little mews coming from under a shrub. Newton had been listless for several days and he'd been vomiting. The vet said he'd probably eaten something poisonous. He injected him with antibiotics and subcutaneous fluids, but the little cat was too far gone and he died in my car on the way home. I pulled over, tears of anger streaming down my cheeks. The rat poison Bill Carter had set out to deter rattlesnakes had probably killed Newton. My stomach always churned when I thought about Carter, and by the time I pulled myself together and drove home I felt ill.

We buried Newton under the shrub where John had found him. A few weeks later, Elsa led John to a coyote bush not far away, where he found our beloved Scamper, our latest missing feline, also poisoned. Scamper, a female tabby, had been with us since San Diego, traveling in the VW bus to New Mexico, Washington D.C., and Mount Hamilton. Scamper looked like she was sleeping, but of course she wasn't. John felt too sad to face burying her at first, but the next day he constructed a wooden box and dug a deep hole under the bush where he had found her. Sitting nearby with Doña on my lap, I read *The Tenth Good Thing About Barney,* by Judith Viorst. I doubt that Doña understood what we were doing, but she liked the story. John and I agreed not to acquire any more animals until rattlesnakes returned to the property. They would be like the canary in a coalmine, only opposite. Instead of alerting us to danger, they would be the harbinger of balance in the ecosystem.

Eventually, the effects of Bill Carter's rodent poison did wear off, and rats, mice, and rattlers all joined the list of fauna living on our land. When the snakes began to appear, John set up his archery course for rifle and pistol practice and honed his target-shooting skills. I joined him a few times. John had taught me how to shoot his .22 pistol at a range in Virginia. Now I added a .22 rifle to my skill set. We both respected the balance of nature, but neither of us wanted a rattler — or a mountain lion — to approach our daughter as she played in the grass. He promised me he would only shoot critters that posed a danger to Doña.

During the years we lived on the land, only three rattlesnakes came into our clearing, and John shot all three with his pistol. One ended up in our freezer. He roasted it on the grill and offered pieces to each of us. It tasted, according to him, "like chicken."

*   *   *

When it rained hard, I sometimes took the children to the public library where they could stretch out and look at books, color, play with Legos. One afternoon while we were seeking respite from the weather, I decided to use some of the library's resources to research the history of our land and the surrounding area. I learned that this part of California had originally been made up of Spanish Land grants, honored by the new government when California was ceded to the United States following the Mexican-American War. The ranchos nearest us had colorful names like Rancho Ojo de Agua de la Coche, Rancho San Francisco de las Llagas, and Rancho Las Uvas. The latter parcel had been owned for many years by Catherine O'Toole Murphy Dunne, who passed it to her son Martin J. C. Murphy. Catherine Dunne received the ranch when she married the elder Murphy, and she had become the largest landholder in northern California by the time she died. I didn't know it yet, but one of my children would one day attend Martin Murphy Middle School, named for the man who had once owned our land.

Had Catherine ever walked along our road, stood on the top of the hill and looked down over the tree-covered land? Tasted the miner's lettuce? Slept under the stars and awakened to a red and orange fairyland? I supposed not, but she might have ridden her horse up to our land to inspect her property. I liked to think about that. I loved reading about all the people who had lived in this valley. In 1882, an entrepreneur named Hiram Morgan Hill married Diana Helen Murphy, the daughter of Martin Murphy. Wanting to attract developers to the Santa Clara Valley, Hiram Morgan Hill built a railway station in the town that bore his name, and publicized The Valley of Heart's Delight, printing thousands of handbills promoting the climate and rich soil.

And there we were, nearly a hundred years later, staking our savings and our livelihood on a piece of land. We were young, idealistic and hopeful. Each morning, I looked gratefully out at the trees and the shrubs and the flowers, and listened to the birds who shared the land with us.

We were indeed living in the Valley of Heart's Delight.

11

SPRING BREAK

I LOVED LIVING ON THE LAND, and I loved living near our friends, but I don't want to give the impression that everything was sunshine and roses all the time. For one, John was an introvert. The presence of Quincy and Dorrie's frequent weekend visitors drove him inside our tiny trailer or off the hill entirely. He would invent errands to run or deadlines at work, climb into his car, and disappear.

Another way John responded to the jollity and activities of Dorrie's family or Quincy's friends was to be rude. He would sit in a chair beside the trailer working on a solitary project, like whittling a toy for Doña, or solving one of Martin Gardner's mathematic puzzles in *Scientific American*. He would refuse all offers to participate in group activities. The objects of his annoyance had no idea why he wouldn't join in, or why he was so grumpy; at other times he acted normally and seemed to enjoy the communal experience.

I enjoyed the weekend visitors. We saved big projects for when we had these extra hands, and the efficiency and enjoyment of working together allowed us to accomplish many impressive tasks together. The shared meals that followed such a day of industry were usually accompanied by music, and I loved that too. I played mediator between John and the others when I could, or found useful things for him to do that took his mind off the party going on at the other side of the clearing. I didn't play an instrument, but I sang along with joy.

The rest of the week, our land was peaceful. John happily puttered about our camp in the mornings, feeding animals or filling their water containers, tinkering with Sarge's engine, or building something. After I came home from school in the late afternoons, I savored the ambiance of the woods and fields, planting or weeding or watering the garden, hiking or playing with Doña, cooking, or relaxing in the hammock.

Until Quincy arrived. He usually came home from work before dark in order to do the evening milking and feeding, and, like John, he had a number of projects going. As he mucked out animal pens, filled water troughs, or measured lumber, Quincy liked to accompany his labors with a soundtrack of country music or sporting events. He had purchased a pocket-sized transistor radio for that purpose, and he would tuck it in his shirt pocket or clip it to his belt. Ear buds weren't a thing yet, and the headphones of the day were bulky and hot. Whatever country songs KFAT radio transmitted to the airwaves would break the silence, quiet the birds, and interrupt my reverie. Weekends without visitors were even worse. Quincy seemed to need to fill the silence with sound. Out came the radio again. And this time we were all treated to the sounds of some kind of ball game.

In the interest of communal harmony, I rarely said anything, and I eventually learned to enjoy country music. I found it more difficult to be pleasant when Quincy's radio broadcast sharp-voiced announcers chronicling each play of a baseball, basketball, or football game. One of the characteristics of my husband that had originally appealed to me was that he had no interest in sports, and our Thanksgiving dinners had never been marred by the presence of a television set surrounded by a circle of cheering fans. I never understood the draw.

When Quincy listened to his favorite teams, the 49ers or the Giants, working out of doors within hearing of his radio felt like a penance. Especially that time when the Golden State Warriors were in the finals for the championship. Not only did we have to listen to the games, Quincy carried on an intense conversation with the players, the coach and the umpires, shouting his disagreement with plays or calls and breaking into loud cheers when things were going his way.

Quincy and his radio were on my mind one day as I drove to the Santa Clara County office building in San Jose. One solution to us grating on each other as we were doing would be to move forward on the land division and help Dorrie and Quincy move to the top of the hill. It was April, still too soon to move their school bus up the road, but not to get the paperwork started for the land division. I had decided to spend as much of my Easter Break as necessary to educate myself about land divisions and building permits.

I had spent an hour in the garden before leaving the land that day, and hoped to get back to it in the evening. The soil was rich and loose. I'd pulled a wheelbarrow full of weeds and planted some early vegetables — radishes, lettuce, carrots, and onions. Since my baby plants had been destroyed by Carter's horses, I planted seeds directly into the ground, which was warming up nicely, yet was still damp from the heavy rains we'd had all winter. I'd already harvested one crop of radishes and lettuce, and was planting more in the empty rows they'd left.

My first visit to the public works department did not go well. I arrived just before noon and drove around for fifteen minutes looking for a parking place. By the time I had Doña and her toys loaded up, and my bundle of land-related papers gathered, an exodus was taking place at the building. I persisted, looking up the room number on the directory by the stairs, then patiently followed Doña up the stairs as she took them deliberately and slowly, one foot at a time. When we reached the correct door, the clock on the wall read 12:30.

CLOSED FOR LUNCH 12:30 — 1:30 read the sign on the door. Not having a telephone at home, I had not phoned the department to learn its open hours. I sat on the floor beside the door, took out Doña's toys, and waited. The dark wood walls smelled of furniture polish and musty attic — a fragrance that I would encounter often over the next few years, and which to this day I associate with our lengthy quest to build on our land.

A line had formed behind me by the time the office opened and, upon reaching the counter, I learned that most of the people in line had appointments. I made one for the following day and we went home. The following day, I arrived for my appointment at 10:00 and explained our situation and asked how to apply for a land division and secure a use permit to put a 40-foot trailer on our land.

"You can't do both at once, dear," said the smarmy man in a sing-song voice, smiling at this ignorant woman who didn't know procedure. "You'll need to complete the land division before you can apply for any permits. Start out by completing this packet of papers and bring it back."

It took the rest of the week to collect all the information required on the forms and signatures from Dorrie and Quincy and John. On Friday, Doña and I once more entered the hallowed halls of the county offices and made our way up the broad staircase. I handed the packet of papers to the clerk, who flipped through them quickly.

"I see your contract with William Carter," he said at last, "but I can't find the title. You'll need to go to the County Recorder's office and get a copy."

"But they haven't received it," I explained. "We keep asking Carter to file the property transfer, and he keeps saying he will, but he hasn't."

"Well you can't divide a tract of land that you don't legally own, ma'am," pushing the packet of papers back across the counter. "Come back when you have title — and bring a copy."

I collected applications for a geologic survey and a well test, a list of vendors who sold 500-gallon water tanks, and a phone number to schedule a fire inspection after we laid the water pipe between the well and the tank.

This was going to take a while.

12

POULTRY 101

A S A CHILD, I HAD CHICKENS IN MY LIFE. After sailing to New York from England, my parents and I traveled by train to a large poultry farm in Zephyrhills, Florida, where for the next year we lived and worked with my mother's aunt and uncle. As a two-year-old, I dressed the hens in doll clothes and put them to bed (or tried) in the little wooden crib that my father had built. I learned to collect eggs and place them gently in a basket, but I also liked to chase the young chickens (called pullets) around the garden when they were let out to forage.

When I turned five, we moved to Australia, where my grandfather reigned over the family chicken coop. He would not tolerate dress-ups or playing tag with the laying hens, but he did allow me to collect eggs, carefully supervised, and to scatter grain inside their pen. I was also sometimes present when he chopped the head off our dinner, and enjoyed playing with a tendon on a severed foot that made the claws move. Creepy as that may sound, my children would one day do the same.

I loved living with chickens again. Keeping a flock of clucking creatures that ate kitchen scraps and bugs, provided eggs for the table and fertilizer for the garden, seemed like a remarkably synergistic endeavor, and appealed to my sense of order. Unfortunately, it wasn't practical for me to have my own coop just yet. Dorrie already kept a flock of chickens in a converted pigeon coop, and they laid enough eggs for the five of us. Instead, I would assume some of their care until Dorrie and Quincy moved up the hill at the end of the rainy season. I enjoyed waking up to the rooster's alarm and listening to the flock's conversational muttering and periodic announcements that a new egg was waiting for us. The first time I collected eggs, the smell of dusty lime that Dorrie sprinkled in the nest boxes took me right into my childhood; and I almost found myself looking around for Granddad.

Eventually we would be raising our own chicks, and culling the flock to remove the males and non-laying females. Butchering would be in our future, but I didn't dwell on that. We named some of the chickens, and I began to recognize differences in their personalities and egg-laying proclivities.

Droptail was our clown chicken. Part of the starter flock that had come from Dorrie's family farm, she was a mature layer, a confident Rhode Island Red. Alert and wary, she was the first to sound the alarm when a hawk flew overhead, or one of the dogs got too curious. Her tail hung down like a folded peacock fan. We assumed it had been broken early in life. She had a way of cocking her head sideways when she listened to something. I enjoyed having "conversations" with her — she looked like she listened to everything I said.

Perhaps the most memorable characteristic of this venerable chicken was that when Dorrie and Quincy let the flock out to forage, she would head for the front left tire of the school bus, settle herself on top of it, and lay an egg. Then she would happily jump off the wheel, preen her feathers, cluck contentedly, and announce her achievement to the world. After making sure we had all heard her, she happily scratched and scavenged among the grasses and shrubs for the rest of the day.

We tried a number of things to keep Droptail from laying on the tire, including locking her in the hen house, but she complained loudly, clucking and jumping at the door repeatedly until, exhausted, she would lay her egg wherever she lay. She was obviously so unhappy about this solution that eventually we gave up and simply collected her egg from the school bus tire each day. Fortunately, Quincy had invested in mud and snow tires for the school bus before driving it to the property. Because the treads were deep, Droptail's egg usually stayed put for a while. We all took to listening for her "I did it!" song, then running over to the bus to retrieve her egg before some other chicken roosted there and knocked it off. All the other chickens eventually learned to lay their eggs in the henhouse, but Droptail never did.

Along with Dorrie's flock of Rhode Island Red and Plymouth Rock hens came one chicken who stood out due to her looks: Flora Fashionista. A black and white Polish hen and, like others of her breed, she sported a large high crest of feathers on her head, full and circular and quite impressive. Once kept as a pet, Flora had been sent along in the flock Mummy and Pooby transported from San Luis Obispo to Morgan Hill. Smaller than the other chickens, she was large for a Polish, and knew it. She strutted about with great dignity and flair, her white crest bobbing wildly as she scratched around for bugs.

"Watch her closely for a while," Pooby warned when he delivered the chickens. "She thinks she's hot stuff, but she's actually at the bottom of the pecking order." Gazing in her direction, he gestured at the feeders. "Sometimes the chickens will peck at her when she's eating or drinking and not paying attention to them."

We did keep a watch on her for the first week, and chased off the offenders or let them all out to forage, which seemed to relieve the tension. After a while, the other chickens stopped attacking her and she was accepted into the flock.

One week in April, while we were picking up supplies at Gunter Brothers, Dorrie impulsively purchased a dozen turkey poults and some ducklings. "We'll have a couple of turkeys for Thanksgiving, and sell the others," she announced as we made our way to the check-out counter. "The pigeon pen is large enough. We can keep the turkeys and ducks in with the chickens, at least for a while."

The babies were only ten days old, and even I knew they would need to be kept warm for several weeks before they could be put in with the others. On our way home, we stopped at a personal storage company and bought a large box. When we arrived home, I appropriated John's metal clip light from the tool shed to provide heat. Turkey poults are really ugly, and we discovered they are also dumb. We had to show them how to eat the starter mash, pressing their little heads down so their beaks were all the way in the food. Sometimes a turkey poult would give up too easily and sit down in a corner. We would then carry the bird over to the feeder and make a place for it.

Once they got the hang of it, a feeding frenzy occurred every time we put the fresh mash in the box. In a few weeks' time, the turkeys were twice the size of the ducklings, and becoming bullies at feeding time. The six poults could easily take over the whole feeding station, leaving the ducks sitting in the piled-up shavings around the edges of the box.

The next time we went into Gunter Brothers, we explained the situation, and Merv suggested that we feed them separately. "And move them as soon as you can into separate brood boxes. It's only going to get worse as the turkeys get bigger," he warned. "Besides, the turkeys need more protein than the ducks, and less calcium than either the ducks or your chickens. Chick starter feed isn't good for them."

Dorrie hadn't known that and obviously neither had I. We had been feeding all the birds chicken food.

Merv suggested turkey starter feed for the poults, and duck starter feed for the ducks, or chicken starter feed thinned down with oatmeal to lower the protein level for a while, and supplemented with brewer's yeast to add niacin, which ducks need more of than any of the three.

Trying not to think about the impact on our feed budget, I procured another box and another light, lined the box with shavings, and moved the ducks into it. I wrote the recipe for duck feed on a card, and stapled it to the box.

I had noticed that the ducks made a poopy mess right after eating. We started to replace their shavings almost every day. They also outgrew their water dishes. They could still drink out of them, but they couldn't swim in them, which is what they wanted to do. We replaced the flat dishes with proper waterers, quart bottles with screwed on metal lids with small circular openings for the chicks and ducks to put their beaks into. We took the ducks out of the box once in a while to play in Doña's pink bathtub in which we put an inch of water. They loved it … but then I had to scrub the tub with soapy water and bleach to clean out all the duck poop they deposited in it — a nuisance and a waste of water. I wasn't sure this was such a great idea.

Eventually we started letting the growing birds out to forage. Within days, several chicks, ducklings and turkey poults drowned in buckets that had filled with rainwater. I hadn't realized the little guys could fly that high, and started storing all the buckets upside down. Still, on the whole, our young poultry herd thrived, and our homestead grew.

Then Mrs. Fierro's chicken arrived on the scene, and our problems started all over again. Her arrival was both sudden and unexpected. That morning we had realized that we were all low on gas. John and Quincy and I decided to drive to work and school together, looking for open gas stations on the way. We stopped in San Jose to take Doña to Mrs. Fierro's, then went on to Sunnyvale to drop John and Quincy at ESL. Dorrie had agreed to pick up the men after her shift and bring them home.

I didn't have time to chat with Mrs. Fierro when we got there, or to help Doña transition into her care. I just handed her over and left. We hadn't found any open gas stations in Morgan Hill, and the stations I went to in Sunnyvale after delivering the men to work were out of gas. I finally found an open station in San Jose near Spartan Stadium. I had just enough time to put $1.00 worth in my tank, find a parking place, and race to class.

After lunch, I drove south to retrieve Doña, and discovered that the honeymoon was over. Mrs. Fierro, in love with our little girl the first week of classes, said that Doña had cried most of the day, and that nothing she had done would make her happy. She went on quite a bit, complaining that Doña expected too much attention, and she wouldn't pick up her toys.

Since Mrs. Fierro described normal toddler behavior, even with the best of morning transitions, I figured that she had just been having a bad day. Suddenly, she left the room and came back carrying a box holding a large red hen.

"You take our chicken?" She asked, when she returned. "My family not want it anymore."

She explained that she had bought four baby chicks for her children the previous Easter. The children loved them at first, but once they were fully-grown, they lost interest. Mrs. Fierro had been letting the hens forage in the garden and collecting their eggs, which they laid randomly here and there. The week before, a neighborhood dog had killed three of the chickens, and really upset the family. She didn't want this one to have the same fate.

"Please will you take to your farm?" Her look was pleading.

I wanted to keep Mrs. Fierro happy. I took the chicken and, on the way home, I told Doña the story of the Little Red Hen. I told myself Doña would like having her own pet chicken, as I had. I drove up the road to the property with Doña and Mrs. Fierro's chicken, singing "Old MacDonald had a chicken, *ee-yi-ee-yi-oh.*"

Meanwhile, the soon-to-be barnyard fowl began making little mewling sounds that Doña thought were "cute."

I put Mrs. Fierro's chicken into the coop with Dorrie's flock. Flora Fashionista immediately attacked her, then several of the other hens began chasing her around the fenced-in yard. Not sure how else to stop them, I let them all out of the enclosure to forage. The home flock left the newcomer alone for the moment.

I left Doña with Dorrie later that day while I drove back into town to meet with my master teacher. When I arrived home, Dorrie sat on a stump, watching Doña chase Mrs. Fierro's chicken around. The hen was so tame, it would let Dorrie pick it up and put it in Doña's arms. She did so while I watched. Doña immediately put the chicken in her red wagon. It reminded me of my own childhood chicken adventures. Watching Doña made me happy. We would have to think up a name for this chicken. We couldn't keep calling her "Mrs. Fierro's Chicken" forever.

After Doña went to bed, I took four lemons I had bought at the farmer's market and made some lemon curd. While I stirred the slowly-heating mixture, I started plotting a children's story about a pet chicken that went to visit a farm. I didn't have any classes on Fridays. I would have three days to get the trailer tidied and my homework finished, and still have time to type a draft of my story. On Monday, I would be back to student teaching and my writing would take a back seat to preparing curriculum.

On Saturday, I awakened to the sounds of plaintive cries from the chicken pen. John and I both ran to the pen to let Mrs. Fierro's chicken out of the yard. The sight of the deep wounds on her head and back made me wince. While I dressed them with iodine, Dorrie said some of them probably came from Rudy the rooster trying to mount her. I was in a quandary about what to do. I realized that Rudy was not going to give up easily, but she ran away every time he came near her, and that encouraged the other chickens to chase her too.

And she hadn't yet laid an egg. On a working farm, Dorrie said, every chicken had to pull her weight. If Mrs. Fierro's chicken wouldn't lay, she'd have to go. Neither John nor I had much stomach for butchering, let alone murdering a chicken that had been raised as a pet. We let the rest of the chickens out to scavenge, and put off our decision. It was early days yet. Surely she would lay an egg soon.

We needed propane and fencing material. After breakfast, Dorrie drove into town in Quincy's pickup. Dorrie, Doña, and I sat in front. Quincy's brother, Buzz, and Dorrie's sister, Lindy, who were visiting for the weekend, rode in the truck bed. John and Quincy stayed home to plan building projects.

On the way to town, Dorrie kept the windows open so we could talk to Lindy and Buzz. The warm May air blew across the cab, lifting my hair. Singing snatches of folk songs, *Blowing in the Wind* and *If I had a Hammer*, we entertained Doña and the people we passed on the way. I saw someone lean back on a rake to watch us.

Dorrie asked Merv about our first litter of rabbits, which had all been born dead. He said that wasn't unusual for a new mother, especially one who had been moved recently. He suggested we breed her again, then cover the front of her cage with burlap so she felt safer. I felt reassured by his remarks. It didn't take long to load the truck at Gunter Brothers, and Lindy and Buzz climbed into the back beside our supplies. This time Dorrie put the radio on and we sang along with John Denver's new release, *Annie's Song:*

You fill up my senses like a night in the forest
Like the mountains in springtime, like a walk in the rain.

We were young and in high spirits, and we sang enthusiastically. We felt like legitimate residents. We'd stopped worrying what the townspeople thought of us.

When we got back to the property, we hauled the propane tank into place at the back of our trailer and rolled the wire over to Dorrie's compound. We enlarged the chicken pen, made a separate area for the turkeys and the ducks, and, at the end of our workday, made supper together. That night we retired to our various castles — the school bus, the trailer, and two tents under the big oak tree. It had been a wonderful day and, as I climbed into bed beside Doña, I reflected on it. Our life in the country was beginning to take form, and it felt wonderful.

On Monday, I picked Doña up after school and went to the public library to research poultry management. I read that when you introduce a new chicken to an established flock, it's best to keep it in a separate cage inside the chicken yard at first. One author recommended introducing two or three chickens at a time so that the inevitable pecking didn't fall on just one bird. When it's time to let the new chickens out of the small cage, that author suggested doing it at night. I also learned that we could get eggs from a chicken without the aid of a rooster. I felt pretty stupid when I read that. I'm sure Dorrie (and probably everyone else) knew that already, but for some reason I had thought the hens needed to be fertilized by the rooster for her to lay eggs. On the way home, Doña fell asleep and I began designing a second chicken coop. We would buy some more chicks and give Mrs. Fierro's chicken a flock of her own.

Too bad I hadn't done the research earlier. When we got home, I climbed out of the car to a pile of red feathers and a very dead chicken just inside our fence. Her death had been so unexpected and so dramatic that I just stood there, hand over mouth, paralyzed with horror. What had she been doing inside our enclosure, and who had killed her?

As I stood there, glued to the ground, our adolescent German Shepherd, Elsa, peeked out from under the trailer with blood on her muzzle. She slowly crawled, her stomach close to the ground, looking guilty and ashamed. She must have been under the trailer when Dorrie put Mrs. Fierro's chicken inside our fence. I could imagine Elsa emerging to investigate the new sounds, then ambushing the hapless

100

chicken. Dogs like to chase chickens — it's a fact of life — and I learned an important lesson that day: even if you don't believe they are a danger, always keep dogs in separate enclosures from the chickens.

After my paralysis lifted, I became totally undone by the scene in front of me. I collapsed on a nearby bench and ran my shaky hands through my hair, trying to decide what to do. Should I bury Mrs. Fierro's chicken or wait until Doña woke up?

While I mentally dithered about the developmental value of introducing the concept of death to a toddler, I heard my father's voice. "You brainless child," he reprimanded. "What were you thinking, leaving a dog free on a farm? It should be chained up or kept in a pen."

I started crying. Yes, I'd screwed up. Again. But surely this was also a case of miscommunication. I learned later that Dorrie had put her in there to protect her from the other chickens. Dorrie didn't know Elsa slept under the trailer — besides, her dogs never bothered the chickens. How was she to know Elsa would? For that matter, how was I to know? I could have made the same decision. I took a deep breath and ordered my father's voice to leave me alone. It didn't help.

Just then, Buzz drove up in his big red four-wheel drive Scout. He jumped out, took one look at the pile of chicken and feathers, glanced at me, then picked up Mrs. Fierro's chicken by one leg and carried her down the hill. I swept up the feathers and unloaded the car. Everything was clean and tidy by the time Doña awakened. I put a blanket down on the grass. Buzz entertained her while I got us a couple of beers and some snacks, then I told him the whole story. It felt good to share my misgivings about being responsible for farm animals with so little knowledge. Buzz didn't care. He would be gone the next day. But he did seem sympathetic.

"You can learn this stuff," he said, after quietly listening to my confession. "Get some books, subscribe to Mother Earth News. Don't depend on Dorrie to teach you everything. Actually, she doesn't know everything." He took a swig of beer and looked stern. At that moment, long red hair crowning his tanned face, he reminded me of an Oracle from Greek mythology. "Find some 4-H people in town. They'll teach you everything you need to know about chickens. Rabbits and goats, too. Children raise those animals for the County Fair. Surely you can too."

I decided he was right. Still feeling discouraged, though, I couldn't get started on any productive work the rest of the day.

Finally, I put something together for John and Doña to eat and drove to my Spanish class — a good diversion. For several hours I didn't think about Mrs. Fierro's chicken. But on the way home, the sadness pressed in on me again. I would have to explain to Mrs. Fierro what had happened to her chicken. Living on the land was not turning out to be as simple or romantic as I had imagined it would be.

As soon as finals were over in June, I went back to the county offices again. I spent several hours dragging Doña between three different buildings at opposite ends of San Jose. I went to Engineering Services, the Planning Commission, the Sanitation Department, and the County Assessor, asking each one for everything they could tell me about how to move our land division forward and get a use permit for a trailer. I learned about building site reports, site approvals, septic tank permits, well pump testing, percolation tests, road easements, assessment maps, and who our neighbors were on all sides. But, since we still didn't have title to our land, I wasn't any closer to getting a use permit. Finally, I collapsed into a little park near downtown, took the picnic lunch out of my knapsack, and let Doña play.

The next day I went to the lawyer Quincy had hired in San Jose to pick up the reservoir easement verification form. Before going home, I drove south to the San Martin Office of Sanitation to find out what I could do about the rejection of our applications for a geologic survey and a water analysis, which I had submitted in May. The sanitation officer told me that our well was suspect due to the low water table, something Carter had failed to mention. Before we could move forward with the geologic survey and the water analysis we would need to submit the results of a pump test. That would indicate how much water we could expect to get over a certain amount of time. Could we do this ourselves? No, we needed to use an "authorized" well tester. The clerk gave me a list of names. More money.

Shortly afterwards, John brought home a deconstructed windmill lashed to the back of Sarge. It was rusty and dirty, but you might have thought it was the Crown Jewels the way John strutted and bragged about his find. "We can forget about getting electricity out here through

PG&E," he boasted. "We'll use wind power to pump our water. And you'll be able to use your electric typewriter!" He took the parts out of the bed of the truck, set them on his outdoor work table, and covered them with a tarp.

"We'll have electricity soon," he reassured me at dinner that night. "Real soon."

13

AN UNEXPECTED CHALLENGE

DREYFUS, DORRIE'S PREGNANT GOAT, WAS DEAD. She lay on a tarp beside the trailer, her neck broken. I reached down to stroke her. Her light brown fur felt soft, her body still supple. Dorrie and Quincy sat on the tarp beside her, holding hands. Their eyes were damp.

I waited to feel sad, but the bile that rose in my throat was bitter. I was angry. Dreyfus's kids were due to be born in less than a month. Now we would never get to hold them, to bottle-feed them, watch them grow. I felt cheated. I wanted to punch someone. Dorrie reached for my shaking hands. I knelt down and put my arm around her. John crouched beside me, his tears flowing.

"Dorrie, I'm so very sorry. What happened?"

"Dreyfus got out of the pen and grazed across the clearing. We found her down the hill. She must have slipped on the dry grass. She was getting really big and awkward."

I saw the crushed grass where they had dragged her body back up the hill, and smelled the fresh hay scent, but I couldn't believe that she was actually dead. She looked like she was just sleeping. Why had she fallen? Weren't goats supposed to be sure-footed? Reverentially, John laid his shirt across her upper body, covering her eyes. Quincy folded the tarp over the rest of her.

Now the sadness came, and with it the tears. I had fed Dreyfus just the night before, and wondered what her kids would look like. Would they have the same white ears and nose as her mother, and the tiny caprine horns? I imagined welcoming the first goats to be born on our land, maybe even watching them being born.

Now, trying to diffuse the emotions that threatened to overwhelm me, I breathed from my belly, then clenched and unclenched my hands. But the tears still flowed. I was lightheaded. I closed my eyes and put my head between my knees.

This wasn't how it was supposed to be. In the first four months on the land, we'd already buried two litters of dead baby rabbits, a dozen chicks, several ducklings and turkey poults and Mrs. Fierro's chicken. Now we had a dead goat and two dead kids. Our animals seemed to be cursed. Or were we just inept?

The situation felt surreal. John and I had been away for most of the day, attending a wedding in Santa Cruz. It had been a beautiful event, and we stayed until the very end, visiting with friends we hadn't seen in years. Driving home over the Santa Cruz Mountains, we had marveled at the magnificent trees on either side of the road and opened our windows so we could enjoy the warm summer air. Those feelings of contentment and well-being had now been shattered. Just then Doña cried out from the Pinto. She had fallen asleep on the way home. Wiping his eyes, John went to get her.

Dorrie wiped her own eyes and continued her story. "We drove into town this afternoon to run errands. After loading hay and grain and groceries into the truck, we thought we'd treat ourselves to dinner at that little deli we'd noticed on Monterey Highway: Mission Trails. We were only gone a couple of hours."

To my mind, this was all about fencing. Our acrobatic animals had learned that if they stood on the top of the wire fence, they could push it down the metal posts and eventually walk right over it. Or sometimes the makeshift gate failed. We closed it by inserting a post into a ring of wire top and bottom, and the goats had figured out how to push the top ring off the post. They'd been getting out of the pen and into mischief as long as we'd lived on the land.

Angry words formed in my throat. "For Christ's sake, why didn't you guys fix the fence? You've certainly had long enough." I swallowed them.

This wasn't the time to think about blame or regret. We'd clearly have to re-engineer the goat pen, but first we had a problem to solve. What should we do with the goat?

I looked around for John and Doña. The light shone in our trailer and the door was closed. John had taken refuge. I hoped he was settling Doña back to sleep. Dorrie, Quincy, and I gathered in their school bus to figure out what to do, trusting that he would join us when he could.

Dorrie wanted us to hang Dreyfus' carcass up right away, cut her throat, and bleed her.

"Why?" I asked, aghast.

"To preserve the meat."

In addition to growing up on a farm, Dorrie had hunted with her father and brother. She had a working knowledge of field-dressing deer. She had seen goats and pigs slaughtered and butchered at her parents' ranch, although she had never personally participated in the process.

"Otherwise the blood will get into the muscles and ruin the meat."

I retched at the thought of cutting Dreyfus' throat. And I didn't think I could eat a goat whose name I knew.

"But will the meat even be edible? She's — what — five years old?"

"It will have a strong flavor, like venison, but we can slather it in barbecue sauce and serve her to our guests tomorrow. It'll save us buying hamburgers and steaks."

Oh God, the party! For several weeks we'd been planning a barbecue open house to celebrate our move to the land and coincide with John's 35th birthday on June 15. We'd invited a ton of people — friends, family, neighbors, and all our regular weekend visitors — to come and see our homestead. A dead goat hadn't been in the plans.

Dorrie had planned to hire Gully Foster, who owned a mobile abattoir, when the time came to butcher any Billy goats that were born in the future, but it was a Saturday. Isn't it always a weekend when things like this happen? It was late, and it was still hot. We didn't have time to drive to town to see if Gully was available, and, even if we managed to reach him, we would have to pay for his services, as well as rent a meat locker. We had no refrigerator large enough for a full-grown goat. All of these thoughts swirled in my head as I pondered what Dorrie was suggesting and tried to understand what she was going through. I guessed she felt especially guilty because Dreyfus, a mature milk goat, was a gift from her parents, meant to be a valuable asset on our farm. She had been named Dreyfus for the investment company of the same name. Dorrie's parents considered the pregnant goat to be an investment in their daughter's homesteading venture. Perhaps Dorrie believed that saving Dreyfus' meat would minimize the loss.

Coming to terms with herd management had been a tough lesson for John and me. As our small animal population had burgeoned, we had painfully learned how to kill and butcher chickens and rabbits, and even managed to eat them. We had not yet participated in castrating or slaughtering any larger animals. I didn't look forward to it.

Besides being an experienced hunter and farmer, Dorrie was training to be a nurse. The rest of us thought she well prepared to lead this project. After some back and forth, she agreed to make the initial cut, but she didn't think she had the strength needed to remove the pelt. I naively imagined that hanging the goat and bleeding her was all we needed to do that night. I urged us to go ahead. John had indeed put Doña to bed in the trailer while the three of us were talking. When he returned, he helped Quincy locate a high branch near enough to the trailer that we could hear Doña if she awakened.

The men searched through their rope supplies and selected a nylon line that they judged to be strong enough. I had watched John throw lines over tall trees in the Sierras to hang our food bag high in the air, safe from bears, so I wasn't surprised to see him successfully lob the rope over a high bough in the big oak and fasten a pulley to it. I wondered how well he would manage the next steps, however.

John and Quincy hoisted Dreyfus by her hind legs, head down, not an easy task. A full-grown Toggenburg female weighs from 130 to 135 pounds, and the kids probably added another ten pounds. John fetched the large cast iron soup pot that I had planned to use as a planter, and set it under her head to catch the blood and internal organs. Dorrie brought a large bowl from her trailer and asked us to catch as much of the blood as we could in that. She wanted to use it to make sausages and fertilizer. Her practicality amazed me. She was such a gentle person, and it was her goat, but she appeared calm, the calmest of any of us. We had all been kind of flailing around, looking at her for direction, and she had risen to the occasion. I didn't realize it yet, but living on this hill would develop that kind of strength in the rest of us too.

While the men were preparing the hoist and hanging Dreyfus from the branch, Dorrie sharpened her knife. She said a prayer of thanksgiving for the lives of the mother goat and her babies, and for the meat we would enjoy. She then cleanly cut the jugular vein, holding the head down so the blood would run into the bowl Quincy and John were holding above the iron pot.

I took a deep breath just before Dorrie made the cut and held it for a very long time. Seeing the dark red blood and smelling its metallic scent made it real. By this time, the light had faded. The men wanted Dorrie to continue her cut and remove the intestines and internal organs, but she demurred.

"I don't think so, guys. I'm pretty sure my father skinned his goats before gutting them."

"Let's just leave the carcass hanging overnight, then," suggested John. "We can wrap it in a tarp to protect it from the dogs or coyotes or mountain lions."

Quincy didn't like that idea, and I didn't either — I didn't want a coyote or mountain lion sniffing around outside our door. But we weren't sure how to proceed from there. Hopefully, I offered my book and magazine collection. I thought I had seen an article about butchering goats in there somewhere.

"Someone needs to drive into town and buy some ice," Dorrie said. "It's going to be a hot night, and that could spoil the meat. We'll need enough ice to chill the carcass once we skin it and gut it. Several large bags I think."

John volunteered to do that. While he drove to town, Dorrie, Quincy, and I met in our trailer to do the research. I pulled the curtain across the bed and reminded Dorrie and Quincy to keep their voices low so as not to awaken Doña. I lit my Aladdin lamp, brought out a bottle of wine, and began to search through my books and magazines while Dorrie rummaged for glasses. I had compiled a small library of farm management books and a series called *Foxfire* that contained interviews with elders in rural communities on topics ranging from blacksmithing to whittling. Quincy found an old livestock magazine with an article titled *Butchering Sheep, Deer and Goat* that illustrated the steps involved. We took the lamp, our wine, and the magazine outside and pored over the article until we understood what we were facing.

The author confirmed Dorrie's recollection: goats and sheep should be skinned before gutting. To my surprise, Dorrie wanted John to do that part. A year earlier he had gone elk hunting with a friend in New Mexico. In spite of his aversion to killing, he knew how to shoot a rifle from his time in the Air Force and, egged on by his friend, he had brought down an elk as a kind of rite of passage. His friend had then shown him how to gut and skin the animal. John had the strong hands this task required.

When John returned from buying the ice a short while later, Quincy and I joined with Dorrie to encourage him to take on the next step. He said no at first, but finally agreed. Quincy brought out several smaller knives, and Dorrie sharpened them while the men cut down the carcass and laid it on the tarp spread out across the ground. We set the big pot aside for the time being.

I held the magazine and read the instructions out loud. "Begin by cutting around the hind legs just at the knee joint. Then slit the skin up along the center of the leg, toward the genitals."

Dorrie held up the lamp so I could see to read. Quincy hung two other kerosene lamps from a branch so John could see better. Dorrie coached, translating what I read by pointing to the carcass and encouraging John.

Between the four of us, we managed to get the skin off the front of the goat with only one or two small tears. Once John had the knife, he took his job very seriously. He painstakingly removed the skin on the back of the legs and the back itself, working up the goat inch by inch, his knife blade flat so it cut through the fat layer under the skin rather than the skin itself. He stopped several times, to rinse his hands because they got slippery or to change knives because the one he was using became dull. Dorrie sharpened knives as needed. I stepped in to help once I saw how it was done, and John held the Aladdin for me.

As John cut through the fat beneath the pelt, we held the already-cut skin away from the carcass so he had a clear channel for his knife.

Once he finished that task, he and Quincy hung the goat back up and worked together cut off the head. Dorrie carried the head across the clearing to the school bus. God only knew what she planned to do with it. But it wasn't the time to ask. She came back with a bucket of clean water for rinsing our hands.

It was nearly midnight when we moved on to gutting. I took over, since that task was most like the fish, chicken, and rabbit cleaning I was used to. In some cultures, goat fetus is considered a delicacy; I seriously hoped Dorrie wasn't going to suggest we eat the babies. She didn't. With help from Dorrie and Quincy, I cut the bulky uterus and its contents free, and, wordlessly, John and Quincy took it down the hill in the soup pot to bury, as deeply as they could, without opening it or viewing the contents.

Dorrie picked up the lamp and I carried on. Removing the bladder, the genitals and the gall bladder was tricky. Blood covered my hands and arms, and the metallic odor revolted me. I kept retching as I worked, rinsing my hands often. The only way I could keep myself from throwing up was to breathe slowly through my nose and into my diaphragm.

The article said it was really important to do this part of the butchering carefully, holding the edges of the bladder closed so urine didn't soil the meat, and being especially careful not to pierce the intestines. Dorrie coached me and caught the intestines, stomach, liver, heart, and kidneys in Doña's plastic bathtub, then set them aside for sausages. She took the knife from me then cut out the lungs and the windpipe, and set them aside to feed to the dogs. We were done.

As we looked over our handiwork, John and Quincy came back up the hill looking somber.

Because Dreyfus wasn't a young goat, we should have aged the meat for several days in a cold meat locker. We couldn't do that, but at the very least we needed to keep it cool. We wrapped the carcass in some painting drop cloths John found unopened in our storage shed, laid it on a tarp in the back of the VW bus and covered it with all the ice John had purchased, wrapping the tarp around it to keep the ice in place. It was three in the morning, and we were exhausted.

We stripped off our bloody clothes and took turns standing under two solar showers we'd bought from a camping store. When hung from trees, they used solar energy to heat water in insulated bags. Directing the lukewarm water through plastic tubes and out the plastic nozzles didn't produce a very satisfactory shower, but we felt cleaner.

We made a pact to meet in the middle of the clearing at sunrise with shovels. We had a large trench to dig. That afternoon we would be joined by thirty of our closest friends, and we were going to roast a goat.

The next morning, Dorrie's family arrived in three cars from San Luis Obispo — a three-hour drive away. Hugs and laughter all around, and then Dorrie explained what had happened to Dreyfus, and there were a few moments of respectful sadness. In short order, Dorrie's parents, Mummy and Pooby, turned to preparing Dreyfus for roasting. As the years passed, I would learn that very little unseated this couple. I had left Doña with John in the trailer to dress and feed her while I greeted Dorrie's family. I helped to lay out the breakfast buffet, then turned to watch Dorrie prepare the marinade. I marveled at her energy. I was worn out from the efforts of the night before and early this morning, and emotionally drained.

Following Mummy's instructions, Dorrie mixed lemon juice, olive oil, garlic, salt, and pepper in a bowl and we rubbed the inside of the cavity with half of it. She then put scallions, rosemary branches, and whole cloves and the squeezed-out lemon rinds inside. Finally, Pooby helped her fasten Dreyfus's chest closed with wire. Meanwhile Dorrie's two sisters set up shade tents against the hot morning sunshine.

With Pooby supervising, Dorrie's three brothers put the metal spit rod through the goat's anus and parallel to the backbone, then wired the rod to the carcass and used several skewers to secure the rest of the body to the spit. It was a long process, as they had to thread wire around the backbone, through the flesh, then around the spit. Hilarity all around as one dirty joke after another was shared. I enjoyed watching the twins, Harry and Larry, work. Bearded and with medium long hair topped with identical brimmed hats, they looked like they had just stepped out of the set of *Little House on the Prairie,* and they worked almost without speaking, as if they could sense one another's next move. Once they lifted the goat, spit and all, above the coals, which had been burning for two hours, they and their brother Eric took turns turning the spit and basting the meat with the rest of the lemon-oil mixture. Eric said they had roasted a goat the same way the year before, and the meat had tasted "stronger than beef or chicken, but delicious. Gamey … kind of like venison," he concluded.

John's parents arrived while this was happening. Having met Dorrie's family the day we installed our little trailer under the big oak tree, they were greeted as old friends. Bea stopped at our trailer only long enough to collect Doña, then pitched in to help Mummy wash breakfast dishes. Doña wanted to help. Bea set her on the ground with a mug and a tea towel. Meanwhile Quincy's brother Buzz arrived on foot with a six-pack of beer in his hand. He had skidded off the road near the gate and had left his vehicle in the weeds to deal with later.

Dorrie's sisters carried several loaves of bread over to Dorrie's ancient wood stove. I heard peals of laughter as they wondered just where to put the loaves inside this unfamiliar oven, and how to control the temperature. With breakfast out of the way, Dorrie enlisted their help preparing sandwiches and soup.

Our usual weekend work crew, now party guests, arrived around 10:00 a.m., jean-clad and bearing food. Most of them, seeing Buzz's 4 x 4, had left their cars at the bottom of the hill. Their heads appeared one by one above the steep pathway as they arrived at the top. Quincy put them to work setting up tables and drink stations and, when they were done, most of them stood around the fire pit, watching the goat cook and making more lewd jokes about the spit. Soon the musical instruments came out, and music provided the backdrop for the rest of the day.

Most of our guests had never been to the land before. They were ferried up the hill by others more familiar with the road, or drove up alone, faces incredulous as they rounded the final bend and saw the trailer, school bus, animal pens, out-buildings. No one seemed prepared for their first glimpse of our homestead.

In December, when John and I had sent out our annual Christmas letter with photos of us on the land, we had mentioned that we would celebrate John's birthday with a party. Since we had no telephone, some people came on the strength of that pronouncement alone. As each new family arrived, John left whatever he was doing to greet them. For some reason, my usually antisocial husband was delighted by all these people. Every half hour or so he would load up Sarge and take a group of guests on a tour around the homestead and up the road to Dorrie and Quincy's future home site. Each new arrival was a surprise and a pleasure, and, by the end of the day, over forty people were milling around the property. Two couples, college friends, drove up from San Diego. It was wonderful to show our friends our homestead.

The biggest surprise, for me at least, was the arrival of my parents and my younger brother, Keith. We'd owned the land since October, and had been living there since February, but this was their very first visit. I'd issued the invitation hopefully, but until the moment they actually arrived I didn't think they would come. Dorrie and Quincy knew my parents didn't approve of our venture, and, after Dorrie recognized who they were, she must have passed the word, because one by one her siblings stopped what they were doing to watch our reunion.

Dad was driving his new Toyota pickup, and it was loaded with food, Adirondack chairs for us, and the folding bench and table set they usually took camping. I don't know if he was thinking about ballast, but it probably made their drive up the road a bit easier with all that weight in the back.

Mom remarked on the steep and winding road. "I was that scared, Marlene, I made your father stop at one of the sharp curves and I got out and walked around. What happens if someone comes down the road when you're going up?"

"You get used to it, Mom," I reassured her. "People who live up here are pretty thoughtful about pulling over. I hardly even notice the curves anymore."

I wasn't sure what else to say. When Mom brought out her picnic basket, I knew I would soon be eating roast chicken and potato salad and immediately gave her a hug, told her I was grateful for her presence. Keith asked where John was, and I pointed him in the direction of Sarge.

I didn't quite know how to behave around my parents. Each time I'd visited them since the day I'd told them we'd bought the land, we had limited ourselves to talking about Doña. I told Mom I was glad they were there, and offered to show her the inside of the trailer, but she declined, busying herself with setting out our lunch. Saying I would be back shortly to eat with them, I slipped away to greet other guests.

The afternoon and evening passed all too quickly in a blur of faces, hugs, food, delicious smells, music, more food, and wine. Doña, now seventeen months old, toddled from one group to another, mooching food from their plates and inviting them to play. The goat arrived on the serving tables around 3:00 and the sad story of Dreyfus falling down the hill was told yet again. Some people were slow to taste the meat, but as braver souls filled their plates with chunks so tender they fell apart, and declared them "delicious," they stepped up to try this new delicacy. I thought it was a bit chewy, but gamely ate a small portion. The barbecue was declared a success.

Conversation groups had settled all over the clearing, in and under the big oak tree, along the pathway down the hill. Everywhere you could see, people were sitting or reclining in the soft brown grass, some with their hats over their eyes, others lying on their backs gazing at the trees and the hills, others talking earnestly with old friends and new. I was touched by the variety of people who had chosen to celebrate our new life — and John's birthday — with us. I loved this kind of gathering, which living in community seemed to encourage. I ate too much (chicken and goat, fresh bread and soup, potato salad, tabouli salad, Jell-o salad and carrot cake), drank too much, and talked until my throat was sore.

My parents had set up their picnic table a short distance away from everyone else. When next I joined them, they were sitting on a large blanket playing with Doña, who had decided to skip her

115

afternoon nap. Some of our friends knew them from our wedding, or even from when I was in high school. They had breached the family outpost and got Mom and Dad talking about old times.

Most of the day, I busied myself visiting with our guests, but circled back from time to time to make sure my family felt welcome. I heard raucous laughter from Dad and Keith as my school friends shared who knows what stories about us. Thankfully, my parents didn't share their opinions about our move to the land — at least not while I was present. I invited Mom to ride with me to the credential office in Sacramento the following week and help me with Doña. She turned to Dad, who nodded his approval. She smiled then, and seemed pleased that I had asked.

As dusk arrived, everyone realized simultaneously that they didn't want to drive down our road in the dark. The resulting exodus happened quickly. People folded their blankets and chairs, found their hosts and said farewell. A line of cars inched their way back down the road. Soon only a handful of family members and close friends remained, loading cars, feeding animals, putting away food and tables and shade tents. Mom, Dad, and Keith piled their belongings into the back of Dad's truck, hurriedly said their goodbyes, and stuffed themselves into the cab.

As my father turned his car onto the driveway and headed down our winding road, I heard my mother cautioning him to "Be careful, Rowland," then "Don't go so fast!"

I wondered if I would ever see them on our land again.

As the sun disappeared over Quincy and Dorrie's hill, our clearing returned to normal. John and I lit oil lamps and collapsed into chairs to enjoy the beautiful evening. Sitting in my new Adirondack chair, I nursed Doña with a renewed sense of peace and tranquility. I believed that our friends and family had blessed us in some way, that their showing up was not just curiosity, but also an affirmation of what we were trying to do.

I looked across at the school bus, watching Dorrie's family exchange loving farewells and prepare to disperse once again. I couldn't have imagined that would be the last time I watched that touching scene from the front of our trailer.

14

THE ADAMSES MOVE UP THE HILL

JOHN AND I HAD KNOWN FOR MONTHS that the Adamses would be moving to the top of the hill once the rain stopped and the access road dried out. However, once the weather improved, the move came abruptly, and took less time, than we had expected. They moved their homestead up the hill only a week after the goat barbecue, and just a few days after John and Quincy had words over a pile of rusty nails.

We used a lot of repurposed wood when we built animal shelters and sheds, and each of us spent time on weekends taking rusty nails out of boards. John and I, aware that Doña frequently took her shoes off, were careful to put all the nails we removed into a tin can that we kept on the workbench. Quincy and Dorrie generally let the nails collect in piles on the ground, then picked them up at the end of their work session, or when the pile got large enough to be annoying. John worried about the nails they left lying about, and had asked Quincy several times to keep his part of the property clear of them. On this particular day, he decided to make a point. Walking to where Dorrie and Quincy were enjoying their morning coffee, he got down on his hands and knees and began picking up stray nails, dropping them one at a time into an old soup can, where they made a resounding *clunk.*

"Don't be silly, John. We can do that later," Dorrie said, reaching toward him with a coffee mug. "Come have some coffee."

"I can't relax, knowing these nails are here. Doña walks over here to visit you all the time," John muttered. *Clunk, clunk.*

Quincy didn't even look up. "Tell her to put her shoes on when she comes over." *Clunk, clunk.*

"We didn't move to the country to make her wear shoes." *Clunk.*

John continued his dramatic act until he had picked up all the nails he could find. Then he stomped off back to our trailer.

The following Saturday, an army of people arrived on our hill, beginning around 10:00 a.m. Pooby had driven his flatbed truck from San Luis Obispo and two pickups followed. After greetings and hugs, Quincy and his brother, two of his friends, and Dorrie's three brothers started taking down fencing and putting animal shelters on the flatbed, and piling feeders, food containers, and tools into the pickups. Dorrie and the other women started in the school bus, packing dishes and strapping the contents in place.

John and I were inside our trailer. When I heard the trucks arrive and looked through my window, I assumed Dorrie's family had a birthday to celebrate or something. Strange that they hadn't mentioned it. When I saw them loading animal pens on to Pooby's flatbed, I was stunned. Had we missed a memo? Were they that upset about the rusty nail incident? Heart in my throat, I walked over to Dorrie.

"My family was available this weekend," she said, "so we figured we'd just do it. The road is dry and the weather's good. It's time. I'm sorry we didn't tell you. I only found out myself for sure last night. If you want to help, why don't you join the crew over there?" She pointed toward the goat pen.

I went over to the group of people unfastening hog fence clips, pulling up stakes, winding welded wire fencing, and loading vehicles. They welcomed me and showed me what to do. John decided the project looked like fun, so he dressed Doña in overalls and boots and joined the work party too.

All the livestock belonged to Quincy and Dorrie, so everything would be moved up the hill. Someone tethered the goats to fence posts while others rolled fence wire; rabbits and chickens were fastened into their hutches and coops and trekked up the hill in a wagon train of sorts. By 2:00, the clearing and the hill above it had been emptied of fencing and animals.

The implications of their move hit me as I saw Drop Tail and Flora Fashionista being fastened into carrier cages. We would no longer be waking to the clucking of happy chickens, or be able to hear their cheerful "I laid an egg!" announcement. We would be alone on the land with no next-door neighbors and no animals. I felt lonely just thinking about it.

As I worked alongside Dorrie and Quincy's friends and family, I tried to look normal, but my emotions were on a roller coaster. I had imagined the four of us would manage the move together, perhaps over several days, and I would have time to get used to the idea.

After all the animal pens and buildings had been moved up the hill and into their new locations, Quincy removed their toilet from the front of the bus and reinstalled the driver seat. Dorrie and her sisters stowed everything from the counters inside the cupboards and hollow benches. With a dramatic flair, Quincy climbed into the school bus and drove toward the driveway.

Instead of going straight up the dirt path from the clearing like everyone else had done when they transported the animals and enclosures, he chose a longer, but less steep route, that curved around the side of a hill from the garbage dump a little way down Hawkins Lane. It had been graded once, but over time had become a mile-long stretch of tall brown weeds that on the left hid the edge of the narrow road and on the right filled the space between the bus and the hill with sharp stickery stems and fronds.

John and Buzz walked ahead of Quincy with shears, clearing weeds as they went. Pooby stood beside Quincy's open window, giving directions to keep him from driving off the edge. Several others followed the bus, shouting random suggestions. I stayed way behind them, Doña on my chest in the Snugli. My sleepy girl murmured sweetly as she drifted off. I had intended to put her down in the trailer, but I feared for Quincy's safety, and nervously followed the procession as it wound its way slowly upward. In retrospect, there was an element of humor in the chain of people it was taking to move one school bus up the hill, but at the time I wasn't laughing. With a sense of relief, I followed the crowd over the crest of the hill and down the gentle slope to the Adams' new home site.

By the time we made it to the top of the hill, Dorrie's brothers had cleared the pad where the school bus would sit. As Quincy backed the bus into place, they used angled chocks to level it into its new location. When they were finished, the vehicle nestled into the trees and looked right at home. I felt tears welling up as I watched them work. I would miss looking across the clearing at this friendly old bus.

Dorrie's mother and sisters had, as always, prepared food for a crowd, and now they set out a feast. We each filled a plate and found a place to sit. Once everyone's hunger was sated, out came the guitars, the harmonica, and the flute, and soon it felt like a party. It always did when Dorrie's family was involved. We sang and talked and passed Doña from lap to lap, but amidst all the joviality my head — and my stomach — was still churning.

Dorrie finally joined us. Mummy and Pooby were trying to decide if they were going to stay the night or drive back home. Soon the light began to fade. Doña fell asleep in Dorrie's arms, and we sat transfixed by a magnificent sunset over the nearby hills. The evening chill settled on us once the sun disappeared below the horizon, and people began to gather their things and either disappear into their tents for warmer clothes or get into their cars and leave. Mummy and Pooby, driving the slowest vehicle, decided to get on the road. Dorrie's sisters and Quincy's brother would stay until morning. Her brothers helped with evening chores, then packed up, said their good-byes, and were gone.

Dorrie patted my arm clumsily and we walked to the bus together. "I hope you'll still help us with our chores," she began. "It's only half a mile, and you can drive up if you want."

I made a face. "Not likely. That road scares me. We'll walk."

"I'll help you build animal pens when you're ready," Dorrie continued. "And then I can help you with *your* chores when you need it."

"We'll figure it out," I agreed.

"Nothing's really changed except we won't be in each other's pockets all the time. And our husbands won't be getting on one another's nerves so much."

Thinking of Quincy and his annoying ball games, I realized that I had occasionally wished for this day. My mom always said, "Be careful what you wish for."

I lay Doña on Dorrie and Quincy's big bed in the back of the bus, and placed pillows next to her so she wouldn't roll off. Dorrie looked down at her cherubic face.

"I'm going to miss this little one sooo much," she said, leaning down to kiss Doña's forehead.

Dorrie's sisters came into the bus then, and we joined them at their tasks, climbing in and out of the bus, clearing and folding tables, washing and drying dishes, all of us talking at once.

The following morning, I baked bread, and we walked up the hill with two steaming loaves as a housewarming gift. The work wasn't finished and for the rest of the weekend, John and Quincy worked together strengthening animal cages, stretching fence wire, and organizing the storage shed that Pooby had carried up on his flatbed. We never did learn if Quincy or Dorrie had told anyone about the rusty nail argument. It wasn't mentioned again.

John and I walked back down the hill that night holding hands, Doña riding on John's shoulders. Dorrie had assured me we would be able to continue living and working together in community — still next-door neighbors, but half a mile apart — out of sight, but definitely not out of mind.

As our clearing came into view, John stopped to look at our home, a tiny little trailer surrounded by dirt, denuded of fences, outbuildings, and animals. The clearing was once again a blank canvas.

With a grin and a wave of a stick that he picked up off the ground, John christened our homestead "Bum Flats."

15

SACRAMENTO BOUND

J UNE 24 DAWNED SUNNY AND BRIGHT. When I opened the curtains, I was reminded that the surrounding hills had turned the golden brown typical of California in the summer. The tall grass that grew in the swale below had also become brown and dry. When I opened a window to let in the cool morning air, I could hear seed heads rattling in the breeze.

I dressed quickly. No time to waste. This was the day I would apply in person for a teaching credential under the expiring legislation. I had been pursuing this goal all year, and finally, I could see the finish line.

I dressed Doña and selected food and toys to entertain her for the drive to my parents' home. While I had been busy attending college classes and student teaching, she had turned from a chubby baby into a long-legged toddler. Her light brown hair fell in curls around her face and neck. I felt a catch in my throat as I fastened her into her car seat in the back of the car. She was so beautiful, and she was growing so fast.

Driving north, I realized I felt nervous about seeing my parents again. Had their attendance at the barbecue signaled a kind of truce? Having failed to keep me from moving to the land, did they continue to believe my rejection of suburban life had been directed at them personally? Mom seemed pleased that I had asked her to go to Sacramento with me. Being a teacher was normal; something she understood. But what about Dad? I was looking forward to a day alone with Mom, without Dad's negativity to color our conversations. Perhaps the long drive would give me a chance to convince her that our lifestyle choice wasn't intended to be a criticism of *their* lifestyle choices.

Predictably, my father was impatiently pacing the living room waiting when Doña and I arrived, about half an hour later than I'd estimated. He hated any amount of tardiness. Face grim, he handed me a map of northern California with a route highlighted in yellow.

"I do know how to read a map, Dad," I began, but finished off with a grin. "Ok. Go on then."

I decided to be content that he was letting Mom go with me. Pointing to the map, he told me to drive north on Highway 101 to San Francisco, then take Highway 80 the rest of the way. I fastened Doña back into her car seat, and helped Mom with her seat belt.

I'd never driven to Sacramento. Since we'd be on highways, I assumed we'd be traveling at highway speed. But when we got to Highway 80, it turned out to be a two-lane country road with cross streets, traffic lights, and cars backed up in lots of places. Sometimes the signs read Highway 80 as we expected, but other times they said 12 or 50, and we went miles without seeing a marker. At four feet, ten inches, Mom could barely see out over the dashboard, but she studied the route carefully and announced that there was really only one way we could go. She didn't think it mattered what the road was numbered. Each time I lost confidence that we were going the right way, she assured me we were fine, and showed me the map.

As we made our way north, I gradually began to realize that Mom was actually a good navigator, contrary to family mythology and my father's many insults. All my life I'd heard him call her "hopeless," and listened to her tremulous voice as she gave him directions during family outings. Her nervousness had seemed to justify his criticisms, but I wondered if it had been his criticism that unnerved her rather than the map-reading itself. When I commented on her skill, she told me she'd learned to read maps when she had been in the British army.

"I didn't know that," I admitted.

"There's a lot you don't know about me, Marlene," she said, with a Cheshire cat smile.

She had dressed up for our adventure: a bright yellow dress with a checked jacket to match, round yellow earrings, hair curled. She made a sharp contrast to me. I wore a faded granny dress and long dangling earrings that I'd bought in London and wore almost every day. My red hair had been recently cropped — a radical change from the long hair I had worn since childhood, and a concession to the summer heat and living without a shower. Mom usually had something negative to say about how I looked, but that day she complimented my new coif, and I tingled with the unfamiliar praise.

It took two hours to get to the outskirts of Sacramento, and another half hour to find the credentials office — which turned out not to be in Sacramento at all, but by the river in West Sacramento. Mom found the street on the map and got us to the correct building. Doña had slept most of the way, but now she raised her arms in the universal signal for "I want to get out of this car seat."

"Leave her with me," Mom said. "I'll take her for a walk and feed her a snack."

As I parked and prepared to go inside the building, I was feeling optimistic. Driving to Sacramento was a nuisance, but necessary. After I had spent most of the fall semester student teaching at Mount Hamilton School, my student teaching supervisor had declared that the school was not a valid student teaching site. I was furious — my mother-in-law had provided me with an excellent teaching experience. He probably just didn't want to drive up the winding road to evaluate me. If I had to do a third semester of student teaching, I would miss the September deadline. I hoped my strategy — submitting my credential application in person directly to the Commission, instead of through the university — would be successful. According to my mother-in-law, the law only required one semester of student teaching.

I carried an envelope in which I had placed the 12-page application with supporting documentation: transcripts, resume, recommendations — and even my Graduate Record Exam score. More than anything, I wanted to place this envelope in the hands of a human being, and be reassured that it would be read and evaluated before the new law went into effect.

Mom seemed to understand the importance of my pursuit. She called out softly as I walked away from the car. "Good luck, Marlene. Stay calm."

Sylvia, my appointed credential analyst, was friendly and cheerful, and immediately examined my papers. Her long black hair and dangly red earrings shook from side to side as she checked off each document on a form, her long red nails clicking against the desk. I held my breath in anticipation, and at last she looked up.

"This is fine. Everything seems to be here, so it will be processed with time to spare."

Much relieved, I managed to keep from hugging Sylvia. I blurted "Thank you" and rushed out of the building to tell my mother. She was holding Doña's hand, while my beautiful daughter, chortling at her achievement, walked along a low wall surrounding the entryway. I hugged Mom and told her what Sylvia had said. Suddenly I realized we could actually enjoy the rest of our outing now. The school term had ended. Vacation had officially begun.

I suggested we eat at Frank Fat's Chinese Restaurant on L Street, recommended by my supervising principal. Mom directed me back toward the city. She loved Chinese food, and I wanted to please her, to make her more receptive to my speech. Unasked, our server brought a bowl of cut-up cooked vegetables for Doña to eat while we were waiting for our meal.

Here was my chance. I took a deep breath.

"You know, Mom, it must have been a shock for Grandma when you and Dad emigrated to America after the war."

I handed Doña a slice of carrot, not looking at Mom's face.

"Yes, I suppose that's true. But there was no work … houses had been bombed. There was no place to live." She took a cloth napkin from around a knife and fork and tucked it into the neck of Doña's dress.

"I'm not saying you weren't justified. Just that Grandma might not have agreed with you." I turned to look sideways at her. "The thought of you leaving must have upset her."

"She did try to talk us into looking for work in Manchester." Mom looked thoughtful.

"Did you?"

"No. Your father was keen to come to America. Streets paved with gold, you know. He wanted a fresh start. For you." Her face was stern.

Did her expression mean it had been my fault?

"And he got one." I looked full into her face, but now she avoided my gaze.

"Mom, John and I are trying to do something that's important to us. For Doña. All we ask is that you let us try. It's nothing against you and Dad. It's about *us*."

She didn't answer, but nodded her head. Was she holding back tears? After a long pause, she patted my arm.

"I know love. I do. It's just that we worry about you, and about Doña, living out there in the hills, with that terrible road and God knows what wild animals." She laid her hand over mine. "Please promise me you'll be careful."

Now it was my turn to nod my head silently.

.

16

SLIPPERY SLOPE

AS I DROVE HOME FROM MOM AND DAD'S after returning from Sacramento, I tried to get my head around our new circumstances. After months of living in community with the Adamses, John and I would now be alone. We could make a fresh start, build a whole new homestead from scratch, drawing on what we had learned over the winter. We could use the entire clearing, and the hills front and back, in any way we wanted. I could relocate the garden so it got more sun. I could ask John to cut a pad into the old goat paddock, too steep really for an animal enclosure, and install the water tank the county required before we could get a building permit. There were tons of projects we could do that we had been putting off, including bulldozing a pad for the 40-foot trailer we had recently purchased, sitting empty in a trailer park in San Jose.

That night we lay awake, talking, thinking, and planning. As we talked, I found myself listening for Quincy to drive up our road. I knew that Dorrie would be late; she had been scheduled until midnight every night this week.

"Where's Quincy?" I asked John, as we gently rolled Doña toward the wall to make more space in bed for us. "Shouldn't he be home by now?"

"Quincy went out for pizza with his team," John said. "He'll be late, but he said he'd be home in time to feed the animals."

I pulled a sliding window open, and listened for a car engine. No sound. The air was still. A red-tailed hawk screamed *kee-eeee-arr* as it flew across the sky, its warning cry rising higher and higher, then dropping at the end. Then the hawk grew silent again, presumably while it devoured its prey. Dorrie and Quincy would each be driving the steep road to their new home for the first time after a long day at work, and in the dark. Even though we'd cut some of the long grass that had grown up during the rainy season, and Pooby and the others had driven vehicles up and down it, all day, the road would still be a challenge to drive. In spite of my hurt feelings, I wanted them to be safe.

As John and I discussed where we would put the chickens, and the rabbits, and the goats, and where we should relocate the garden, we stopped every time we heard a sound, thinking it might be Quincy.

"We need to put the water tank on the highest spot," John said,. "Off to the right at the top of the driveway would work. If we cut a flat pad — wait, is that an engine?" We peeked through the curtain. Just then a great horned owl hooted its presence in a nearby tree. That call always sounded to me like "Who's awake? ... me too." I wanted to hoot back. But mostly I wanted Quincy to come home so I could go to sleep.

At last Quincy came around the last curve, past our driveway. He stopped at the bottom of their road, just past where John wanted to put the water tank. He downshifted then started up the incline, driving very slowly. I held my breath, listening for some clue that he had made it to the top. Eventually we heard the cacophony that meant their "watch geese" were greeting him, and, soon after that, a symphony of bells announced he was feeding the goats. I relaxed then, and soon went to sleep.

John was sleeping too by the time Dorrie returned home, but the unmistakable sound of her BMW wheels slipping on grass awakened us both. I sat up in bed, trying to hear better. The sound came from the road that curved around the side of the hill, the one Quincy had driven their school bus up. Not surprisingly, she was having problems getting traction. Remembering all the people it had taken to get Quincy's school bus safely up the road, I couldn't imagine why Dorrie would choose the more hazardous route.

"Why the hell would she take that road?" I asked, mostly to myself. But John responded.

"That one isn't as steep as the one that leads straight up from our camp. Maybe she feels safer going that way."

Ok, that road wasn't as steep. But she would still need to deal with the dry grass and weeds, and in the dark it would be difficult to see the edge of the road. I imagined the worst. It was fully dark now. There was no moon. What if she fell off the road? I held myself perfectly still and prayed that she would be very, very careful. Her engine stopped, then started again. Perhaps her wheels had gained a purchase on the road. I knew that Dorrie understood the mechanics of slipping wheels — she had taught me how to drive in mud, after all. I should have more confidence in her. After a few more minutes, we could no longer hear her progress. She must have gone around the back of the hill. I knew that Quincy would be listening for her too, and I wasn't doing anything helpful. After the silence persisted, I gave up my vigil and went back to sleep.

We awakened to Quincy beating on the trailer door.

"Dorrie's car went off the road," he began, and we were suddenly wide awake.

"*What!?* Is she ok?" I climbed out of bed and pulled on a kaftan.

"Yes, she's cuddling with the dogs in the bus, drinking a glass of wine."

As he explained what had happened, my heart raced at the thought of what *could* have happened, and nearly had. Just as I had feared, Dorrie couldn't see where the left-hand side of the road ended. A short way up the first slope past the garbage dump, first her front left wheel then her back one had slipped off the pavement. As I imagined myself inside her car, trying to make decisions, Quincy told us she had climbed across the gearshift and out the passenger side of the car, then stumbled up the hill on foot with a flashlight, arriving at the top covered with scratches from stickers, stones, and dry grass.

"I'm so grateful she had the presence of mind to stop the engine and put the emergency brake on," he said, his voice thick with emotion. "And that I replaced her flashlight batteries last week."

I noticed then that Quincy's hands were shaking, and his face was pale. We all knew that beside that stretch of road was a steep drop into a ravine, and it sounded like the BMW was hanging precariously over it.

"It's a miracle she didn't go all the way over," Quincy said, putting his hands over his face.

I put my arms around him, patting his back as if he were a child. "But she didn't," I crooned. "She didn't and she's safe." Back inside her car in my head, I wondered what I would have done in her position.

Quincy then asked if John would help him pull the BMW back onto the road in the morning before work.

"It seems impossible that she's thinking about this after all that's happened, but Dorrie wants to drive to the hospital tomorrow. She's worried about missing work and specifically asked me to get you to help, John."

The two men sat down on the edge of the bed and worked out what equipment they would need and what time they would meet. Wanting to be part of the solution, I said I'd make breakfast.

✳   ✳   ✳

It took us a while to get organized. First, Dorrie and Quincy had fed their animals, then they drove Nuts down to our trailer. When they sat down to breakfast, their eyes were red and they both looked somber. I imagined they had been rehashing the events of the previous night.

The men ate quickly and headed for the Quonset hut to collect towing cables, ropes, tools, gasoline for Nuts. Dorrie and I located gloves, sun hats, sunglasses, and bottles of water. She picked up Doña and began singing to her while I searched for the Snugli. At 19 months of age, Doña had become very active. I still wore her on my chest when

I wanted to keep her out of mischief or leave my hands free to do other things.

Dorrie and I had been assigned to put chocks under the BMW's wheels as the men towed the car from its precarious position and I wanted to keep Doña safe in her carrier while we did that. But I couldn't find the Snugli. I didn't know it was missing from its hook until after I rinsed the dishes and dressed Doña. While Dorrie, Quincy, and John gassed up Nuts and stowed the supplies, I anxiously circled our campsite. I searched the trailer, the Pinto, the VW bus, the storage shed. When I returned to the trailer without the Snugli, John handed me the metal-framed child carrier that he usually used.

"Here, put this on. We're ready to go."

I hated the Gerry pack. I reminded John I had a sore shoulder, but he was already adjusting the straps and gesturing for me to turn around. He fastened the stability strap across my chest and lifted Doña in. Delighted, she, immediately grabbed a chunk of my hair, put her feet against my back, and pushed herself upward.

"Fasten her harness, John, so she doesn't climb out."

He tried to fold Doña's arms and nudge her hands into the safety harness, but she curled them into tight little fists and shoved them down by her sides. I felt her shaking her head vigorously.

"No!" Her new favorite word. "No-no-no!"

"Ok," her obliging father agreed. "But no climbing Mommy's back, Ok?"

Doña must have nodded some kind of assent, because I felt John lean in to kiss her and tell her she was a wonderful child. When I wore her on my back, Doña usually climbed up my long hair as if I were Rapunzel, but now that I'd had my hair cut there would be less for her to hold onto. Hopefully that would keep her in the carrier and not climbing up my back.

We walked down to the well where Quincy had parked Nuts. Dorrie took the Gerry pack from me with Doña in it, and set it on the front bench seat. The carrier had a hinged support that allowed it to sit securely on a horizontal surface. There were no seatbelts. I had to hold it.

133

The sun was high in the sky already, and the drama of the previous night had been vanquished by daylight and by our belief that we could solve the problem quickly and get on with our day. But we were getting hot sitting on the exposed seats, and it felt like forever for Quincy to drive the ponderous vehicle to the top of the hill on one road and back it down another. Doña wiggled and whined all the way to Dorrie's BMW.

I stood on the road bouncing Doña and singing nursery rhymes while Quincy got Nuts into position, waited for John to hook on the towing cables, and pressed the accelerator.

"Oh, the grand old duke of York (bounce)
"He had ten thousand men (bounce, bounce)
"He marched them up to the top of the hill (bounce)
"And marched them back again (bounce, bounce)"

The old vehicle's worn wheels spun uselessly.

After a few tries, John suggested he get Sarge and hook the two vehicles together, for greater pulling power. While we waited, I let Doña out of the carrier. Dorrie gave her piggyback rides and engaged her to search for rocks to use for chocks. We were close to the garbage dump that we had inherited from Bill Carter. The dump held pieces of furniture, carcasses of various animals—some bleached white from years in the sun, others in various degrees of decay — a pile of bricks and broken chunks of concrete. It smelled sour. Doña wrinkled her nose, which made me laugh. Selecting a small piece of concrete, I took Doña's hand and started back up the hill.

Finally, we heard Sarge chugging backwards down the road. I looked up to see John, leaning out of the cab grinning, totally in his element. There were no side windows on Sarge, or doors, either, so we could see him clearly. Whenever John got behind the wheel of his old truck, especially when wearing his blue overalls and floppy hat, he reminded me of Jed Clampett in *Beverly Hillbillies*. I smiled, both at the sight and at Dorrie, who lifted Doña up in the air and "flew" her towards the Gerry pack on my back.

"Should I buckle the safety harness?"

"No. John made some kind of a deal with her. She's being good."

134

We took our positions behind the BMW.

With the two trucks hooked together, the trucks were able to get traction and slowly, painfully, inch the BMW forward. They stopped often to reconnoiter and, each time they did, Quincy instructed us to put our chocks under the wheels. Since Doña wasn't fastened into the carrier's safety harness, I had to twist an arm around my back and remind her to hold on to the aluminum tubes around the top to keep from falling out when I leaned over.

When the men started forward again, we retrieved the chocks we'd put under the wheels ("Hold on, Doña!") and walked up the hill behind them until they stopped, then put the chocks under the wheels again. Finally, Dorrie's car had been lined up straight, directly behind Nuts, with all four wheels firmly on the ground. The men put on their handbrakes to get out and make sure the hitch held tight.

I examined the road. Ahead of us, tall brown grass had been crushed flat by Nuts' and Sarge's broad wheels. Coming up from behind were two narrower tire tracks. On the right side of the road, a dirt bank rose twenty feet straight up. On the left ... well, there was nothing on the left, except a ravine with a dry creek at the bottom. The ground just dropped off. Above us, unfettered trees and shrubs had grown together from the edges of the road to form a kind of tunnel that camouflaged the danger. I understood why Dorrie had gone off the road.

Dorrie used the break to go back to the garbage dump and get larger pieces of concrete. As she approached with one, John called down to us, "The car's straight. Come on up and you can ride on Sarge the rest of the way."

Quincy shouted his agreement. Dorrie discarded the concrete and began walking toward her BMW, two car-lengths ahead of us. She pointed out some poison oak growing out of the side of the bank as she passed me, then looked ahead and shrieked, her face contorted, "Get away! Quick! Get away!"

Like a monkey, she clambers up the bank to my right. Clings to the poison oak. Reaches a hand down for me to grab.

I stare at her car. What does she see? Why did she climb that wall? There's nothing on the ground. No snakes. No spiders. No scorpions. Nothing.

I'm glued in place. Time stands still as I try to figure out what she sees.

"Marlene! For Christ's sake — MOVE!" Dorrie yells. Now she's staring at her car.

What is going on? I look back to the BMW. Is it moving?

Shit! It IS moving. It's coming toward me.

Jesus! Dorrie's BMW is rolling backwards and I'm directly in its path.

"Get up here, Marlene — now!" Dorrie shouts again, still extending her hand.

Should I climb up the bank? It looked easy enough when she did it.

Doña bounces up and down in the carrier, singing The Grand Old Duke of York.

I can't do it. She's too heavy.

I look around.

Time slows even more.

My ears are buzzing. Quincy is shouting, but I can't make out what he says.

Maybe I can outrun the car.

I can't turn around. If I turn around, Doña will be between the car and me. I can't move. It's like I'm glued to the ground.

The car is nearly here. It's going to hit me. I back away, one step, two, three … feel a sharp pain in my chest and hear a loud crack! as 2000 pounds of metal slams into me. I am spread-eagled over the trunk, but I can't feel my body. The car rolls down the road, picks up speed. Suddenly the wheels turn left. We roll off the edge of the road. I am glued to the trunk by its backward motion.

Dorrie's car is taking me into the ravine.

"Dear God, keep Doña safe. I don't care about me. Just keep my baby safe."

I'm ready to promise anything, but there isn't time.

I close my eyes. I can't watch. But I can't stop my ears, my nose, my mind's eye.

We tear through manzanita, sagebrush, poison oak.
I hear the rustle and swoosh of dry grass.
Crack! Bang! Smack! Crash!
The car breaks trees and brushes, hitting rocks and discarded furniture thrown into the ravine.

As we careen through the underbrush, I slip from the trunk, grab the back bumper to keep from being pulled under. It doesn't work. Jesus, Dorrie's car is going to run us over.

In spite of what I'd said to God, I don't want to die.

My mouth and nose fill with dirt and grass. Something pierces my chest. I hear a metallic crack and feel a sharp wrench as the Gerry pack catches on something, then breaks loose. Hell! Is Doña still under me? No — please no!

Suddenly, we stop. Roll back and forth, then stop again.
I snort out dirt, am rewarded with the smell of newly-mown grass.
I spit out dirt and weeds, try to clean my lips with my tongue.
I feel the crush of grass and sticks wedging me under the car.
My eyes sting.
My chest throbs.
My right leg is twisted under my body.
It is dark under the car.
Scarily quiet.
There is no sound of a baby.

TWO

RECOVER AND REGROUP

1975

- Xerox PARC debuts the first GUI or "Graphical User Interface"
- Steven Sasson at Kodak invents the digital camera
- Bill Gates and Paul Allen develop a version of BASIC for the Altair personal computer and found Microsoft
- Steve Wozniak and others found the "Homebrew Computer Club"
- Hewlett Packard releases HP-25 Scientific Programmable Calculator

17

YEARNING TO GO HOME

JOHN AND QUINCY SPRANG FROM THEIR VEHICLES and raced to where Dorrie peered into the ravine, calling my name. I called back, terrified, wailing, "I'm here, I'm here. Where's Doña?" I had forgotten she had been on my back, and kept asking for her. "Please — is Doña ok?!"

Quincy scrambled downhill through the underbrush, guided by my voice. He found me under the car at the bottom of the hill. Meanwhile, John was searching for Doña. He had seen her being catapulted out of the carrier by the impact of the car hitting me. She had flown through the air, but he couldn't see where she had landed.

"That way," Dorrie called, pointing in the direction where she thought Doña was, and starting to run toward it. "I hope she's ok."

Just then they both heard Doña calling "Mommy," over and over. No crying. Just "Mommy."

Following her voice, John found her nestled safely in a bush close to the top of the hill. Except for a few scratches, she was unhurt. John told me later that when he saw her, he mentally replayed the series of events that had led to her sitting, unconstrained, in the Gerry carrier on my back rather than secured firmly to my chest in the Snugli. He murmured an unaccustomed prayer of thanks.

After a quick inspection, he announced, "She's fine, just fine!" Bursting into tears, he collapsed on the road, cradling Doña in his arms.

With Quincy down the hill and Doña in John's arms, Dorrie, the student nurse, was the only one left to run to Bill Carter's trailer, break a window to get in, and use his telephone to call for an ambulance. Quincy sat beside me. I lay on my back, my head between the back tires, the rest of my body wedged completely under the car. "Where's Doña?" I asked again. Nothing else mattered to me.

"She's fine. John has her." Lying on the ground next to the car, Quincy spoke to me slowly and gently. Remarkably, I giggled. I realize now that I was probably in shock, but the news about Doña had calmed me. I hurt, badly, especially my chest, and I couldn't move, but everything was okay now. Now that I knew Doña to be safe, I could settle. I trusted the three of them to get me out of there.

I wiggled my fingers and toes as Quincy instructed, and tried to tell him what hurt. "My back," I began. "My leg … My chest … It hurts to talk. And it's dark. I can't see anything. Am I blind?"

Finally, more urgently, "I can't breathe, Qui." For some reason I used Dorrie's pet name for him. I became frightened. "My chest hurts. I can't take a proper breath. Help me."

Quincy crawled under the car to get a better look at me. Presumably he saw the branch sticking out of my chest, but he didn't say anything about it. What he said was "Open your eyes."

I had kept them shut all that time. It was still dark under the car, but at least I knew I wasn't blind. I felt embarrassed, but only for a few moments. As I continued to try to breathe deeply but couldn't, I moved from anxious to hysterical. I kept gasping and crying, which Quincy knew would make things worse. He spoke quietly to me, telling me everything would be ok. Help was coming. I began shivering. Quincy, perspiring from the exertion and the heat of the late June day, took off his shirt and put it over me. Then he crab-crawled backwards from under the car and yelled to John.

"Marlene can't breathe," he yelled. "What should I do?"

Quincy had never been in the military, had never taken a first aid course. He and Dorrie had not yet had a child. Yet, following instructions called down by John, who had done all of those things, he instructed me in childbirth breathing techniques.

Once John understood that I could actually breathe, but couldn't take a deep breath, he assumed correctly that I had a collapsed lung. Standing up and demonstrating, still holding Doña in his arms, he taught Quincy "choo, choo" and "pant, pant, blow" breathing, both of which I had used during labor. I couldn't see them *choo-choo*ing, but I heard them. Pretty funny. I giggled again, then breathed in fast. Giggling hurt. John shouted "choo choo, choo choo. Like that!" to Quincy, and Quincy repeated: "choo choo, choo choo, choo choo." John told him to encourage me to breathe high in my chest, and to take shallow breaths. Quincy told me to breathe in lightly, hold my breath for a few seconds, and breathe out with longer, relaxing exhalations.

From his perch on the hill, John coached Quincy to keep me talking, to help me visualize a clean hospital bed with starched white sheets and flowers on the nightstand. Never mind that I hated hospitals and had agitated to take Doña home from the hospital only two hours after her birth. Quincy's calm voice, the patterned breathing, and the visualization worked. Lying under the car, dirt in my hair and feeling something crunchy in my mouth, my chest pierced by a tree branch and my back bent around the broken metal struts of the Gerry carrier, the thought of a clean hospital bed sounded wonderful. His guided meditation began to calm me. In a bizarre change of focus, I thought about my recently waist-length hair. That trip under the car might have scalped me (or perhaps broken my neck) if my hair had become tangled in a wheel. But it hadn't. I would be ok.

It must have taken at least an hour from the time Dorrie left to find a telephone and the paramedics to make it up to where we were, but I didn't have any sense of the passage of time. Quincy kept me awake by talking to me, and convinced me I should stay put until help arrived.

When they did finally arrive, the paramedics slipped a rigid stretcher under me and pulled me out from under the car. Someone gave me a shot. I babbled on about all kinds of things after that — my hair, my daughter, the mother rabbits with the dead babies. They did something painful to my chest and I screamed. One of the paramedics told me he was going to take my gloves off so he could see my hands. Why had I been wearing gloves? I couldn't remember. He rolled me onto my side and took the broken Gerry carrier off my back, handing the pieces to Quincy. They strapped me to the stretcher. As they started up the hill, I closed my eyes again.

*   *   *

I awakened to hear John arguing with the ambulance driver.

"I want to go with her. And I want our daughter to go with us. No, she's not injured, but she needs her mother."

Loud voices. Lots of movement behind and beside me. The engine started. We were moving. Bumpy road. Starts and stops. Winding roads. I clutched the side of the stretcher to keep from falling off. I felt very tired. In a fog I heard John talking to Doña, telling her Mommy was going to be ok. I tried to stay awake, but I couldn't.

The next time I woke up, I appeared to be surrounded by people putting things around my arm and in my arm. They moved me from the ambulance to a gurney, and rolled it down the hall. I kept closing my eyes against the bright lights; every time we went over a bump or turned a corner, I screamed. I didn't seem to be able to help myself. I apologized to the nurse walking beside the gurney.

"It's alright. You've been hurt badly. You are a very lucky young lady," she said.

I wasn't feeling very lucky. They took me to a room where the technician told me to move to the X-ray table. I laughed, then cringed from the pain.

"You'll have to move me," I said, but it came out all blurry. "I can't move my leg."

"What hurts?" he asked.

"Everything!"

Finally, he got an orderly to help roll me onto the table. That wasn't bad, but then the technician rearranged my leg. I screamed, then I passed out. I woke up several times before they were finished

144

with me. Everything seemed blurry, and their voices sounded to me like we were under water.

Finally, I awakened in a different room. I had been propped up in a bed, wrapped in bandages and hooked up to a bundle of bottles. A nurse came through the door, put a thermometer in my mouth.

"You were very lucky, miss," she said, wrapping a blood pressure cuff around my arm and reaching for my hand.

"Mmmmm," I said around the thermometer. "Where am I? Where's my daughter?"

"Wheeler Hospital, Gilroy," she replied. "Intensive Care. Do you want to see your parents? They have your daughter." *What were they doing with Doña? How did they even know I was there?* Picturing the angry lecture I'd get from Dad, I shook my head 'no.' The nurse did ask John to come in at my request, but he immediately turned white, leaned against the wall, and left without saying a word.

After that, I told the nurse no more visitors.

*   *   *

My first week in hospital passed in a blur. I had a vague awareness of people coming and going, murmuring among themselves, changing my dressings and the bottles that hung above my head, but I slept most of the time. Five days after the accident, I made the first entry in my journal: "Tonight I'm feeling weepy."

I wrote that I felt fuzzy and confused from the meds and I didn't like it. I refused a Demerol shot one lunchtime. By dinner, pain washed over me in waves, inhabiting different parts of my anatomy in turn. But at last my head felt clear.

A nurse tried to help me get more comfortable, propping me up on pillows and adjusting the breathing tube in my mouth. Did I want a shot to help me sleep? I shook my head, no.

After the night nurse took my vitals, I pantomimed my request for a book. Something fat by Daphne du Maurier arrived on a cart. I read until I felt sleepy, then closed my eyes, but sleep didn't come. Propped up on the pillows, I couldn't get comfortable. I lay there a long time, listening to voices and the clatter of dinner carts down the hallway outside my room.

I embraced the ebb and flow of the breathing machine, the throbbing pain that occupied first my knee, then my chest, then my lower back. My skin itched. My breasts were full of milk, tight, aching. I actually liked feeling those sensations better than the fuzziness. They made me feel alive; made my injuries seem real, tangible. Until then the whole event had seemed dreamlike, illusory, unreal.

I tried to turn on my side, but couldn't. My right leg had been wrapped in a beige elastic bandage, suspended in the air, attached to a hook in the ceiling, waiting for the orthopedic surgeon to come back from water-skiing. I wondered how I had managed to sleep like that for five days — I always slept on my side at home. Then I remembered the Demerol. Would I be able to sleep without it? I pressed the call button, asked for hot milk.

I missed Doña, her soft little body curled up in bed beside me, her warmth, her chubby cheeks. I hated knowing that she felt abandoned, frightened, sad, confused. Where had her mommy gone? She had never drunk out of a bottle, or gone to sleep without nursing. How was she coping? Her mommy wasn't coping well at all. I wanted her there with me. The charge nurse had said children couldn't visit. Period. I would talk to Dorrie. She was almost a nurse. Perhaps she could get around the rules. Meanwhile, I asked John to bring me one of her stuffed animals to cuddle. It would at least smell like her.

A candy striper brought a cup of hot milk and a straw. I burned my mouth at first, then took smaller sips with just my lips. The warm liquid tasted good and made me sleepy again, but the pain was getting worse, and I found it difficult to stay on top of it. I would ask for something to help me sleep. My eyes filled with tears as I watched the volunteer leave the room. I didn't want to ring the call button again because the intercom was so loud and other patients were asleep. I sat there, propped up on pillows, listening to the ambulance sounds below and feeling sorry for myself.

I played back the accident in my head, thought about using it in a novel, but there were too many holes in my memory. Why had the car come off the tow bar? How did Doña get out of the baby carrier? Then I remembered how my foot itched, my toes twitched, how helpless I felt. I couldn't change my position. I hurt. I wanted to go home.

My surgeon, Dr. Nadler, inventoried my injuries as if he were reading a shopping list. "You lost a fair amount of blood from all the scrapes and contusions you suffered sliding down that hill," he began. "You also have a traumatic pneumothorax — that's a collapsed lung — fractured pelvis, cracked sacrum, separated sacroiliac, fractured tibia, displaced patella, and a traumatic lumbar spinal subdural hematoma which we will start to drain tomorrow."

I had no idea what he had just said. The Latin words made my brain hurt. I asked him to write it all down. He took out a notepad and scribbled some notes, then put them on the table beside my bed.

"You're a very lucky young woman," he said. "It will take some doing, but we can fix all these injuries and have you back home in a matter of months."

"Months? That's the good news?" I shouted, although it came out as a croak, followed by coughing. And that word, again, lucky. Whispering, "I have a baby. I have to go home!"

He just smiled. "You need to be patient. You have been very lucky but you need to give your body time to heal."

Eventually I read what Dr. Nadler had written, how many injuries I had. He'd left out the poison oak that was making my entire body itch, turning my skin scaly and rough, and my engorged breasts, which the nurses bound tightly every day until I screamed. They assured me this was the only way to stop my body from producing breastmilk. But I didn't want to stop making milk. I wanted to feed my baby. Angrily, I unwrapped the bandages when the nurses left the room.

The laundry list of my broken body parts was overwhelming. I *had* been fortunate, I supposed. And perhaps I had been unrealistic, thinking I could get through this without pain medication. I refused Demerol at lunch time, but I finally buzzed for something to help me sleep. When the nurse came back, I asked her to remove the extra pillows. She brought Valium, which she said would make the leg spasms settle down. She rearranged my pillows, but wouldn't take them away.

"You have to sit up," she said, "or your lung will fill with fluid."

I asked for my journal and worked on some poems I had started before the accident. Writing used a different part of my brain than pain, and it helped me relax. I fell asleep with my journal in my hands.

I awakened with intense chest pain. I took the Demerol as instructed. It made me foggy and didn't really seem to help the pain.

"I have to get back to the land," I told the nurse.

"You need to be patient."

That word again. I hated being patient.

During my return to the drug-induced fog, several friends, my parents, and John all telephoned, but I couldn't make head or tails of what they said. I'd been unhooked from the dedicated positive pressure ventilator by this time, but Dr. Nadler had left orders for me to use a Bennett breathing machine before bedtime. After dinner, the nurse showed me how to use it. The machine slowly blew air into my lungs and I had to blow it back out again. It was kind of like being helped to blow up a balloon. In the morning, I had a little less pain in my chest. The nurse changed all my dressings after scrubbing me clean. That felt awful and wonderful at the same time. I cried when it was over. But after a candy striper massaged my shoulders, I finally drifted into sleep.

Two weeks after the accident, Quincy and I filled out the accident report and sent it to the state. John had been carrying the papers around with him all that time, but couldn't bring himself to sit down and do it. Quincy said John was blaming himself for the accident, and it was affecting his work.

"He's more cantankerous than usual," Quincy quipped, his eyes twinkling. "If you can believe that."

I appreciated Quincy taking care of the accident report, which we needed for the insurance claims. But really, John should have done it. *He* was my husband. I told myself John was traumatized by the accident. And he did, after all, drive 20 miles north each day after work to my parents' home, where Doña was staying, which put him 60 miles away from the hospital. From what Quincy told me, my parents also blamed John for the accident, and just barely tolerated him in their home. I needed to get out soon, before our family broke apart in enmity.

One day, an orderly wheeled me downstairs so I could have the stitches taken out of my chest and take a sitz bath. That turned out to be a bowl that you sit in, not quite what I expected or wanted. The warm water did feel good though. As she reapplied Calamine lotion to my poison oak and rewrapped my swollen breasts, the nurse informed me that three weeks earlier I'd had a tree branch sticking out of me. It all seemed like a bad dream now.

I felt exhausted when I got back to my room. As I dozed, John and Dorrie slipped silently through the door and pulled the curtains around my bed. Dorrie carried a humungous brown paper bag. In it sat Doña, her legs folded tailor fashion. She smiled broadly, like she had a wonderful surprise for me, which of course she did. Somehow, they had sneaked her past the nurse/guard at the door, instructing her to sit very still and not say a word. As soon as I saw her little face smiling up at me, I came wide awake, my pain vanquished by the joy of seeing my daughter again.

Doña was quiet at first, and sat on John's lap, eyeing me warily, but finally put her arms up in my direction. What a treat it was to hold her! Together we looked at a photo book, and talked about Ganma and Gandad, cat, dog, etc. I read a picture book that John had bought from the gift shop. She snuggled into the crook of my arm and rooted around, wanting to nurse. Tears came to my eyes as I gently told her Mommy's milk was "All gone."

When it was time to leave, she tried to get me to "wak" away with John, but was finally persuaded to go with him without me. She looked so precious, holding out her hand toward me as John went out the door. I had missed her terribly, and my heart broke with the knowledge that our special nursing time had come to such an abrupt end. Dorrie gave me a gentle hug and said she'd be back soon.

I slept so well after John and Doña's visit that I wrote three query letters before breakfast the next morning. I had sent some poems with Quincy to mail to *Mother's Manual*. And now I had some new ideas for articles. I enjoyed spending the morning writing, but the exertion of X-rays and a change of room brought on chest cramps after lunch. The physical therapist taught me some breathing techniques to use, and they helped me relax out of the pain for a while.

My new private room was a lovely big corner suite, with windows that looked out to the parking lot. My orthopedic surgeon, Dr. McClintock, was my first visitor.

"I am very happy with the pictures of your fractured tibia," he began. "The traction was meant to take pressure off your spine, but it also has kept your leg immobilized and the break is starting to heal."

"How much longer do I have to have my foot in the air?"

"I should be able to set the bones and cast your leg in another week or two. We'll have to see how the swelling in your back is doing. Perhaps just another week of traction."

"And then I can go home?"

"You need to stay immobilized here for several more weeks at least. And no, you won't be able to go to the writer's conference in August," he answered in response to my next query. "The pelvic fracture won't have healed by then, and you'll have a full leg cast on. You need to be patient and allow yourself time to heal." Familiar words. I was sick of them.

I hadn't thought I could be any more restricted in movement than I already was. That news sent me into doldrums. Now I understood why my parents had arranged for such a nice big room — I would be in it for a long time.

Since everyone who cared about me had decided I couldn't navigate life on the land for a while, John had started looking at houses to rent in Morgan Hill. There were no rentals, but his parents had agreed to pay the down payment on a small house, as long as we made the mortgage payments. Meanwhile, John's dad had announced his retirement from Lick Observatory, and his mom decided to retire from teaching. They would be leaving Mount Hamilton at the end of July and moving into the 40-foot trailer we had bought the previous spring. We wouldn't be able to use it anyway until I had healed. They would make the payments on our trailer while we made payments on their house. It all seemed very confusing to me

My father had made plans as well. Without speaking to either of us, he had decided I should stay with them to recuperate. When John told Dad he had found a house in Morgan Hill, and that Dorrie would be taking care of me and Doña, Dad got really angry. I always knew when he was angry because I knew what it looked and sounded like even when he was silent. John couldn't read the signs. Fortunately, Dad's fury went over John's head, and they didn't get into an actual argument. I knew

Mom and Dad were worried about me, but there was so much blame in their voices whenever they called or visited that I dreaded seeing them. When they did visit, I made up reasons for them to leave early, like I needed to sleep. They had never cared for John, and the accident had only made them dislike him more. Sometimes my frustration at the way they were treating him, and my inability to do anything about it, would bubble over and I would cry myself to sleep.

By July 8th, according to my journal, I felt marginally better, so long as I took my meds. My legs had stopped twitching. The pain in my sacrum and knee was manageable after two Talwans (Pentazocine). At night they gave me Valium. I tried to go without it sometimes and it didn't work, but I kept trying. Every few days the nurse would take me out of traction and lay me on my stomach, propped up with pillows so I didn't hurt my back or my pelvis. The poison oak blisters had nearly healed, leaving my skin scaly and dry. Now she rubbed lotion on me to speed the healing. My milk had dried up, so no more painful wraps.

From my journal:

I never thought I'd say it, but hospital routine sustains me, keeps boredom from getting intolerable. The morning stiffness and pain are relieved by the cheerfulness of opened draperies and having my face washed and my teeth brushed. After breakfast I languish until it's my turn for my sponge bath, that combination of agony as I have to move my painful body and ecstasy as the warm cloths and refreshing lotion soothe my body.

In the summer, Gilroy smells like pizza. Wheeler hospital was only a few miles from the Dole packing plant and South County Foods, the biggest processor of garlic in the state. Trucks and railway cars delivered tons of tomatoes, onions, and garlic for washing, mashing and canning. Those combined fragrances still give the city a unique character that people passing through town remember for years.

From my bed, I had a clear view of the sky outside my window, and of the street signs for Sixth and Eigelberry streets. I loved the few moments each day when a ray of sunshine crossed the floor and warmed my bedding. Even when the thermostat was adjusted for comfort, my room was a cold, lonely place. But I gratefully inhaled the food perfume that wafted in through the cracks in my window. It reminded me of the real world outside the hospital — and I wanted to rejoin it.

A friend from San Jose State sent me a poster, and one of the candy stripers climbed onto my bed to tack it to the ceiling. On it, a scroungy-looking kitten clung to a rope, hanging over a pool of water. "Hang in There!" the caption read. As I lay on my back staring at that damn cat, smelling pizza, desperate for home, I bemoaned my situation. Wrapped in elastic bandages, I was trapped by my broken body, my cast, the traction equipment, and my bed.

Hang in there, indeed. What choice did I have?

It was difficult for John to come all the way from my parents' home in Belmont during the week, but Quincy often stopped by on his way home from work. Sometimes he came in the morning, too, smuggling in a thermos of fresh goat's milk or a handful of peas still in the pods. Dorrie brought a bounty of fresh fruit and vegetables every few days, instructing me to eat heartily because hospital food was notoriously bland, and the fresh food would help me heal. She had that right — I hated the food they served, and looked forward to the fresh strawberries, blackberries, and tomatoes she washed and sliced and delivered in little square plastic boxes. Dorrie had secured a summer job at the Nursing Registry in San Jose, but she and Quincy agreed that once I went home, she would resign and stay with me until her classes started in September. I felt truly grateful for her offer.

A few weeks after Quincy and I filed the accident report, he told me that his auto insurance combined with my medical coverage through John's job at ESL would cover all my medical bills. Also, he told me that Carter had dropped his charges against Dorrie for breaking his window, which I hadn't known about. He also had — at last — filed the transfer of title papers with the county. All of that news helped to cheer me up.

A few days later, John brought me a copy of *Mother's Manual* with my article in it about our trip to Africa with Doña to view the solar eclipse. I loved seeing the article in print — the highest-paid article I had ever sold. A check from John's parents arrived that day too, for the down payment on the house. That weekend Quincy, Dorrie, and John brought in a notary and we all signed the title transfer papers for our land — at last! Now that the land was officially in our names, I could start working toward getting a use permit for the big trailer. It never occurred to me that we would alter our plans for the future. We would return to the land and we would build a home.

Sometimes, when I had no visitors, I lay and replayed the accident over and over. One day, I thought about how I hadn't been able to find the Snugli, and how Doña would have been crushed by the car if she'd been fastened into that cloth carrier. On one of those long days, Dr. Nadler drained the plate-sized hematoma on my back for the second time. It was spooky, but painless to have him drawing blood out of me and not be able to feel it. He said the nerves in my back had been damaged by the metal struts of the Gerry carrier, and I might never get any feeling back in them. He did hold out the possibility that that with onsite nursing care I might be able to go home soon — I burst into tears. I was alive, and Doña was alive, and I would soon be able to go home. My heart soared with joy.

John visited late one night, after I'd already gone to sleep. He told me he was having a hard time sleeping at my Mom's. He said that Doña cried for me in the night and put her pillow over her head when he tried to comfort her. He felt helpless. I didn't know what to suggest, how to help him. I'd already taken my pain meds and I felt a little fuzzy. He stayed a long time, needing to talk. He hadn't yet found a house for us to move into. He showed me his new HP-25 calculator, then we opened a stack of mail together and snuggled on my bed. Finally he had tried to open up to me, and I found myself too drugged to respond.

I continued to ask when I could go home. I had things to do. A baby to take care of. Most of the staff just ignored me, but one day, after she had released me from the traction for a few hours, one really nice aide massaged my back and showed me how to stretch my legs in ways I couldn't while hooked up to the equipment. She also taught me how to do pull-ups on the trapeze bar over my head to keep my arms strong. She said she could swap a hanging shelf for the trapeze if I wanted. I could put books on it, notepads, and even a typewriter. I asked her to please do that. Dorrie brought my typewriter the very next day.

My Aunt Rose had been keeping me supplied with romance novels and Redbook magazines. After I got the typewriter set up, I sent her to the library to track down material about children and separation. I wanted to know how I could help Doña cope with my absence, and learn what long-term effects it might have. I asked Dorrie to check out Bowlby's classic, *Separation and Loss,* from City College. I planned to research and write an article about separation and what a parent could do to help. Writing the article would help the time pass and make me feel useful.

On her next visit from Mount Hamilton, my mother-in-law brought several children's books and a tape recorder. She suggested I record myself reading the stories, which fit right in with Dr. Bowlby's suggestions for parents who had to be separated from their children. Reading the stories kept me busy for hours and made me feel closer to Doña. John took the tapes to her and played them at bedtime. He said my voice seemed to calm her and help her sleep.

My hospital bed began to look like an office — papers and books everywhere. I busied myself reading and writing, doing exercises, eating well, and feeling almost — not quite — content for another few weeks. But I kept asking to go home.

By then it was late July. Doña was 19 months old, and becoming a bit much for my mother to handle. No one told me at the time, but later I learned that Doña was throwing temper tantrums almost daily, and Mom had reached the end of her rope. During the week, John juggled work with driving north from ESL to my parents' home to visit Doña. He had been kicked out of my parents' house and was bed-surfing in Sunnyvale, but they "let" him help with bedtime. He tried to drive south to Gilroy to visit me on weekends, but he also needed to make up lost work hours. Sometimes he telephoned during the week, but our conversations were often interrupted by hospital routines. I missed him terribly.

Finally, the doctors agreed that I could go home, as long as I had nursing coverage until the cast came off, and someone to take care of Doña. My high school friend Arlene had agreed to drive down from Eureka to help me move from the hospital, and on the strength of her R.N. and Dorrie's L.V.N. I was released.

The part I remember most about the last few days in the hospital was the dawning awareness that many people cared about me. I had never been injured before — not even a sprained ankle or broken arm. The helplessness I felt sometimes threatened to overwhelm me. As I slowly began to emerge from the drug- and pain-induced fog, I realized that there were always people in my room, longtime friends, fellow students, colleagues of mine or John's from work, neighbors from around Chesbro Reservoir that I hadn't even met yet, Arlene, Aunt Rose and my parents and in-laws. Not just visiting, but reading to me, feeding me grapes, making me laugh. John Charles, an artist with a uniquely-furnished studio in downtown Morgan Hill, had offered his electric hospital bed. Fran and Walt Peters, neighbors from Chesbro Lake Drive, brought fresh food to my hospital room and entire meals once I moved to the house downtown. And always, Quincy and Dorrie, whose car had caused this terrible thing to happen to my body. They were my touchstone, always ready to run errands or hold my hand.

I had never been good at accepting help, but now I had no choice. I wasn't always clear about that, and I wasn't always good-tempered about it. During the next months, I gradually learned that I needed other people to help me get through this. I couldn't do it alone. Their support kept me from succumbing to despair.

The next lesson I had to learn was that I still had a long way to go before I'd be "back to normal," if ever. It was a big disappointment to discover that no one who cared about me believed I should return to the land. Ever.

My leg was encased in a plaster cast from my ankle to my hip, and I had been given strict instructions not to twist my torso at all until my pelvic and back injuries had healed. I could lie on my back, sit in a reclining chair, or walk a few steps to the bathroom, leaning on a person or a walker. No crutches yet, as they put too much strain on my swollen sacrum, and no upright wheelchair. There was no way I could negotiate the rutted roads, winding paths, or trailer steps at the property. Yet. In my heart, though, I knew I would return to the land. Leaving the hospital would have to be enough for now.

18

LINDO LANE

ON THE DAY I LEFT WHEELER HOSPITAL, I awakened so early that I couldn't rationally begin getting ready. I forced myself to stay in bed until 6:30 a.m. I rang the bell and asked for help to get out of bed and to the bathroom. Marie, the gentle aide who gave such wonderful massages, maneuvered me in and out of the restroom then left me in the reclining wheelchair, pillows protecting my back, while she went to help other patients.

I gave myself a thorough sponge bath, then played ring toss with my underpants until I managed to get them over my feet and up over my full-length cast. I couldn't hope to get my jeans on, but the previous day Arlene had brought me a loose dashiki kind of garment that she had purchased before leaving Arcata. When my breakfast arrived, I sat upright in a chair, fully dressed, hair combed. I was so excited I felt I would burst.

When the nurse arrived to give me my meds, she chided me for not waiting for help, and for sitting in a chair.

"You're not out of the woods yet, Missy," she scolded. "Your back isn't healed properly. You shouldn't be twisting and turning. Let your husband help you when you get home. Be patient." *Patient. How I hated that word.*

Putting her arms around my torso, the nurse lifted me out of the chair and back into bed.

Swallowing my anger, I assured her I would try to be patient. "I'm sorry," I said. "I'm just excited about going home." Then, as soon as she left, I opened the drawers beside my bed and packed up all the toiletries and office supplies I'd stockpiled. I felt gleeful, like a naughty child.

I inched my chair over to the window, looked out once more at the street signs that had been my talismans for two months. Then I parked myself where I could see the entrance to the hospital and waited for Arlene and John. It was 8:00 a.m.

I thought I'd die of boredom, I waited so long. Finally, at 9:00 a.m. Dr. Nadler signed my chart after making me climb back into bed. Dr. McClintock came in at 10:00 a.m., said he would call in a prescription for pain medication and Valium to help me sleep. John or Arlene would need to pick it up. He handed me a piece of paper on which he'd written the phone numbers of a naturopath and a chiropractor. "You might find these people helpful as you rehabilitate," he said, his old eyes twinkling kindly. "They can help you deal with the pain. You'll be feeling it for some time yet." Then, with a flourish, he signed my release papers.

Arlene came at 11:00 a.m., examined my chart, then carried all my bags and flowers out to the car. I reached out my arms to hug her, but she was all business, figuratively wearing her nurse's hat. John finally arrived, having spent the morning unpacking boxes and setting up the Charles' hospital bed in our living room. I tried to hug him too, but he also was focused on the tasks at hand.

When we got to the car, Arlene helped me out of the wheelchair into the front seat, which John had pushed back as far as it would go and laid flat. A sharp pain shot through my back and down my leg as Arlene maneuvered me, and I shrieked. She said something quietly to John, then wheeled the chair back to the front of the hospital and drove off. Before climbing behind the steering wheel, John jury-rigged the safety belt so it would go over me and my cast and still fasten. I smiled in spite of the pain. He had always been a stickler for seat belts.

The slow drive home reminded John of another trip in the Pinto nearly two years earlier in Washington D.C. I had been in labor with Doña, and John was driving me and my midwife, Tina, to Georgetown University Hospital. We were traveling from Alexandria, Virginia and it was a weekday morning, rush hour. Five bridges allow access from Virginia and Maryland to the District of Columbia, and that morning two of them were closed. Today, as John negotiated traffic and detours, I called out in pain at every jerk of the car, just like I had done all those years ago.

Now, as John made his way along the pothole-filled road from Gilroy to Morgan Hill, he reminded me of that journey. "Remember how you told me to "stop right there" and get you out of the car? I left the car in front of Emergency and came back to a parking ticket."

I admitted I'd forgotten all about that.

"And how the hospital typewriter didn't have a tilde? Doña's name on the paperwork, and eventually her birth certificate, contained an apostrophe between the n and the a. Forever."

Engaged by his colorful narrative, I relaxed, and the pain eased somewhat. I was going home at last. I couldn't wait to see the house John had found, and to get on with my life.

Arlene was waiting for us at the house, the front door wide open, a glass of water and two Valiums in her hand. Once again, she was all business. She opened my door and gave me the pills, then began unloading all my flowers and books and plastic bags from the back of the Pinto. Finally, she unfastened the seat belt and motioned for John to take me in. As he lifted me and my heavy cast out of the car, up the two stairs to the living room, and deposited me clumsily onto the bed, I couldn't help laughing through my gritted teeth.

"You're like the Alms Uncle carrying Clara to the patch of lupines on the mountain in the Heidi book," I said unsteadily, already succumbing to a Valium-induced haze. Neither of them had a clue what I meant.

Arlene arranged my pillows and bedding to support my leg and back, then asked if I wanted anything to eat. At last, she was relaxed and smiling.

"Sure," I said, "I'll have a burger and a beer."

And then I went to sleep.

So, in this manner I moved to the little house on Lindo Lane, where I was carried from room to room, or allowed to use a walker, which I found both humiliating and difficult. I'd never seen anyone use a walker who wasn't very old, and the embarrassment of having to use one only added to my frustration at being unable to return to the land. Mom and Dad brought Doña down a few days later, rather grumpily, and Dorrie took over her care.

John found it painful to see me incapacitated. He resumed his routine of sleeping late, leaving for ESL immediately after breakfast, and returning late at night. I tried to keep him home longer, asking him to brush my hair, read a story to Doña, or sit with me and talk, but he said he had missed so much work since the accident he felt pressured to make up the time. It felt like an excuse, and disappointing that he wouldn't spend at least a few days at home with me.

A few days after I left the hospital, Arlene and Dorrie drove up to the property together. While Dorrie took Doña to feed the animals, Arlene packed boxes of clothing, food, and kitchen equipment from the trailer, which she then organized into the house on Lindo Lane. Many years passed before I realized that Arlene had spent her 28th birthday sorting through my disorganized belongings.

Each day as I awakened and submitted to the indignities of being dressed and deposited on the couch, I bemoaned all the time being wasted.

"When can I go back to the land?" I asked everyone who would listen. "I want to plant my fall vegetables."

No one would give me a straight answer. I became so depressed I couldn't even write.

After Arlene went back to Arcata, the days and weeks crawled by. Dorrie took over the task of caring for both me and Doña. She bought groceries, did the laundry, brought treats to cheer me up. I was still in pain, and couldn't hold Doña unless she sat still. She found it difficult to see me and not be able to cuddle. Dorrie took her along whenever she left the house to shop, milk the goats, feed the animals, or work in the garden. She'd return late in the day to prepare our dinner, bathe Doña and put her to bed. They spent many hours together, and developed a loving relationship that lasted for years. Meanwhile, I missed out on precious time with my daughter and felt like a waste of space.

Slowly, minutely, I learned how to maneuver the walker around the house. I started to prop myself at the sink to wash a few dishes, prepare simple meals, set out PlayDoh on the kitchen table. Each week I could do a little more, and Dorrie started leaving me alone with Doña for an hour, then two, then half a day. Finally, my cast came off and I began learning to use crutches. Dorrie returned to school and work, and Doña and I were alone together for long periods of time.

This was a time of healing for all of us, a time for us to forgive ourselves for the errors in judgment we had made that caused the accident, a time to build a set of interconnecting relationships that would allow John and me to return to our adventure in the hills. We had a couple of conversations about the accident, then we left it alone. I felt strongly that any blame should be shared between the four of us. I certainly didn't hold Dorrie or Quincy accountable for my injuries.

We understood more clearly now the dangers inherent in living on the land, and the ease with which one wrong decision could wreak terrible consequences. We were so very young, and we had very little direct experience with the tasks required to develop a piece of land into a farm. The families who lived along our rural road made repeated visits: first to me in the hospital, then in town to the house that John's parents had purchased, and finally to all of us when I finally returned to the land. We discovered a community of people who understood the draw of the land, and who had lived on it longer than we had. They were happy to help us learn the ropes. Next time we had a difficult task to accomplish, we promised, we would ask for help.

In order to keep me entertained while under house arrest, Dorrie and Quincy began coming over to take their showers and do their laundry. After a while, they began to prepare celebratory meals at the drop of a hat. The First Day of School, the First Day of Fall, Halloween, Thanksgiving, and Christmas all would have their celebrations, their decorations, and their gatherings. They formed work parties and cleared our back yard of debris so we could start a garden. I watched from the back porch as they built raised boxes and poured in bags of soil and manure they had carried down from the land. John built a high picket gate across the driveway so that our German shepherd and his parents' dog, Duchess, also a shepherd, could come and live with us. I loved watching everyone work, but my life was still on hold.

OUR FIRST VISIT TO THE LAND

MARLENE ON A HORSE

GRADING THE ROAD

MOVING MANURE

FAMILY PORTRAIT

OUR HOME ON THE ROAD

DOÑA FEEDING THE CHICKENS

SNOW ON OUR HILL – APRIL 1976

GARDEN WITH CHILDREN

ON THE HAMMOCK WITH FRIENDS

MARLENE AND DOÑA

DORRIE AND QUINCY
LOOKING GOOD

BOB SETTLING INTO HIS NEW
HOME

DOÑA HELPING MOM
SPRUCE UP AN OLD BENCH

BABY JOHN IN A SANDBOX

NINA AND CHILDREN COOLING OFF

JOHN CUTTING STRUTS FOR THE DOME

DIAMOND, ELSA, AND WILLIE GUARDING THE ROAD

BABY JOHN AND BABY CHICK

QUINCY IN A
CONTEMPLATIVE MOMENT

DEAN PUTTING SOCKS ON
DOÑA

BABY JOHN IN THE
PINK BATHTUB

THE MORGAN HILL TRADING POST JEEP

DOÑA IN THE STORE WINDOW

BOB AND WILLIE

FAMILY ON THE
DOME FRAME

REPURPOSING THE BATHTUB

MARLENE TAKING A WALK

WATTLES AND KIDS

MARLENE'S FAMILY TODAY

19

WIDENING MY HORIZONS

ALTHOUGH JOHN HAD WORKED HARD to make the house welcoming for me coming home from the hospital, he had been moody and distant since I'd actually arrived. No matter how often I asked, he wouldn't sit down and talk about his feelings. I felt shut out and unsure what I could do about it. Dorrie still came over each morning before school to get me up and dressed. John would wait until she left the house, then he would come through the living room to the kitchen, eat his breakfast standing up, then leave. He seemed to find it difficult to look at me, and he didn't want to help me with dressing or personal hygiene. I needed his help and support, but he couldn't seem to provide it. I thought about consulting a therapist, but suspected he wouldn't agree.

Trapped in the little house on Lindo Lane, I turned to the tiny local newspaper, the *Morgan Hill Times*, to stay in touch with the outside world. I read it cover to cover every day, and bored John when he did come home with details of the comings and goings of Morgan Hill socialites, politicians, and members of the business community.

Doña needed more stimulation than I could offer from my walker. I could pull her onto my lap and read to her, and I could sit beside her at the kitchen table when she drew or painted, but it still took real effort for me to stand up and move from one place to another. When she lost interest in whatever she had been doing, she looked for things to do to get my attention. One day she unrolled an entire roll of toilet paper, then pulled the end down the hallway to the living room to show me. Another day she opened the cupboard in the kitchen where the bags of flour and sugar were stored, and emptied the contents onto the floor. It didn't make sense to get angry with her — she was behaving like a normal two-year-old — but I did.

In desperation, I advertised in the paper that I would be holding a weekly playgroup at my house, and three moms joined me for tea while our toddlers totally destroyed any semblance of order in the front room. What had I been thinking? The playgroup did help, though, with our loneliness and boredom. Doña looked forward to her new friends arriving, and would stand by the front window behind the sheer curtain as we waited for them to arrive. I had been so lonely that, just like Doña, I would often sit at the window waiting for someone to walk by. I would talk at length to the mailman. Having other mothers to converse with felt wonderful. But once a week wasn't enough to keep Doña's mind and body occupied — or mine either.

I advertised in the newspaper for high school students to play with her in the afternoons, the most difficult times, and for a few weeks that went well. At the end of the month, however, when John saw the checks I had written, he objected to the cost.

"The payment on Mom and Dad's mortgage is taking most of my salary, Marlene, on top of our land payment and our share of the animal feed. There is simply no money for extras."

I felt chagrined. I had not even considered our financial situation. Perhaps money was the source of his malaise. I apologized for not checking with him first. I had been lonely and bored, and now I felt unappreciative as well.

The solution came the next day when I received an invitation to a series of La Leche League informational meetings in San Jose. La Leche League had been founded in 1958 to support new mothers who wanted to breastfeed their infants. At that time, less than 10% of American women were breastfeeding when they went home after the birth of their child, and most stopped after a few weeks. I had joined La Leche League in Washington, D.C. shortly before Doña's birth, and attended meetings regularly as long as we lived there.

I had also attended LLL meetings in San Jose when we lived on Mount Hamilton. The stress of student teaching and living with my mother-in-law had triggered a drop in my breastmilk production. Jody, the leader running those meetings, had been understanding and helpful. She suggested several relaxation techniques and loaned me a guided meditation tape to play each time I sat down to nurse Doña. My milk supply soon had returned to normal.

I called Jody, told her about the accident and my challenges keeping Doña entertained and happy. I asked her if she thought any of the mothers in her group might want to bring their toddlers over to play. She drove down the next day with her own two children. While the three children played happily, Jody reviewed the addresses of current and former members of the group. She suggested that we hold the next series of meetings in Morgan Hill.

"Several of our members live down here," she announced. "And I see four or five others on the list who live in south county. They would probably be willing to come down for a meeting, and perhaps also for a playgroup between meetings."

We sat companionably for another hour, drinking tea and watching our children play, and thinking of other activities the mothers might enjoy. Then she made an unexpected suggestion:

"Why don't you train to be an LLL leader, and start your own group in Morgan Hill?"

La Leche League had collected current information about birth and newborn care, developed a four-meeting format to help mothers educate their families and friends about breastfeeding, understand the supply-and-demand nature of producing a consistent supply of breastmilk, and improve their personal nutrition — and that of their families — in order to meet the needs of their babies. Jody pointed out that I'd attended at least six complete 4-meeting programs, and that I knew the answers to the most common questions mothers asked.

"*The Womanly Art of Breastfeeding* has the rest of the answers," she continued, citing the LLL bible. My personal copy of the book was dog-eared and soiled from all the times I had searched it in the middle of the night, holding a hungry, fussy, baby.

"The training packet is do-it-yourself," Jody continued. "You can take as long as you like to study it and complete the worksheets, then you send it in and a team back in Chicago will certify you."

Doña and I were bored. I agreed. The next four monthly meetings were scheduled to meet at our house, we set the dates for monthly play dates, and I began working my way through the LLL training material. During this period, my advisor, Bev Jensen, visited. "We're starting a new master's program," she told me, "in Early Childhood Education. Several new state funding initiatives call for us to increase our early childhood work force statewide. We need to design certificate and degree programs for community colleges to offer, and they'll soon be desperate for instructors to teach the new standards of care." I knew what Bev was leaving unsaid: "Come back to school and join the program."

"I'll look into it," I promised her. "When I'm back on my feet."

*   *   *

I had been persistent in my requests to move back to our homestead during the early months of my recovery. John thought that building a chicken coop and buying some chickens might satisfy me for a while. Using a coyote-proof design he found in a *Mother Earth News* article, he built a pen that would fit on the back of Sarge and that he could transport up the hill to our land when we were ready to move back. By the time he had drawn the plans, purchased the lumber and wire, and constructed the coop, I could help from the edges, using a walker.

Bea and John were leaving Mount Hamilton, and Bea had gone through stacks of supplies and curriculum material that collected over 20 years of teaching. In one of her boxes was a large incubator, designed to keep a dozen eggs warm until they hatched, and to permit several children at once to look at the eggs or the chicks. She gave that to me, and I set it up on the kitchen table. I asked Dorrie to bring down a dozen eggs that she believed to be fertilized. Doña loved watching the eggs while she ate breakfast, and we checked off each day on a calendar. I marked Day 21 with a large red X. That's when I expected the first egg to hatch.

The chicks emerged on schedule, all twelve of them. After a few days, we moved them from the incubator to a large box with sawdust in the bottom and a light at the top. Their *cheep-cheep-cheep* became my constant companions, and when they all had feathers John moved them to the pen outdoors. I now had a daily chore: feeding the chickens and replacing their water. I couldn't manage cleaning their bedding just yet, or removing their larger waterer from the pen to clean, but Doña and I would go out morning and night just to watch the poults scratch around and take them scraps from the kitchen. On weekends, John or Dorrie or Quincy would clean out the wood chips and replace them with fresh, and whoever was around when the waterer got empty would fill it back up again.

Soon I began to think about rabbits. John agreed to build a rabbit hutch, and I started reading about rabbit management. I'd never raised rabbits on my own, but it didn't look hard when Dorrie did it. Dorrie brought me the address of a 4H family who had posted a card on Gunter Brothers' bulletin board, and I telephoned them. They would be selling their hutch and all four of their rabbits after the county fair in late August. We would be downtown farmers.

In mid-August, John flew to Los Angeles to demonstrate ESL's new image processing program at an electronics show. Quincy had just left for England on a similar mission, so both Dorrie and I were left alone. The last week before leaving, John worked long hours at ESL in preparation for the show, and when he came home, he was often in a bad mood.

"I should have gone to England instead of Quincy," he explained. "He's better than me at big shows, and I know England better than he does." He was dreading the dog and pony show he would have to stage in L.A. and the days of customer support that would follow.

To cheer him up, I suggested we go out for dessert. John and Sue Charles had invited us several times. I called them and accepted their latest offer. Doña and their daughter, Donna Tina, were the same age and played well together. Using my walker, and John's help supporting me from behind, I made it up their three steps and into the house fairly easily.

Sue served vegan chocolate cake topped with goat milk ice cream she had made from milk Dorrie had given her. As we ate, I told the Charles' they could retrieve their hospital bed in a couple of weeks, when I would hopefully get clearance to use crutches and return to our big bed. Our visit felt so *normal*. I felt reassured that I would soon be up and about.

Dorrie had to go to an orientation at City College the next day, so when we got home, John called his sister Jo and asked her to come and stay with me. He left for work before dawn. Jo was great — she dressed Doña and took her out back to water the garden, then she took her for a walk in the stroller until her niece fell asleep. She hung up the new curtains in the living room and started in on dinner. I asked her if she'd like to move in for a while, but she just laughed. Dorrie was starting school the following week, and would be limited in the amount of time she could help me or care for Doña. I didn't feel ready to be on my own just yet.

That night I called Mom and asked if she would stay with me while John was in L.A. Dad brought her down the next day. John stayed for a while, working in the yard with Dad, but it was awkward because neither of my parents would speak directly to him, instead directing messages through me. Finally, *humph*'ing and stomping, John left to go to the property.

He'd rented a piece of equipment the previous week to grade the road. He needed to remove the fence and stakes surrounding the trailer so that Pop could move the trailer back to Mount Hamilton. He and Bea had postponed their vacation due to my accident, but were still planning to leave when they could, and they needed to have their trailer back. After John left, Dad finished raking leaves and packed them into plastic bags. Mom cleaned the kitchen and made a lovely dinner. After we ate, Dad drove back to Belmont and I settled Mom into our guest room. John flew to L.A. the next morning.

It was a difficult week. Doña refused to sleep in her new bed, which was a pallet on the floor. She couldn't sleep with me in the hospital bed. I couldn't lift her into the porta-crib. When he was home at bedtime, John lay down beside her and read or sang to her, so Mom tried that. It worked pretty well, but it wasn't a solution I would be able to continue once she went home.

The following Saturday, Dad came back, this time with my brother Keith driving Mom's car. They mowed the lawns and Dad took us all to lunch at Martin's Old Time Ranch in San Martin. We ate delicious chicken and dumplings and fresh baked biscuits.

"We used to stop here on the way to Hollywood to play cricket," Dad told me as we ate our meal. "It was my favorite part of the drive."

Dad bowled for the Golden Gate Cricket Club in Berkeley, and they played a cup game every year against the Southern California Corinthians, a team made up at least partly of Hollywood notables such as Boris Karloff and Aubrey Smith. They alternated playing in Hollywood and Berkeley. One of Dad's teammates in this friendly match was Colin Fletcher, the pioneering backpacker and writer, who often invited both teams and their families, including me, to his home in Berkeley after a match. Other teammates were doctors, orthodontists, lawyers, and nightclub singers. None of this meant anything to me at the time, but now I marvel at how the game of cricket became an equalizer, allowing my father, a working class man from the north of England, to play and socialize with a class of people who would have shunned him in their native England.

We returned home from lunch to find Pop's truck and trailer in front of the house, and Pop unloading stuff from the trailer that Arlene had missed. After he left, Aunt Rose and Uncle Alex arrived; my parents had invited them for dinner. Mom made an amazing rabbit stew. Dorrie had been keeping our freezer filled with chicken and rabbit and Mom had happily reached for the rabbit when she saw it.

"I haven't cooked rabbit since we lived in Australia," she told me. "Your grandmother made the best rabbit stew — I never do get the seasonings right." But I thought Mom's rendition tasted just fine.

That night, after Rose and Alex left, Dad and Keith bunked in the living room and Mom slept with Doña in the guest room.

Sunday, Mom and Dad put up our new drapes in the master bedroom while I coached from the bed. In the middle of our industry, Quincy walked in, on his way from the airport to the property.

"How was England?" I asked.

"The milk was warm, and I had to queue up a lot." Quincy was not a happy traveler.

He had brought me a package of chocolate digestive biscuits, which I immediately opened and passed around. Dad and Keith left in Dad's truck shortly after Quincy, leaving Mom's car at our house. She and I geared up for another difficult bedtime. Quincy had delivered a message from John that he would be demonstrating their new product in San Diego before he came home, so he'd be gone an additional week.

"Couldn't he at least have called?" my mother asked. I didn't have the heart to tell her he rarely did.

On August 20, Mom drove me to Dr. McClintock's office in Gilroy. He cut the plaster of Paris monstrosity into two vertical pieces. Then, after X-rays and a luxurious soak of my leg in hot water, he put the back piece of the cast back on as a splint, and wrapped my leg with a very long ace bandage. My knee was still swollen and, even after he cut my cast off, I couldn't bend my leg. Dr. McClintock said a bone chip floated loose in the joint, but pretty low.

"Eventually it will settle," he said, "and full movement should be restored."

He gave me exercises to do, but told me to keep using the walker another couple of weeks. No crutches yet.

The next day was really hot. Mama and I spent most of it in front of the fan, trying to keep cool and to entertain Doña. I took off the splint to do my exercises, but accidentally knocked my foot off the coffee table, and the weight of it dropping to the floor forced it to bend, making me screech. It surprised me, how much it hurt after all this time. I had to use both hands to lift my foot slowly back up again and rest it on the table. I decided to forget about exercises for now, and wrapped my leg again in the splint and elastic bandage.

I missed John, and so did Doña. She called him often on her little plastic telephone, and asked if the cars she could see outside our living room window were her Daddy. Now she cried for Daddy at bedtime. She didn't want to be with my mother any more, and I appeared to be totally useless to her.

The heat wave continued through the rest of the week. On Friday, Mom drove us to Safeway, and we dawdled through our shopping, enjoying the air conditioning. I leaned on the grocery cart as if it were a walker.

We returned home to two telephone messages. The first was from Adult Education. They agreed to offer the course I had proposed: Children's Literature for Parents. I would be teaching at the high school, just a block from our house. Mom walked to the Adult Ed office to pick up a personnel packet for me to fill out. She took Doña to the park while I did so.

The other phone message was that John would be flying home that afternoon. *Thank God*, I thought. He had been gone for two weeks — two weeks too many. That evening, Quincy dropped John off on his way home, and Mom made her last meal. John happily did bedtime with Doña and then we shared a bed for the first time in months. It wasn't glorious or sexy, since I still had a heavy half-cast wrapped in an elastic bandage on my leg, but I turned on my side and John curled up around my back, and it felt cozy.

The next morning, John hitched a ride with Mom to Sunnyvale to retrieve the Pinto from ESL, and he took Doña with him. Grateful for the gift of a whole day alone, I began to write my article on Separation and Maternal Deprivation. I felt optimistic. *Baby Talk* had accepted my article about using a Snugli to keep babies happy while on vacation. It would be in their September issue, titled "Portable Baby."

After John returned, we slipped into a pleasant domestic routine. He seemed happier. Apparently he had acquitted himself well at the two electronic shows and with the customer in L.A. He was pleased to see my cast gone, and me standing at the kitchen counter, preparing our meals. He spent fewer hours away, and more hours with Doña and me, even helping me with my exercises. My muscle tone was completely gone and it was nice to have him hold my foot so it didn't crash to the ground when I unwrapped the bandages and took it off the coffee table. He supported my foot while I cautiously bent my knee and then he hung a handbag from my foot as Dr. McClintock had instructed. He cheered me on as I tried, ineffectually, to lift my weighted foot off the floor. Doña was delighted to have her father back, and followed him around, watching him repair things, sort boxes, and putter in the yard. She watched thoughtfully while he helped me with my exercises. I wondered how much she understood.

I felt mobile enough by the end of August to can eight quarts of peaches and make some jam. I also wrote another article for *Baby Talk*, about feeding toddlers real food from the table. John built a bookshelf to hold Doña's growing picture book collection, which I planned to use in the Children's Literature for Parents class I would be teaching in the fall.

After Dorrie went back to school and work in September, I spent my days alone with Doña. Unlike Dorrie, who had played on the floor with her for hours, I couldn't lift my daughter, or chase her when she ran away, or correct her when she threw a toy. She was almost two, and as two-year-olds often do, she expressed frustration in tantrums. The first day we were alone, she pushed my walker to the far end of the house. I had to crawl on my belly down the hall to retrieve it. Time after time I found myself on the floor, unable to get up, feeling angry and helpless. My joy at being a mother was slipping away.

I loved the idea of teaching a class for Adult Ed, but I needed to earn real money; I'd lost so much time already. In order to do that, I would have to put Doña back in child care. Once Dr. McClintock gave me clearance to use crutches, I called Heidi's Learning Center in Gilroy to see how much it would cost for Doña to attend their toddler program for a few hours each day. I explained to the owner, Nancy Hendrickson, about the accident and my physical limitations. I also told her that I had recently received an elementary teaching credential and would be willing to exchange teaching for childcare. That was providential — Nancy had been looking for a primary level teacher. She suggested I come to the school for a tour and she would see what we could work out. The following week, I asked one of the playgroup moms to stay with Doña and I crutched to the bus stop near our house, which stopped just a block away from Heidi's.

Heidi's Learning Center was located in an old church at the corner of 7th and Eigelberry Streets, just a block away from Wheeler Hospital. Nancy used many of the concepts of the Open School movement popular at the time, including giving children control over when and where they completed their assignments. I saw children lying on the floor, sitting alone or clustered in small groups, working with a wide variety of hands-on educational materials. Some sat at desks, others at tables. One boy walked around aimlessly until a teacher gave him a suggestion and guided him back into focus. The walls were covered with posters and banners the children had made; moveable chalkboards served as dividers between groups of children.

"When a child first comes to school," Nancy explained, "I assess them in each subject area. Then I assign them to a form (rather than a grade), based on their level: First Form, Second Form, and so forth. Each is identified with one of the colors of the rainbow."

The children spent each morning in their form, reading and writing and taking part in a variety of emergent literacy activities with their teacher.

In the afternoons, children moved from area to area within the building as they worked on their personal work contracts in other areas of the curriculum. A child could be in the First Form for Reading and Literacy, but the Third Form for Arithmetic and Science. Teaching of skills and concepts took place in small groups and individually. Periodically, each child was reassessed and moved to a new form if appropriate. In addition to teaching their homeroom students and supervising the afternoon contract activities, each teacher developed specialized units of study in areas that interested them — such as astronomy, geography, or a foreign language — and presented that material to each of the forms in turn. I could readily imagine Doña attending this cheerful school.

Doña joined the toddler program, and received the loving care and attention she desperately needed from the lead teacher, Ann. Both the toddler program and the preschool were located in cozy little houses next door to the Big School. Fencing enclosed the three buildings such that each structure had its own play yard, and each could be accessed via gates to each of the others. I will forever be grateful that, along with practical life activities, letters and numbers and an amazing number of songs with hand motions, Ann taught Doña to use a potty independently and how to tie her shoes.

Nancy asked me to teach a second/third grade combination class. I would earn a modest salary, and Doña's fees would be waived. Nancy was offering me a wonderful opportunity. I started teaching the last week of September, sitting in one chair with my leg on another and my crutches propped up beside me. Doña and I saw one another many times during the school day; she always knew where to find me, and I always knew she was okay. The memory of my discouraging semester of student teaching at Morgan Hill School began to fade as I learned to teach reflectively and responsively, encouraging the children to be self-motivated, independent, and responsible.

Using crutches was a step in the right direction, but I still couldn't drive. Doña and I traveled to Gilroy each morning by bus. I enjoyed the ride, straight down the old Monterey Highway from the stop close to our house. Farms were still the primary occupants of the frontage along the highway at that time. Doña watched for cows and horses and goats, and the occasional deer. Karen, the First Form teacher, lived near Morgan Hill, and after she discovered what we were doing, offered to drive us one way or the other. She and I became friends, and she included me in invitations to impromptu musical concerts, work parties, grape stomping, hot tub skinny-dipping, and other weekend activities.

These social activities usually included the other teachers and their partners and several other people living nearby in yurts and tents and refurbished chicken houses. Sometimes John would join Doña and me at these events, but due to his introverted nature, he didn't usually find them enjoyable. He preferred to stay at work or home and meet us later. I loved meeting all these new people. Who knew there was an alternative lifestyle community in the Valley of Heart's Delight?

20

100 DAFFODILS

B EFORE I COULD DRIVE, Dorrie sometimes took me along when she ran errands in town or further afield. One day she introduced me to the Whole Earth Truck Store in Menlo Park. What a wonderful place! Originally an actual truck, the Truck Store sold just about anything a back-to-the-lander could want out of a large warehouse. A tall counter on the left as you entered invited you to sit on a tall stool and drink an organic juice or smoothie. The tall shelving units further in, filled with amazing goods, invited you to climb back off the stool and start exploring.

These are the sorts of items I remember being offered at the Truck Store: hoof picks, lamp wick cleaners, brackets to hang lamps on the wall, manual latches for old four-wheel-drive vehicles, and hay hooks. Books of all kinds. *Chickens in Your Back Yard*, *The Last Whole Earth Catalog*, and *The Dome Book* were the first ones I purchased. Barrels filled with bulk grain, teas and herbs, and an entire wall of farming tools. I dubbed it a "way-of-life" store.

Stewart Brand came up with the idea. He had friends all over the country who were living on the land, and they had a common complaint: the local feed stores and hardware stores were limited in the kinds of tools they offered. They didn't sell parts for wood burning stoves or windmills or plans to build a methane toilet. He would search for these diverse items and drive around the country selling products out of his truck. He would take orders, find the desired items, and deliver them directly to the communities that wanted them.

The truck idea didn't work very well. Brand developed the *Whole Earth Catalog* next, putting people directly in touch with the sources of tools they needed. The *Whole Earth Catalog* was a uniquely American counterculture magazine and product. Customers couldn't buy any products from the catalog, but had to go directly to the manufacturers, whose addresses and telephone numbers were listed in the catalog. Brand's best-selling tool was the catalog itself, annotated by him, featuring tools and other products that didn't fit into his truck, reviewed by people who had actually used them. He sold millions of copies of the three editions, and then he created this one-of-a-kind retail store in Menlo Park for those of us lucky enough to live nearby. I decided that when I could drive again, I would become a regular customer.

One Saturday in late September, I asked Dorrie to take me to the land to see what remained of my garden. She wasn't sure driving on the bumpy road was a good idea, but she did it anyway, even stopping on the way to buy a bag of daffodil bulbs. She had packed a picnic and once we arrived, she laid out a large blanket on the knoll. She helped me into a comfortable position on the blanket, reclining on pillows but leaning on one arm so I could see the clearing and my garden, which looked a little sad. She set out our lunch, starting with Doña. Sitting under the tree, eating a sandwich and feeling the slight dampness from a rare fall rain through the heavy woolen blanket and my jeans, my eyes filled with tears. I loved this place like nowhere I had ever lived.

John and I had been on the land only four months when I had been carried away in an ambulance, and it had taken four months for me to return. How long would it be before I could live here again, walk in the woods with our daughter, milk our goats, collect eggs from the chickens, feed us with food harvested from the garden I had so lovingly planted?

I sobbed with disappointment and sadness. Dorrie held me briefly, then reminded me that we had daffodils to plant. She handed me a small shovel and a dry brown daffodil bulb. I planted it where we sat, then scooched myself a few feet from the blanket and planted another. Doña wanted to help. I showed her how to put the third bulb in the hole. When I got tired, I rested, and Dorrie dug some holes. I scooched up and down that hill so much that I wore holes in my pants. It took a very long time, several hours, but Dorrie and Doña and I planted 100 daffodils that afternoon. And as we drove back down the hill to town, I pledged to be back to see them flower in the spring.

THREE

EVOLVING

1976

- MOS Technology introduces the 6502 processor
- Steve Wozniak and Steve Jobs form Apple Computer and build the first microcomputer in Jobs' garage in Cupertino

1977

- Steve Jobs and Steve Wozniak develop the Apple II using the 6502 processor
- Atari introduces a videogame console, the 2600, based on the 6502 processor

1978

- The Global Positioning System or GPS is inaugurated by the USA military
- Apple launches a project to design a personal computer with a graphical user interface
- Atari announces the Atari 800, designed by Jay Miner

21

FROM TEACHER TO AUTHOR

I DREW MY FIRST SOCIAL STUDIES PROJECT at Heidi's Learning Center from a unit I remembered from my own sixth grade class at Arundel School in Belmont: the Aztecs, and the importance of corn to their society.

Dorrie enjoyed helping with my projects and during the weeks I couldn't drive she drove me around, gathering needed supplies. Since it was early fall, we were able to purchase several ears of fresh corn, yellow and white, from a farmer's stand that she passed on her way from the property. Dorrie harvested some ears of popcorn from my garden where they had been left to dry, and we found dried Indian corn at a local craft store where it was being sold for use in Thanksgiving decorations.

Talking with the children about these three different kinds of corn, I learned that most of them had never seen white or multicolored corn, nor knew that popcorn came from an ear of corn like corn on the cob or creamed corn, which turned out to be their favorite way to enjoy the vegetable. I took the children into the teachers' break room and we heated the ear of popcorn in the microwave. To everyone's delight, including mine, the kernels popped right on the cob.

Together we read several illustrated books about the Aztecs, and the children spent a week drawing four-sided pyramids, temples, and Aztec sculptures. We read that corn — or *maize*, as it was called by the Aztecs — had been very important in their society. They worshipped and celebrated different stages in the corn plant's life with festivals and offerings. The Aztec people gave these stages names, and created images of them in stone and in paintings. As the children's art projects became more elaborate and comprehensive, I brought in a *metate* and *mano* to demonstrate the traditional way to grind corn, and the children learned how to make corn meal, then drew what they had made and the tools they had used. We decided our next cooking projects would be corn bread.

At home, I experimented with grinding corn using the same metal-toothed hand grinder that we used for making whole wheat flour and peanut butter. It could be done, but it would be too hard for the children to turn the crank. By the time the walls of our class area had become totally covered by Aztec art, Dorrie and I had visited the Whole Earth Truck Store in Menlo Park to purchase a bag of dried corn and a stone grain mill. The stone wheels would crush and grind the corn kernels more effectively than the metal wheels. I demonstrated how to grind and sift the corn. Soon the children had produced several cups of cornmeal suitable for baking.

At our second cooking session, we made two batches of cornbread from the same recipe — one using standard degerminated cornmeal purchased at the grocery store, and the other from the whole grain cornmeal we had ground ourselves. That was a very popular activity. The children wrapped up a square from each batch to taste test at home. While we were eating the results of our labor, one of the children asked if we could make tortillas next. I agreed, but explained that we would have to *nixtamalize* the corn first.

The ancient Aztecs had discovered that cornmeal, even when ground very fine, didn't absorb enough moisture to make a cohesive dough that could be flattened and baked. In order to solve that problem, they ground corn grains against rough pieces of limestone found in river beds, in the process mixing powdered lime into the grains. When ground that way, the resulting corn flour absorbed more liquid and made a malleable dough called *masa*. Today, people in Mesoamerica and elsewhere accomplish the same thing by adding lime or calcium hydroxide to a pot of boiling corn and soaking it overnight. Then they rub off the skins and grind the soaked corn in a hand grinder or food processor. When corn is processed this way, it is known as *nixtamal*.

The day after the tortillas went home from school, I had four requests from parents for recipes. At our weekly land potluck, temporarily moved to the Lindo Lane house, I told everyone about the success of the Aztec corn curriculum.

"Perhaps you and the children could make a corn cookbook for the parents. You know, incorporate some of their art into it, as well the history of the Aztec people." That was Dorrie, who knew exactly what I had been doing and perfectly captured the main concepts I hoped to teach.

"You could move on to the Incas next," added Jan, Bob's friend from ESL. "They used some kind of rare grain that grew in the higher altitudes. Quinoa, I think it was called. I wonder if you could get hold of some."

"And barley — the Scots used barley for all kinds of things, including booze," contributed John, grinning.

Quincy had been looking pensive, staring at the grain grinder fastened to one end of our kitchen table.

"Marlene," he said gravely. "I think you should write a book. A real book."

Quincy wasn't the first person to suggest that. On one of our visits to the Whole Earth Truck Store I had asked if they had a book that had recipes using different kinds of whole grains. I explained that since we didn't have refrigeration to keep our whole grain flour from going rancid, we bought our grains whole, often buying much larger bags than we needed.

As he rang up my purchases, the cashier shook his head. "No, we don't have anything like that," he answered. "But if you wrote one, we could sell it."

Tricia taught 5th and 6th grade at Heidi's. They were doing a unit on ancient civilizations in the Fertile Crescent — Egyptians, Sumerians, Babylonians, Persians, and Hebrews. All of these societies grew and ate both wheat and barley. Barley was also used by the Sumerians as the basic unit of measure and by the Babylonians as monetary currency. I decided to teach a unit on barley to Tricia's class, then wheat to the remaining 3rd and 4th graders.

I proceeded with those plans, using recipes from books that I found in the library and creating activities that showed how these ancient people used barley in a variety of different ways. Since barley is thought to have been the first domesticated grain, I also took the children for a walking field trip to a vacant lot a few blocks away from the school. There we found grass as high as some of the children — I cut several grain heads and we took them back to class to inspect. Our sample consisted primarily of oats, but some barley also. The children took the grain heads apart and looked at the grains within. I told them that the Hebrews had been known to eat raw grain, and also to parch unripe grain to take on travels. A few children took a tentative taste of the raw grains.

Meanwhile, Quincy's suggestion had been growing on me. If I could publish a book, the royalties would help us move along more quickly with permits and the land division. I took my copy of *Writer's Market* to school, and combed the book publisher's section, looking for likely places to query. Using the format recommended by Rebecca Greer in her 1973 *Writer's Digest* article "How to Query an Editor," which had worked well for me so far, I sent off letters to three publishers just before Christmas. I included a copy of the corn booklet with each one, and proposed a similar treatment for each of ten grains. I pitched this as a book for teachers, about 200 pages, with background information about each grain and its history, and curriculum plans for each grade. Then, as I had learned to do in three years of freelancing, I forgot about it.

In January, editor Paul DeAngelis wrote from St. Martin's Press, saying he loved my corn chapter and found it to be well-written. He promised to pitch my book to the acquisitions editor at his first opportunity.

In February, Paul requested two more chapters with thirty to forty ethnic recipes for breakfast, lunch, and dinner. St. Martin's Press wanted a cookbook, not a teacher's curriculum guide. I felt disappointed, and didn't tell anyone about it for a few days. Finally, the pragmatist in me said, *"Who cares?"*

"If they want to publish a cookbook, I'll write a cookbook," I told John. Then I told everyone else. And then I started writing.

I rewrote my sample chapter on corn, starting with an essay on the ways corn had been used in various cultures, and how to grow and harvest it. Then I moved on to recipes I researched at the library, and tried out at home adapting them to modern kitchens, families with children, and available ingredients. I included interesting stories whenever I could find them. I did this for wheat and barley and sent the three chapters to New York.

One weekend when John was traveling for business, our friend Bob Fabini offered to take me to visit a friend of his in the mountains, an artist. "Maryanna would make a good illustrator for your book," he suggested. He wanted to visit a nearby Buddhist retreat, and Maryanna had invited me to stay with her while he did so.

I liked Maryanna Kingman right away. I had worried that she would find drawing pictures of plants rather boring, but she said she enjoyed scientific illustration and promised to send me some samples that I could share with the publisher.

*   *   *

I hoped that by the time I healed well enough to move back to the land, we would be able to do so in the 40-foot trailer John's parents were living in. That would require a use permit, which we didn't yet have. John wasn't taking any chances. One Saturday in late September, he left the house on a mysterious errand and returned a few hours later with his father, who was pulling a rather sad-looking blue travel trailer behind his pickup. They moved the VW bus out of our driveway and backed the trailer in. When they were finished, they both grinned at me like a couple of Cheshire Cats.

"Your new home, Madam," announced Pop, gesturing at the 16-foot trailer with a flourish.

I made my way over to it and opened the door. The acrid smell of smoke assailed my nose. A large hole showed the sky through the ceiling, and it appeared the trailer had been on fire. All the cabinets were smoke damaged, and the floor had buckled.

"*Eeeeyou!*" I exclaimed. "You don't think we can live in *that*, do you?"

"I do indeed," John said enthusiastically. "The bones of the trailer are good. Pop and I will tear out all the old cabinets and build new ones. I'll put a new sheet of plywood in the ceiling and seal the roof. Then we can create the trailer kitchen of your dreams and you can make cushion covers and curtains. It'll be fine."

Over dinner, Pop and John explained that John had been keeping an eye on the trailer for several weeks. It had appeared on the side of the road near Alviso, and no one had come back to claim it.

"I put a note on it a couple of weeks ago asking the owners to contact me," he said, shoveling spaghetti into his mouth and chewing quickly so he could continue. "Pop and I went to look at it last week. It's basically in good shape, under the burned bits."

"No one answered John's note," Pop continued while John cut some French bread and handed it around. "So we figured 'finders' keepers.'"

"It's ours now," John concluded, smiling at me. "And we have a project to keep us busy this winter."

On October 15, Dr. McClintock finally announced that I could forgo the use of my walker and crutches if I could get around without them. I could also drive again.

That night, I put Doña in the Snugli for the first time since the accident, and cleaned the house with her on my back. After that I dressed her for bed, read several stories and put her into her bed. I limped a lot, and by the time I collapsed into the rocking chair, my back hurt, but the freedom felt wonderful.

I called my drivers and told them they were off the hook for the following week.

John was stoked. "I finally have my wife back," he cheered.

After Doña fell asleep that night, I retyped a rejected story for resubmission and planned my lessons for Heidi's for the rest of the week. It has always been my nature to over-extend myself, and that one sentence explains how I do it. I had been told I could drop the crutches and what did I do? Cleaned the house and put Doña to bed. Neither of which I had done for months. Then, instead of resting, I sat up even later to retype a story proposal and plan curriculum. Not too surprising that the first entry in my journal on October 16 was "Tired."

For the rest of the week I behaved as if my body was totally back to normal, and each day it signaled the opposite, with aches and pains and nervous exhaustion.

But with no one to tell me to stop, I just kept going. I wanted to be strong and healthy again, so I forced myself to act as if I were. I'd had it with being an invalid. Along with teaching at Heidi's Learning Center, I had enrolled in two evening classes in the new master's degree program at San Jose State. Bev Jensen had visited me twice at home, bursting with exciting news about the expansion of child care services in California, and the need for master's level instructors to prepare the workforce. I wanted to be one of them.

Traveling between San Jose State and Morgan Hill had worn me out the first week of classes. I used my walker to get to the bus stop and from the bus stop to class. No wonder I got tired. However, I gradually built strength and endurance. At first, I used the elevator to get to the third floor of the Education building, but after a few weeks I began to arrive early and climb the stairs — first just one flight, then two, using a cane instead of a walker. Finally, I could walk up to the third floor. But knee and back pain continued to plague me. One night after class, as I limped into the student center where John and Doña were waiting for me, John encouraged me to go to the chiropractor Dr. McClintock had recommended.

Dr. Stuart was a kindly old man, but his office looked like it hadn't been updated since he was first certified. The examining rooms were paneled in dark wood; on racks rested stethoscopes and other instruments I didn't recognize made out of stainless steel and brown rubber tubing. The whole place smelled like formaldehyde and furniture polish. I soon came to associate the odor with comfort and relief from pain.

Dr. Stuart practiced a type of chiropractic called cranio-sacral therapy. Never having been to a chiropractor before, I didn't know that I had lucked into a form of alternative medicine that was ideal for my particular injuries, using gentle manipulations of the skull rather than the bone crushing methods of mainstream chiropractors. Dr. Stuart believed in cod liver oil with a chaser of raw milk, and directed me to the same dairy in San Jose that Dorrie had taken me to. He encouraged me to gently exercise all the muscles I had been neglecting for such a long time.

"Walk every day," he instructed me. "And swim."

He wrote a prescription for a new health club in Gilroy that had a pool, and recommended water exercises and twice weekly workouts on a stationary bicycle.

"Find an attractive walking stick, taller than you've been using, to keep your body straight when you walk. It will also keep your unstable knee from collapsing, and lessen your limp, which is aggravating your back injury."

I found it difficult to take a step back from walking unaided to using a walking stick, but I tried it, and he was right. I was truly back on my feet.

During October and November, John and Pop worked on the trailer every weekend. Pop did some research and decided it was probably a 1948 or 1949 Westcraft Sequoia, although there were no name plates on the chassis to verify that. It was obviously a high-end caravan, entirely paneled in wood. The smoke damage to the paneling responded well to scrubbing with TSP (tri-sodium phosphate) solution. The TSP removed the grease and soot left behind from the smoke, but the smell remained. John's mother suggested we wipe the paneling with white vinegar, then wash it with dish soap dissolved in warm water. Her solution worked beautifully.

Once John and Pop removed the cabinets, and Bea and I scrubbed the walls, I could begin to see the possibilities. The chassis was about the same size as the Bumgarner trailer, but we could design the cabinets and kitchen how we liked. I selected a stove like the one in

Bea's trailer — a Dometic unit that operated on LP gas (propane). Sears also carried a European 3.7cubic-foot refrigerator that could be powered by electricity, propane, or 12-volt battery. We ordered both.

Over the next several months, we acquired curtain rods, foam pads and fabric, and I sewed cushion covers and curtains. John replaced the ceiling panel, then began designing a folding bed and a set of cabinets and shelves that were customized to our lifestyle. It was therapeutic. Soon we had fashioned a cozy home that I couldn't wait to move into.

✳ ✳ ✳

There is a slang expression in the north of England, where I was born, that goes, "On yer bike!" It was usually used as a polite way of telling someone to quit arguing, or to go away at the end of an unsatisfactory conversation.

Later, when I lived in Yorkshire in the 1980s during a teacher exchange, I noticed my cousins and some of my colleagues used the expression in a different way. There seemed to be an implication that the hearer should get on his/her bike and actually do something useful. I read somewhere that this new usage was popularized by a speech given by Employment Secretary Norman Tebbit. In that speech, he described his colorful father, who chose not to riot along with others in the 1930s when he was unemployed, but instead "got on his bike and looked for work." As I began to heal from my injuries and experience the restlessness that comes from being confined indoors for many weeks, I found myself fantasizing about riding my bike again. As in Tebbit's story, getting "on my bike" began to take on a deeper meaning — getting on with my life.

I had grown up in the Belmont hills, south of San Francisco. During junior high and high school, I spent every afternoon cycling through those hills to meet with friends and ride to the various open spaces available to us — Waterdog Lake, Pulgas Water Temple, Alpine Road. Because they had grown up in freedom, and had also used bicycles to get around in their own youth, my parents didn't worry about me or set any limits on where I could ride, so long as I arrived home by dark.

In 1967, John and I had purchased matching Schwinn bicycles, and after we were married we cycled to work each day. Our bikes only had three gears, and we weren't serious cyclists like today's young people, but we enjoyed the feel of the wind in our hair (no helmets then), and being out of doors. We often rode around town on weekends, and continued to do so while attending college in San Diego and Las Cruces. When John went to work for ESL in early 1972, we put our bikes in storage, and moved to a rental home near John's first assignment in Washington D.C.

After the accident, John and his dad had moved most of our belongings to the little house on Lindo Lane — including our bikes. One of my goals as I slowly progressed from immobile in an electric bed to full leg cast and a walker, to crutches and finally to a single walking stick, was to get back on my bicycle. On New Years' Day 1975, six months after the accident, I decided it was time. John had a few days off, and could stay with Doña while I took some short journeys to test my balance and build my endurance.

The first hurdle I had to overcome was a loose chain. Also, the saddle wobbled, and the tires were flat. I had never worked on a bike, never changed a flat tire. Before moving to the property, I depended on John to keep pretty much everything in our life running smoothly. If my car wouldn't start, John would cheerfully come to my aid; if I had a flat tire on my bicycle, John fixed it. If the toilet backed up, or a garden hose leaked, it was always John to the rescue.

Those few months living on the land, and the many hours I had spent lying in bed, had changed my perspective. John wasn't sleeping well, and he was moody. I suspected he still felt guilty about the accident and worried about money, but he wouldn't talk about what was upsetting him. I knew we needed to talk, but meanwhile, he didn't need me asking for help doing things I could do myself.

For Christmas, my brother had given me a book about maintaining and repairing bicycles. I decided to get it out and see if I could at least make a start. I waited until John took Doña with him to run a few errands, then I grabbed the book and went out the back door.

During the months I had been incapacitated, John set up a workshop in the detached garage, where he liked to putter in the evenings. I found all the tools I needed hanging on hooks above the bench. Tightening the nut underneath my saddle was easy. I did that first. Admiring my work, I moved on. Getting the chain back onto the cogs was harder, but with the help of a screwdriver and a pair of pliers I managed it. I pumped up the tires, then pushed the bike down the street to see if it all held together. My confidence was growing.

Back at the house, I tested the saddle, the chain and the tires, carefully pulled my leg over the bar, and started slowly up the street. I didn't ride far at first, only to the high school a block away, where I rode around and around the parking lot until I got my balance. Then I headed for Main Street and the public library, about a mile. Coming back down the slope to our house I felt the wind ruffle my hair and I grinned broadly as I turned into our drive. I was definitely on my bike.

*   *   *

In February 1975, Quincy left ESL to take a position at International Imaging System (known generally as IsquaredS). He was the first of the image processing team to be head-hunted, and he had been offered a salary far above what he earned at ESL. His colleagues were simultaneously grieved by his departure, and awed by his good luck. More than that, he would be leading a department, and would be in a position to influence the direction image processing would take in Silicon Valley.

To mark this watershed event, friends and colleagues organized a party at one of their favorite after-work watering holes, Castle Pizza in Mountain View. This pizza parlor had four of the new video game consoles, featuring *Pong* and *Space Wars*. For much of the evening, the host and his friends surrounded the little video arcade, shouting encouragement to the players controlling the action. I suddenly missed working in technology, missed the camaraderie that I once too had felt with my workmates, missed the after-work gatherings at pizza parlors like that one.

We all sensed this night was the end of an era, but we had no idea of the changes that would come to ESL — and in all of Santa Clara

Valley — over the next decade. Computers were growing smaller; scientific calculators were in development and would soon hit the market, new programming languages were emerging. The times were definitely changing. Sometimes I wondered if we were doing the right thing, raising our daughter away from civilization. With no television, very little contact with families in town, and our idyllic farm life, would she be prepared to live and work in the new world of technology? John and Quincy were highly engaged with that world when they went to work, but didn't speak much of it at home. When they did, it was often to share utopian dreams: a computer on every desk; onboard computers that would help automobile drivers navigate to their destination; a network that connected everyone electronically and would allow toll-free communication across national boundaries and vast oceans.

John's growing discontent with ESL escalated after Quincy left the company. Their department was reorganized and soon several others of the original team left to take advantage of new opportunities in the valley. He looked around for another position, and in March decided to join a startup in Mountain View that was working with NASA to develop global positioning software.

*　　*　　*

Willie, the sausage dog, entered the world on March 13, 1975 in a mud puddle under our VW bus. He was the unlikely progeny of Elsa, our purebred German shepherd female, and a well-hung dachshund from down the street. When we moved into the house on Lindo Lane there had been no fence around one side of the yard. Rather than divide the yard from the driveway next to it, John had built a 6-foot high picket-style gate across the driveway, making a very large space accessible and safe for Doña to play in when the gate was shut.

It was a masterful design, one which contained Elsa inside the yard, and which would allow us to select the sire of her first purebred litter. At least that had been the idea. Unfortunately, the aforementioned dachshund was able to squeeze in *under* the gate, and take advantage of our innocent girl. Willie was the result.

When I first found Willie under the VW bus, he looked like a very unhappy rat, all the way to the end of his long, naked tail. He was a tiny little thing, and seemed even smaller than he was that day, because he was soaking wet. I looked all over for other puppies, but Willie was the only one. Poor Elsa thought she had done something wrong, and retreated under my bed, refusing to take care of him.

I fed Willie diluted evaporated milk with an eye-dropper the first day, then sat on the floor and stroked Elsa while I put him to her teats. Eventually, after lots of coaxing, she got used to the idea and cuddled with him until he went to sleep. After that, she was a devoted mother. It was hilarious to see tiny Willie following the huge German Shepherd around everywhere, and even funnier to watch her feeding and grooming him.

Willie eventually grew into his tail. He developed a Dachshund snout and floppy ears, a thick Shepherd body and short little Dachshund legs. That spring I once again signed up for two night classes at San Jose State. John was traveling a lot for work and attending evening meetings of the Homebrew Computer Club and of MIRA, the Monterey Institute for Research in Astronomy. He wasn't always available to take care of Doña while I went to class, but Dorrie and Quincy did so when they could.

Bob Fabini also sometimes stayed with Doña. We'd moved our piano down from Mount Hamilton and he entertained Doña and himself by playing ragtime music. Bob soon became quite attached to the odd-looking Willie. On more than one occasion I came home from class to find Bob asleep in our reclining chair, Doña curled up in one arm, and Willie in the other. When Bob moved to the land, Willie moved with him.

*   *   *

John and I spent most weekends on the land that spring, sleeping in our VW bus. I couldn't do any heavy work yet, but I loved being up there with everyone. I couldn't wait till we finished the little blue trailer and could move back to the land full-time. I was expecting a second child, and I wanted this baby to be born on our land.

We made our monthly payments for the land to Margharita Langwell now. While I was in the hospital, Carter had moved out of the trailer and sold that parcel of land to Larry Orlando, a lovely man who owned an Italian restaurant in Cupertino and planned to retire on the land.

"Good riddance," I said under my breath when Quincy told me. Carter would no longer be driving up and down our road, glaring at us and making me nervous. Anxious to sell us the land, he had appeared to resent the fact that we actually moved onto it and lived there. I'd never understood that, but now it would no longer be my concern.

Bob Fabini was joining our back-to-the-land adventure, and he negotiated successfully with Orlando to rent the trailer. Bob had been a custodian at ESL when John and Quincy realized his intelligence and drive and hired him to operate the new scanner in the image processing lab. Since then, Bob had joined us for musical events, and often stayed the night and on through the rest of the weekend to work beside Quincy and John. He was a happy person and brought a young man's enthusiasm to every project.

June 16, 1975, my contract with St. Martin's Press arrived by special delivery, along with a check for $3000. John earned that in two months, and once upon a time I earned it in four, but I felt like a millionaire just the same. June 17 was our eighth wedding anniversary. To celebrate, we moved the last of our stuff up to the land and moved into the little blue trailer, which John and his father had installed the previous week. Doña and I promptly came down with the flu.

At my next obstetrician appointment, Dr. Creevy told me I was anemic and I needed to rest. He increased my iron prescription and urged me to take a week off work.

In spite of that advice, John and I drove to San Francisco the following weekend to meet with my editor. We stayed in a Motel 6, but met Paul at the St. Francis Hotel, where we went over the contract and I signed it with a notary present. It felt very grown up and surreal. Later that evening, Paul took us on a cable car to a Hungarian restaurant, and I tasted my first authentic goulash. Exhausted as I felt, it had definitely been a night to remember.

We returned to the property Sunday afternoon to find our weekend workers helping Bob clean out Carter's old trailer. It had been badly trashed and was in disrepair, but Bob seemed delighted to have his own place on the land. John and I helped him clear brush away from the trailer and rake the ground free of weeds to reduce fire danger. Unfortunately, Bob was extremely allergic to poison oak. He developed a serious rash and felt so miserable that he moved in with his parents in San Jose until he recovered.

Meanwhile, I had contracted another respiratory infection and had a couple of sleepless nights. I drove to Gilroy to see if I could get in to see a doctor without an appointment. The doctor on call diagnosed an ear infection and pleurisy and prescribed antibiotics. I didn't want to take them, worrying about their effect on my unborn baby, but I felt so awful, I did. By Monday I felt better, and returned to school. But I soon became ill again, this time with pneumonia, and slept around the clock for several days. John took care of Doña and fell seriously behind in his work. The high we'd been riding after my contract signing had fizzled away.

July followed, hot and dry. I was now five months pregnant and teaching summer school at Heidi's. Dragging my body around the classroom exhausted me. My hemoglobin was low again and I had lost weight since my last appointment. Dr. Creevy doubled my iron prescription and recommended a nap each afternoon. Hah! The summer schedule at Heidi's consisted of multi-grade groups developing long-range projects and enjoying lots of free play. Outside. In the heat. Not much likelihood of a nap.

My group was making a seven-foot high papier mâché Tyrannosaurus Rex. We had finished the chicken-wire skeleton, stretched several pairs of panty hose over parts of the frame to hold the newspaper strips, and were elbow deep in flour and water paste and gooey strips of newsprint.

I fantasized about spending the day on our land instead of building a dinosaur. On top of teaching, I had chores to do, and a long list of projects I wanted to complete before our baby was born.

Nancy had been out for a week with some kind of intestinal flu. I considered asking her if I could take August off so that I could return fresh for the school year. But losing a month's salary would hurt, and I hadn't talked it over with John. And anyway, Nancy was still at home.

Putting my books and papers away as I prepared to fetch Doña from preschool, I looked up to see Nancy's husband Russ standing over me. He had been filling in for Nancy during her absence, and looked pretty haggard. Their children were ill, too, and he looked like he might be getting sick as well.

"Marlene, I need to see you in Nancy's office before you go. It's important."

Russ told me that Nancy's illness had been diagnosed as hepatitis. The vector, he explained, was their cleaning lady, who worked both in their home and at the school and had recently returned from an extended stay in Mexico. The Department of Health had closed down the school until it could be certified free of the virus. Notices would go up that afternoon, and all the children would be sent home with explanatory letters.

The Department of Health representative recommended all employees obtain an injection of gamma globulin, believed to be an effective agent in preventing the disease if taken before onset. Arrangements would be made for me to obtain an injection at no cost. Given my pregnancy, Russ and Nancy had decided to pay me through August and send me home for the rest of the summer. He handed me my last paycheck and asked me to pack up everything before collecting Doña. Her possessions, being collected by her teacher, would be ready when I arrived at the preschool.

"We would never forgive ourselves if you caught this disease and it harmed your baby," were Russell's parting words. "Thank you for your service to the children of Heidi's Learning Center. We wish you the best of everything."

Free!

We had purchased a family-sized rope hammock when we visited the Twin Oaks Commune in 1973. Now John hung it behind our trailer, where I could lie and look down at the valley. Doña liked to take her naps there, gently swinging, cradled in my arms. She seemed happier to be with me than she had at Lindo Lane. I spent the next several days after chores lying in the hammock, reading and sleeping and holding her in my arms, luxuriating in the unaccustomed rest.

Once I regained my stamina, I resumed work on the book.

22

THE BOOK OF WHOLE GRAINS

U NTIL I BEGAN WRITING *THE BOOK OF WHOLE GRAINS*, my writing "career" had consisted of freelance articles in parenting magazines that paid from $15 to $50, with just three exceptions: an article about the soccer player Pele in *Highlights for Children*; a piece titled "When You Are Away" that was inspired by my long hospital stay, published in *American Baby*; and an article in *Mother's Manual* about taking Doña with us on "An Astronomical Adventure." They each paid $1000 and raised my hopes that I could someday earn a living writing.

But a book contract! That was tangible evidence that at least Paul DeAngelis believed I could write a full-length book and that the publishing house could sell it. He made me feel like a *bona fide* writer. I had no idea what all this would actually mean to my future, but I did know what I wanted to write. I began by creating lesson plans for each grain, and laid them out in my plan book. In the proposal I had said I could have the book ready in a year. I wanted to follow through with my promise.

Being laid off from Heidi's in August was a blessing. I had four months until the birth of my baby, and I would be able to devote most of that time to researching and writing. There was no Internet yet, and research was done using index cards to record facts and bibliographic citations, and required visits to several different libraries. I registered Doña for a "Baby and Me" swim class at San Jose City College and, for the two weeks of the class, we went to the nearby San Jose State library every day after swimming. Doña was nearly three, and, thanks to her teacher, Ann, and her nursery school experience, she had developed the ability to sit and engage in an activity for an hour at a time. I purchased several new coloring books, a big box of crayons, and a cassette tape player with headphones. I found several fairy tales and Disney books that had accompanying cassettes, and those helped to entertain her during my long work sessions in the library.

During this period, Elsa birthed a second litter of puppies. As if to make up for her one-pup litter the first time, this time she had ten. We suspected the father was one of Walt and Fran's German Shepherds — several of the pups had the same shaggy long hair as their youngest dog. Doña loved the pups. She began playing with them, putting them in her small red wagon and pulling them around the farm. Soon they could get out of the wagon almost as quickly as she could put them in, and putting them back entertained her for long periods of time. John had emptied out a large wooden crate for Elsa to birth her pups. We covered it with a tarp at night. But puppies began to go missing, one at a time.

When we were down to seven pups, John sat up one night to see what was happening to them. After a while, two pups peeked out from under the tarp and climbed on their siblings until they worked their way out of the crate. They started exploring the area. Suddenly and silently, an owl swooped down and flew away with one of them. We both felt terrible that we hadn't considered the danger from raptors. We moved the pups into one of our sheds, and closed the door at night. When they reached six weeks of age, we took five of them to the SPCA to be adopted. We kept the cutest puppy and named her Diamond.

Researching the history and husbandry of each grain was slow work. Using the card catalog I found a couple of books about food and history, but there wasn't much there. The reference librarian suggested I look at magazines and journals. I turned to the Big Green Books — *The Reader's Guide to Periodical Literature*. They have since been made superfluous by the Internet, but in the 70s and 80s, this index to articles in hundreds of popular and academic periodicals was a valuable research tool.

I began by consulting the bibliographies of each of the books I had located and noted the related articles. The next step was to locate those articles. That's where the *Readers' Guide* came in. They were arranged by subject and spanned several decades, often all the way back to their inception in 1901. Throughout each year, four softcover chapbooks were published. They were then compiled into the thick green hardcover books usually housed to one side of the card catalog in any public or academic library.

It was a ponderous process. I first searched volumes several decades back, reasoning that my topic was not timely, and those books were not liable to be in use by another patron. Before going to the library, I prepared a list of subject headings I wanted to find, for example: corn, maize, corn in Mexico, corn in Aztec religion, grain and Aztecs, grain and Incas. I put the subjects in alphabetical order, then flipped through the indexes looking for related articles. If I found one that looked good, I would write the topic across the top of a 3x5 card, then write down all the bibliographic information. I'd have to repeat that process with every volume of the guide, but eventually I learned which topics were showing up and which weren't, and I got much faster.

The next step was to identify which periodicals were available in that particular library, which ones could be requested through inter-library loan, and which had a cost associated with it. Different libraries had different collections. I traveled up and down the San Francisco Peninsula, spending hours at San Francisco State, Stanford (where I had to purchase a reader's card), College of San Mateo, and San Jose State, as well as the public libraries in Gilroy, Morgan Hill, and San Jose. I became truly appreciative of the public institutions that allowed me to research for free. Reference librarians who located books and magazines from all over the country — as far away as the

Smithsonian Institution in Washington D.C. I drew on these sources as I wrote the introductory material for each grain.

I also found some recipes this way, especially ancient recipes and those from modern ethnic cookbooks, but I found some unexpected sources of ideas also. The Berkeley Food Co-op, for example, put out one-page information sheets on various foodstuffs they sold, including wheat berries, oat groats, quinoa, and hulled barley. Those sheets gave basic cooking times for the whole grain, and how to grind it into grits or meal or flour. Granola and muesli couldn't yet be purchased commercially, but the Co-op provided recipes for both. During the Depression and both world wars, the U.S. Department of Agriculture promoted sorghum as a partial solution to the food shortage, and even published bulletins with recipes for its use. Appliances often come with recipe books; from my mother's collection I found a time table for pressure cooking dried beans and a warning to not cook dried peas in a pressure cooker. Her electric skillet cookbook gave cooking times for whole grain oats (cheaper than oatmeal). Wartime recipe books (my mother's collection again) contained lists of food that could be substituted for ingredients that were hard to find. Historic colonial cookbooks made much use of wheat, oats, barley and corn, although measurements were approximate — a handful of wheat; a teacup of milk; a small ball of butter — and friends who had grown up in other countries shared recipes they had learned from local residents.

Recipe testing became my life. In fact, it became all of our lives. After we moved back to the land in June 1975, I cooked and baked using a camper-sized propane stove and oven. I realized that my baking times and temperatures might not match those of cooks in typical kitchens. To test that, I started sending recipes to my friends — and my mom — with little kits containing the grain or legume or nut required, and any other unusual spice or ingredient they would need. When I visited my parents, I tested recipes. On weekends, I used Bob Fabini's oven, which was of standard size. Everyone soon got used to me handing them 3-x-5 cards with their meal or plate of cookies and asking for their opinions.

While I obsessed over the book, John was racing to beat a deadline. He had promised me that the 40-foot trailer would be in place on the lower saddle before our baby was born at the end of November, and that I would have running water. Our little blue trailer home would then be my study, and a cozy place for visitors to sleep.

In mid-November, 63-year-old Lillie Rist, owner of her own heavy equipment company, used a small bulldozer to cut a level pad and tow our trailer up the road. I was impressed at her strength and skill. She seemed ancient to me, but she sure knew how to drive a dozer.

With help from Pop, Quincy, and Bob, John ran an unapproved electric line through the trees from Bob Fabini's trailer, and a temporary water line above ground from the well to our trailer. There was very little water pressure, but I could turn on a tap and get cold water for tea or a bath. Until we could afford a septic tank, we would continue to use our porta-potty for necessary bodily functions, but grey water from the sink and the tub would be routed through 4-inch perforated pipes down the hill. There was no time to redecorate. We kept the red plaid carpet that Bea had installed, and pulled back the thick drapes that darkened the living room.

John made a trip to Mount Hamilton in a rented truck, and brought down my maple desk, which he installed in front of the biggest window. He managed to get the matching maple bookcases in also, and the rocking chair I had used in Virginia. My heart swelled when I looked at the final result. John had worked very hard to make things perfect for me. Packing the contents of the blue trailer only took a weekend, and we moved down the hill to our new home weeks ahead of schedule.

A few weeks later, our long-time friend Nina Holzer joined us on the land. She and her husband had separated, and she needed a place to live and re-orient herself. She moved into the blue trailer and immediately staked out a garden and hung up a clothesline. Soon she began spending hours writing in her journal and composing poems. She added a liveliness to our social gatherings, and I enjoyed having her nearby. We fell into a rhythm that continued for years, John, Quincy, Dorrie and Bob leaving each morning for work, Nina and I writing in our separate trailers, sometimes enjoying a cup of tea in the afternoon before we geared up to prepare the evening meal. We often ate communally, taking turns to cook, and eating outside when the weather was good. On weekends we worked in the garden, cleared out animal pens, built new things, repaired broken things. Our differing personalities and working styles sometimes led to friction, but we usually managed to settle our differences quickly. Sunday night we let down our hair. Nina would usually prepare a wonderful dessert, and we would gather around Dorrie and Quincy's guitars, or around our piano, which we had moved into Bob's trailer.

In spite of selling his land and moving out of the trailer, Bill Carter continued to show up randomly, sometimes with men in the back of his truck, sometimes waving a shotgun. He never did more than threaten us, but I worried he might do more. As much as I liked my telephone-free life, one day in October I decided I wanted to be able to call for help in an emergency.

Naively, I assumed getting a phone line would be as easy as asking for it. Shortly after we moved back to the land, I called Ma Bell from my parents' home and ordered a brown push-button telephone. Sure enough, the switchboard operator gave me a date and time, and on that day and at that time a telephone company van came driving up Hawkins Lane. The installer took a good look at our trailer, walked all around it, and announced

"But ma'am, you ain't got no poles!"

"Well, no, we haven't, sir. Don't you provide those?"

"No ma'am, we don't. Everywhere we go out to install telephones, there are electric lines and PG&E poles already there. Everyone calls them 'telephone poles,' but they're really 'electricity poles.'"

"So, how do we get those? We don't have any."

"I don't hardly know, ma'am, but this man will know. He's my supervisor,"

He handed me a card. The following week, a very nice gentleman came up the road in a telephone company car, a sedan this time. John had stayed home from work in order to be there when the man came. He thought my story about the installer was hilarious, but realized that we might actually get somewhere with this second visit.

After John explained our situation, the supervisor and John walked the line where John imagined the power poles would be installed if we had legal electricity. Perhaps it was my very obvious pregnancy that made him want to help us, or perhaps he was just a kind man.

"You can purchase four by six pressure-treated poles 25 feet long," he said to John. "You'll need to set the poles 4 feet in the ground. Put one pole in every 150 feet." Then the key information: "If your poles are in the ground when our installers come, they'll put the phone lines on the poles. And you, ma-am, will have your brown push-button console."

And just like that, it was done. The poles were expensive, and it took us several months to save enough to buy them and rent the equipment to dig the holes. It took four men to do the job. John and Pop wrestled a giant auger four feet into the ground, and then Bob and Quincy walked each 25-foot pole into the hole and filled it with concrete. The pole installation took several days, but it was worth it. I had a brown push-button telephone before Baby John's first birthday.

For the impending birth, I had selected a doctor at Stanford Medical Center who supported same-day mother and baby release, as my doctor in Washington D.C. had done when Doña was born. My dream of a home birth on the land had been squashed. Dr. Creevy was worried about my persistent anemia and my back and pelvic injuries. He urged me to consider a Cesarean delivery. I disagreed, fearing I'd be incapacitated and unable to return immediately to the land. I compromised by promising to drive to Stanford as soon as I went into labor so we would have time to make a choice.

Since we had no way to contact Dorrie, who had offered to drive me to the hospital when the time came, we came up with a system of beeps made by pressurized air horns. Dorrie, Nina, and I each had a horn, and we agreed to use them in case of emergency or of me going into labor. Unfortunately, Dorrie was away from the land when my contractions began on December 4, so I ended up driving myself as far as ESL in Mountain View, where John took over. Doña stayed on the land with Nina.

Fortunately, John entered the world the usual way without much fuss, and we went home to the land the next day. After the excitement of my arrival with her little brother had died down, Doña curled up in Nina's arms and went to sleep. When she awakened, Nina took her for a long walk around the property. The walk was so well received, Nina began to take her out regularly, and sometimes would ask Doña to keep her company while she worked in the garden. She had no children of her own, but was wonderful with both of ours. Sometimes, when John had been fed and changed, she would take him and Doña up to her little trailer to give me an hour's break. She also spent many hours in our trailer rocking John while I worked on the book just a couple of feet away.

I researched several days a week, and I wrote every day. I taught myself how to make butter and cheese from our copious supply of goat milk, and we enjoyed these with the various types of breads I baked as I experimented with each grain. By the time John was born on December 4, I had made it more than halfway through the book. Which was good, because things came to a complete halt after he arrived. Doña had been born mellow and, although she went through about six weeks of after-dinner colic, she had generally been a quiet and cheerful baby. She rarely cried, and only fussed when she needed something. John, on the other hand, was a communicator from the very beginning. Most of the time when he was awake, he was chortling with delight or fussing and crying mournfully. He chattered, he mumbled, he grumbled, he fussed, he shouted, and, just when I thought I would go nuts, he'd laugh and smile and totally charm me.

On the day after Christmas 1975, I walked to the top of the hill as the sun set. The fog was rising and slowly claiming what warmth was left in the air. Moments earlier, I had been curled up in my favorite corner of the couch, my afghan tight around my feet. I had looked hopefully at the sleeping girl beside me, and taken a long sip of tea.

This wasn't supposed to be a solo walk; we had planned it as a family outing earlier in the day. But Doña had thrown up and now said she was too ill to walk up the hill. It was probably too much Christmas food.

The Adams' had gone to San Luis Obispo for a few days, and we had agreed to do their chores while they were gone. I tried to talk John into walking up the hill to milk their goats so I could stay with Doña. He was doing something on the table with rusty windmill parts and a screwdriver, and kept putting me off. I retreated into sorting out our world from beneath the holiday clutter. By that time, I had put off making the trek until three-week-old Baby John's before-dinner fussiness was well under way. We all needed a break. We finally agreed that John would stay with Doña and I would walk up the hill with Baby John in the Snugli. It was four o'clock, and I left the sunshine behind as I began the ascent up the shady path from Bum Flats, our dogs Elsa and Diamond, Elsa's adolescent pup, running ahead.

The muddy ruts in the road reminded me, as they always did, of the weekend that Buzz drove his power wagon off the side of the road and we all slogged about in the February mud helping him to get out. Walking up the road to Dorrie's always triggered memories.

My first ascent after the accident, a crutch on one side and John's strong arm on the other ... My thoughts roam to Dorrie's graduation party, which was the occasion for that particular walk.

Many walks with Doña grumbling about the steep hill ... a few early in the morning when she ran ahead of me to see Buffi, Dorrie's new puppy. Nighttime walks to spend an evening drinking wine with Dorrie, or listening to her and Quincy sing, accompanying themselves on guitar ... a walk with Bob and his friend Jan one weekend before John and I moved back to the land from the house in town. Smiling, I remember Dorrie's voice reaching us before we made it up the final hill. There was some discussion about whether she was playing a transistor radio, but it was not Judy Collins, it was lonely Dorrie singing and playing her guitar. Quincy was on one of his many business trips, and she had been alone on the hill all week.

Before I ran out of memories, I reached the top of the hill, and assumed my watchful mode, keeping dogs from eating animals and birds while I fed everyone. Diamond cavorts playfully, yet responds well to my warnings when she nears the Banty hens. For the umpteenth time, I wondered at the many animals and the complexity of the Adams' feeding methods. Climbing up into Nuts with Baby John hanging on my chest like a monkey, I chuckled. What would Bob's new landlord, Larry Orlando, say if he saw me doing this? He had been quite troubled when he spied me, seven months pregnant, riding in the back of Sarge during one of his visits to the land.

The water coming from the tank on the back of the truck is cold, and the leaking hose valve spills it onto my fingers … *garumph*. Baby rabbits are out of water again.

"Diamond, get over here!"

I milked the two goats, made sure everyone had food. Finally, fingers numb, I finished filling the water containers and turned off the valve.

On the way down the hill, the milk sloshing in time to my steps, I heard the sounds of John's hammer echoing against the hills. Hearing it, I felt relaxed and happy. Walking in the hills will do it every time, but having him at home and content helped too. Doña's laugh reached me, and I smiled involuntarily. She must be feeling better. I think about our walk down to Bob's trailer yesterday — gifts and a Christmas tree piled up in her new red wagon as we played Santa together.

As I approached the trailer, the fog drifted in over the trees, and soon I could not see beyond those that are closest to me. I saw the light in the window, heard John and Doña talking and laughing together. My two new Guinea hens were still foraging, singing their lovely "buck-wheat, buck-wheat" song as they scratched in the dirt. Soon they would roost in the large oak and take on their evening role of night-watchbirds. All was well in our little world.

*   *   *

For a time after Baby John was born, time was suspended. December passed in a blur of rocking, feeding, and changing diapers, and then it was January. Too cold for a three-year-old to go outside and play. Doña was bored and needed something to do. I used part of my book advance to re-enroll her at Heidi's Learning Center for half days, and I began my itinerant writer phase.

Each weekday morning, I would drop Doña off at Heidi's, find a coffee shop or restaurant where I could nurse John and lay him, asleep, in the Moses basket I kept beside me. Then I would pull out my notebook and 3 x 5 cards and work on the book until he woke up. I found a couple of places where they didn't mind him making baby noises, and sometimes he would play happily in the basket after he nursed, and I could stretch out my writing time. Once the public library opened, I would go there, not so much to research — although with him in the Snugli even that was possible — as to sit at a table and write while he exercised on a blanket on the carpeted floor.

I had been invited to teach Children's Literature and Child Health & Nutrition to child development students at Gavilan College in Gilroy. I usually took John with me to class. One day, when I slipped in a little writing time in the library after class, a librarian showed me a quiet room on the mezzanine, surrounded by soundproof glass. She invited me to use the room whenever it wasn't occupied by students. I brought my typewriter down from the land and left it there.

At lunchtime, I would retrieve Doña from Heidi's and take her home, feed her lunch, and put her down for a nap. If by some perfect alignment of the stars John also slept during that period, I would get some more productive work done. Nina stepped in when she needed a break from writing.

Dorrie helped out with the children on weekends, and whenever she had a day off from school or work. Bob and Jan helped too. So did Dean and Lance, the teenagers who joined Bob in his trailer most weekends. The Fabini crew had grown. Bob and Jan were a couple now, and Jan spent most weekends and several nights a week on the land. Bob had been matched with Dean in the Share program (kind of like Big Brothers) and Lance tagged along wherever they went. Everyone on the land tested my recipes, and took turns helping proofread the draft. In this way, with the help of my friends, *The Book of Whole Grains* was completed on deadline.

New Year's Day 1976 found John and me taking a short break in the mountains, introducing the children to snow. We'd realized at Christmas that we hadn't been away from home since we first moved to the land. We decided to combine a visit to the artist who was illustrating my book with a mini-vacation. First, we stopped briefly to visit with Mom and Dad in Belmont. and let them fawn over Baby John. After that, John drove north straight through to Stateline, Nevada, where the temperature was somewhere around 18 degrees.

We slept warmly in down sleeping bags in the VW bus, but awoke to frozen water lines. I'd forgotten to bring gloves, so we pushed on to Carson City where we bought what we needed to stay warm, and ate a traditional breakfast at a Denny's restaurant. Looking around me at all the tourists, I felt like we were in a foreign country, so long had I been cocooned on our homestead.

It was wonderful to be alone with John and the children. It felt normal, watching John puttering in our bus, straightening things, fastening the lids on the film canisters we used for salt and pepper, organizing the maps.

We explored Carson City, and then drove to Virginia City — a historic mining town I had visited as a child. We had a nice day roaming around, Baby John in the Snugli. Along with Doña we drank sarsaparilla and chewed licorice root. But it was more fun being a child there than being a parent. By the end of the day, we were both exhausted from keeping up with our two little ones. John drove back to Carson City, where we treated ourselves to a grown-up meal at the Ormsby House, then found a quiet bend in the road to park the bus for the night.

While I put the children to bed, John made some creative repairs to the Coleman lamp and balanced our checkbook. The next day we meandered through Mark Twain country, ending up at Maryanna Kingman's home in Coulterville.

Maryanna was making good progress on the illustrations for *The Book of Whole Grains*. She showed me some of her newest watercolors and gave us a tour of her extensive vegetable garden, which had provided models for some of the drawings. Maryanna and her husband had retired from Silicon Valley jobs to move into this house in the mountains. Her husband sold real estate while she painted, and they had a huge vegetable garden. I guess you could call them back-to-the-landers too.

After dinner, John and I drove around Coulterville looking for a place to park for the night. We had been driving for about 45 minutes when John suddenly turned to me and said "Why don't you bed down with the kids, and I'll drive us all the way home?" I fell asleep in seconds. The next thing I knew, we were driving up the rutted dirt road to our land. John said it was 2:00 a.m. Climbing out of the bus to a moonlit night, I realized that this was where I wanted to be. Our little vacation had been nice, but I wouldn't be traveling away from home again any time soon. Why would I? We lived in paradise.

I forgot that there was a snake in the Garden of Eden. On a Saturday at the end of January, we were busily engaged in chores. John was stacking hay bales, one of his favorite tasks, lifting them from the back of Quincy's truck with a pair of hay hooks. Dorrie was splitting firewood into smallish pieces that would fit into their wood burning stove. Quincy and Bob were mucking out the chicken pen, and I was filling the feeders. It was sunny and we were all in good moods.

Suddenly the guinea hens made their alert cry, *chi-chi-chi*, and the dogs began to bark. Slowly, an old pickup that we didn't recognize came up Hawkins lane. Three very large Mexican men were sitting in the back, each with a rifle. Carter was driving. John and Quincy walked over to the far side of the bus, where they could see down to the road.

"Just wanted to tell you that you'll be movin' off this property pretty damn quick if you know what's good for you," Carter called from the cab.

"Why's that?" Asked Quincy, calm as always.

"This hillside's no place for a bunch of hippies," he retorted. "Do-gooders, smoking that weed and protesting against the War."

Quincy didn't say anything. Truth be known, John didn't oppose the war at that point. We were more likely to be drinking beer or wine than smoking pot, and we certainly didn't think of ourselves as do-gooders. We were just doing our chores and minding our business.

"We'll be hunting up ahead a-ways. Better keep your kiddies and dogs inside the rest of the day. Never know where a bullet will land, do ya?"

And, racing the puny engine on his truck, he spun the wheels until they finally grabbed the road, then continued on up the hill, waving his hunting rifle in the air.

I had heard every word Carter said, and was stunned. I felt violated and frightened. We saw so few people on that road that I had come to believe that we were the only ones up there. Maybe we were. But Carter clearly believed he had rights of ingress and egress. And that scared me. Quincy wasn't sure. He said he'd consult a lawyer the following week. John said he'd take a couple of days off work, while we found out what rights Carter really had.

"But it won't make any difference, guys," Dorrie argued, her voice low and controlled. "We know that Bob sold land on the other side of the hill to Hugh Graves to hunt on. Hugh definitely has the right to drive on the road."

"And he can give Carter permission to hunt up there," finished Quincy.

"Exactly."

We finished our chores and went down to Bob's for coffee, which turned into a mutual comfort session. Jan arrived with her cousin Dave and they left to go sailing; when they returned we ate lunch together.

Later in the day, John and I walked down to Bob's trailer with dinner. Right after we finished eating, John began to make noises about leaving, which was not unusual. He grew impatient with lengthy conversation and with the musical jam sessions we often had after sharing a meal together. He offered to take Doña and put her to bed. Suddenly I didn't want to be walking up the path alone in the dark, so I went with him, carrying Baby John in the Snugli. Carter had achieved what he wanted — I felt frightened to be on my own piece of land.

The next day, Sunday, we caught up with repairs, construction, and chores and ended our vacation week with a potluck at Bob's trailer. We all used our Christmas gifts in one way or another: while BJ — as we had begun to call Baby John — and Doña snuggled under the grannie afghans I'd crocheted, Jan stir-fried vegetables in her new wok. After dinner, Bob figured out how to wear his new harmonica holder while he played the piano. Quincy played the guitar and Dorrie led us in song. We had all received kazoos in our stockings — even Doña — and we played them together.

Returning to the routine of driving Doña to Heidi's early the next morning, after waking up for nighttime feeds, was difficult. John helped me get Doña dressed while I nursed Baby John. I heard a ruckus outside the trailer. I put him down abruptly and ran into the yard. Diamond, Elsa's pup, was chasing a guinea hen. I caught her, slapped her on the rump, tied her to a fence post, comforted Doña, who was heartbroken that I'd hit the puppy, and finished nursing my screaming baby. The day went downhill after that.

By Wednesday, we were beginning to get a rhythm going. I had resumed work on the book, although I found it difficult to make progress. At five weeks of age, BJ was wakeful and fussy. Fortunately, he was also beginning to smile, and to push his chest off the bed and look around, so it was easy to get distracted and to forgive him for sidetracking me.

On Thursday afternoon, I found Willie running loose, chasing chickens. I put him inside Bob's trailer before driving to Gilroy to pick up Doña. I stopped at the trailer on our way back up the hill to drop off groceries for Bob, only to find that Willie had trashed Bob's screened porch — there were broken plant pots, damaged plants, and soil everywhere. Feeling guilty about having shut him in, I brought BJ and Doña in from the car and Doña helped me clean up the mess. Bob wasn't happy about my request when I made it, but agreed to Willie-proof the porch and keep him inside.

Diamond went after the guinea hens again on Friday, in the midst of a rainstorm. I had been brushing Doña's hair, and, when I finally caught Diamond, I hit her with the hairbrush in my hand and broke it. Once again, the guineas escaped injury; Doña was angry with me for hitting Diamond, I was angry at Diamond for chasing the guineas, and I was covered in mud. I decided it was time to find her a new home.

Emotions had been running pretty high all week. As always, it helped to have everyone home for the weekend. Nina had been away on a short break of her own, and she returned Friday night, requesting a bath in our trailer. After she emerged, wrapped in my warm hooded robe, we sat down to a communal dinner. Bob and Jan brought spicy beans, and the Adamses provided a quart of fresh milk and a dozen eggs. We all squeezed in around the table. We fit, although Dorrie was sitting on the edge of the couch and John was perched on a stepladder.

After the food had been served, I brought up the subject of the dogs. All of our dogs, it appeared, were inclined to chase things that ran from them — whether it was chickens, guinea hens, or the neighbors' goats. We agreed that it was time to contain them inside fences. None of us was particularly happy about that, but it seemed necessary if we were to stay friends with one another and our neighbors. I felt better by the time we returned to our respective homes, and it appeared that the others did, too.

*   *   *

In February 1976, we had the first of what would soon become regular visits from the Santa Clara Health Department. John and I had been turned in for violating sewer regulations.

My first response when Mr. McPhaill handed me an eviction notice was fury. I started railing at the unfairness of being turned in to the Health Department. Why would someone — probably a neighbor — do something like this to us?

Mr. McPhaill spoke calmly, and I began to listen to what he was actually saying. He explained that to live in a mobile home we were required to have a septic tank. I told him that I knew that. We had applied for a use permit shortly after we gained title to the land in 1974 and were informed that we had to complete our land division first. We'd been jumping through hoops ever since: geologic survey, well testing, installation of a 500-gallon water tank and a water line between the well and the tank, and fire department approval. Each step had cost money that we had to save, and only led to another requirement. Finally, we applied for the land division, and it was approved. Next, we applied for a septic tank permit, a prerequisite to requesting a use permit for the trailer, and were told we needed a percolation test. John had drilled the required holes for the perc test, which was scheduled for the following week. I had the money for the permit, and I'd priced septic tank installations. Everyone charged more than we had in the bank, but we planned to save for one and get it installed in a few months. We hadn't been able to wait any longer to install the trailer, because I wanted it in place before our baby was born.

I explained all this to Mr. McPhaill, who listened carefully, his eyes on the infant in my arms. He said that since we had applied for a permit already, he would tear up the eviction notice. Then he explained what we needed to do to comply with regulations in the interim. It involved purchasing a very large waste container and attaching it by means of a hose to the grey water outlet. He explained that we could purchase a plastic tank with two wheels at one end and a handle at the other so you could roll it to the car. I stopped listening halfway through his instructions. All I could hear was "more money."

When the container was full, which it would be after a single shower or a bath, we should empty it at the gas station where we already emptied the portable toilet. We would need to do that until the septic tank was installed. He was actually quite kind. He apologized for having to make us go through this, when we were obviously trying to comply with Health Department regulations. His hands were tied, however, when someone made a complaint. Could he tell me who that was? No, he couldn't.

It looked like we were going back to sponge baths and no showers.

In the last phase of moving us back up the hill, John had transported the chicken coop and rabbit hutch and installed them near the blue trailer. Next, I began looking for a goat pen and milking stand. Once again, I turned to a 4H family. They had put an ad in the *Gilroy Dispatch*, offering an already-bred Nubian goat and a milking stand, and a pair of New Zealand White rabbits. When I saw the goat I thought immediately of Dreyfus, but this goat didn't look anything like that ill-fated one. They were totally different breeds. Dorrie told me Nubians had the most drinkable milk. "They don't produce as much as Toggenburgs or Alpines," she explained when I showed her the ad. "But their milk is milder-flavored. Doesn't taste so much like goat." Remembering the many quart jars of milk I had seen collecting in Dorrie's propane refrigerator, I decided a Nubian would be just fine.

And so Wattles came into our life. She was a mild-mannered mature goat, mostly brown, but with some black and white markings, and long floppy ears that draped down on either side of her elegant head with its Roman nose. She was named for the hair-covered appendages of flesh hanging from each side of her throat. She was accustomed to being milked, with large distended teats that I had no trouble emptying. Now in addition to feeding rabbits and chickens twice a day, I began milking Wattles morning and night. By this time, I had learned the secret of getting a goat up on the milking stand — a mixture of oats and barley with a little molasses stirred in. If I put about a cup of that mixture in the feeding trough, Wattles would jump right up. She put her head through the hole in the headpiece to reach the grain, and then I would fasten the latch. The only time she got that special grain mix is when she was being milked.

I found the early morning walk up the hill enjoyable and refreshing. As the sun came up, I would nurse BJ and tuck him into our bed on the floor next to John, then get dressed, take the milk pail from its hook, and walk up the path. Morning milking became my special alone time.

That spring Wattles gave birth to Seventeen, a black and white doe with a very clear marking of the numeral 17 on her pelt. Seventeen was mellow, just like her mother, and she eventually grew into a fine milker. We now had chickens, ducks, guinea hens, rabbits, and a herd of goats. We were finally a farm.

In March, we had a surprise visit from Bill Carter's daughter. She hadn't been on the land since we bought it, and was amazed to see what we had built and what Dorrie and Quincy had done with the inside of their bus. Dorrie offered tea, and we all crowded into the bus to hear why she had come.

"It's about my dad," she started. "He's acting weird."

We looked at one another, our faces unmoving.

"What kind of weird?" asked Dorrie.

"He's carrying loaded guns with him everywhere he goes, and he's sure we're all out to get him — everyone, the family, his friends, his neighbors."

She put her face in her hands for a minute, then looked up. "I'm really worried he's going to shoot someone. I'm really worried about him getting hurt."

She had our attention. Dorrie told her about his random and frightening visits. We hadn't seen him since BJ had been born, but we were always on high alert, just in case he came again.

His daughter thought Bill was suffering from dementia-related paranoia and should be in a nursing home. Would we help her put him in one?

Dorrie and Janet talked for a long time while the rest of us went back outside to work. Dorrie didn't think it was all that easy to get someone committed, but did think that reporting him for having loaded guns in the car, combined with us reporting him brandishing firearms on the land, might at the very least get him arrested. Janet said she would call the police the next day about the loaded rifles in his car. We agreed to file a report about his hostile threats.

23

THE MORGAN HILL TRADING POST

ONCE I SENT THE FINAL GALLEYS for *The Book of Whole Grains* back to St. Martin's Press in June 1976, a wide-open space appeared in my life. I felt unsettled and depressed, much as I do at the end of every school year. But this time I couldn't look forward to a new school year, and I wasn't ready to put six-month-old BJ in childcare.

We had recently learned that dropping a new electric line on our side of Chesbro Reservoir would cost thousands of dollars. I needed to earn money, but I needed to find a way to do that with John beside me.

While researching *The Book of Whole Grains*, I had traveled as far north as San Francisco and as south as Monterey to locate some of the specialized grains. The absence of a natural food store in our region was a vacuum I thought needed filling. Morgan Hill was halfway between San Jose and Salinas on Highway 101, perfectly situated for such a store to be successful.

When John and I had traveled through Britain in the 70s, we had visited many shops on the high streets of towns and villages. My mother had a friend who owned one — a yarn shop. A common characteristic of these shops was the back room, usually hidden behind a heavy curtain, from which one could sometimes hear conversation or the sound of a television. We were invited into Hetty's back room on one occasion, where we found her two grandchildren sitting on a small sofa watching TV while her husband heated water for tea in an electric kettle and prepared their evening meal on a hot plate. A small bookcase held children's books and toys. It was as warm and cozy as their sitting room at home. There were even pictures on the walls. I could picture myself running such a shop, selling natural foods rather than wool and knitting needles. A back room like that would make it possible to keep the children with me when they weren't in preschool.

John had left the start-up in Mountain View, and was working with a friend in Santa Rosa, developing software for embedded systems. Once he drove the two hours to meet with Glen, John usually stayed there for several days. Since I wasn't teaching or writing to a deadline, the children and I sometimes went with him, leaving our animals under Nina's competent care. During one of our visits, I bought supplies from a store called Organic Groceries. It was spacious, well-lit, and well-organized, with an attentive and friendly staff. Dozens of bins and barrels were filled with bulk grains, beans, nuts, and seeds, and an almost equal number of jars held teas, herbs, and spices. A little alcove contained reference books and a bench where customers could sit and read them. Along one wall was a literature rack that held stacks of recipe sheets. Near the checkout counter was a juice bar with high stools. This was exactly the kind of store I had imagined for Morgan Hill.

On a visit to the Whole Earth Truck Store in Menlo Park soon after, I discovered Earth Sign Natural Foods just around the corner. It was a smaller version of Organic Groceries, cozy and friendly. They carried the basic bulk grains, nuts, seeds, herbs, spices and tea, and a small selection of organic vegetables and fruit and packaged natural foods. Something like that would be perfect for Morgan Hill.

I approached my bank about financing such a venture. We owned all four of our vehicles, but even taken together they weren't worth much, and the property wasn't suitable as collateral for a loan.

Ironically, if I already had a store, I could borrow money on the business, but of course I didn't. The loan agent recommended I join the Chamber of Commerce. There were other ways to finance my venture, she said, and they could help me research them.

The receptionist at the Chamber collected a fat folder of information about Morgan Hill, including traffic studies, demographics, and the city master plan showing how future development was expected to play out. She also gave me a flyer advertising a two-day workshop called "Starting a Small Retail Business." It seemed providential to me that the training was only a week away. I signed up.

The workshop was sponsored by the Small Business Administration, and led by a retired pharmacist and a retired insurance broker. They were encouraging and offered free private consulting to anyone who completed both sessions. The first session was based on an SBA booklet titled *Ten Steps to Start Your Business*. Our instructors explained how to conduct market research, write a business plan, locate funding, select a name, file a Fictitious Business Notice, obtain necessary permits and licenses, etc. I would need to develop a projected balance sheet, projected earnings statement and break-even analysis, which required me to figure out my assets and liabilities, projected monthly expenses, and so on. The second session covered vetting and hiring staff, employer-employee relations, fire and health codes, and arranging for required inspections.

Some of this was vaguely familiar to me from General Business and Business Accounting classes I'd taken in college. Who knew they would actually be useful one day? I took copious notes, and made an appointment to meet with the insurance broker once the workshop ended. The list of things to do was long. I felt nervous about my ability to do this, but the speakers were encouraging, and their presentation had made completing each step sound straightforward.

After the workshop and my follow-up session, I felt confident that I could create a natural food store in Morgan Hill that would serve our unique community, provide me with an income, and allow me to keep my children with me while I worked. I shared the idea with John, who was pleased to see me enthusiastic again. I pulsed with the energy that always comes with having a new project to work on.

I could see that my life would be very busy for the next few months, and the first tasks would require analyzing the data I had collected about Morgan Hill's demographics. The children needed somewhere to play beside under my feet in the trailer.

I went to the lumber yard by the railroad tracks downtown and asked if they had plans for a sandbox. Armed with their handout, I purchased the necessary lumber and enough bags of play sand to fill it up. Then I bought lawn seed and edging, fence posts and hog wire, and asked to have everything delivered to our homestead on Hawkins Lane. It was the first time I'd attempted a delivery, but there were no problems. The truck made it up the curvy dirt road just fine, and the men dropped everything where I showed them, within a short distance of the new play yard I had been imagining.

I then contacted Dorrie and Quincy, Bob and Jan and the two boys, several couples whose children also attended Heidi's, and a couple of John and Quincy's colleagues at work who had been up to the land before. I promised cold drinks and a delicious lunch to all who participated in the construction of the sandbox and the lawn enclosure.

The crew accomplished far more than I expected. When they left that evening, they had built and filled the sandbox, raked the soil and planted the lawn seed, edged the lawn and constructed a tightly stretched fence around the whole thing. All that was needed was a gate, and John was already designing that. I felt like Huck Finn. Only one casualty of the project: Bob Fabini sprained his ankle, and was clumping around on crutches for several weeks afterward.

On my way up the hill to milk Wattles one morning, an idea had occurred to me for how I could learn more about running a natural food store. The next time I went to the Whole Earth Truck Store for supplies, I walked around the corner to Earth Sign Natural Foods and asked to see the manager. Entering, I noticed a Help Wanted sign in the window.

"I have a rather unusual request," I explained. "I want to open a store like this in Morgan Hill, nearly 50 miles away, but I've never run a store like this before."

The manager didn't seem to think that was a problem.

"Retail is retail." she replied.

I didn't want to tell her that I'd never run *any* kind of business before. I continued, "I'd like to shadow you for a while, learn where you get your products, how you know how much to charge, how you manage your inventory. Could I work for you for free one or two days a week in exchange for you teaching me some of what you know?"

Remarkably, the manager was willing to take me on as an apprentice. She pointed to the sign in the window and said she was understaffed and could use the help. We talked about days and times, and I left for my parents' house with a tentative schedule. Mama was delighted at the thought of having "her babies" for a couple of days a week.

So, for the rest of the summer and into the fall, I spent Tuesday and Thursday afternoons packaging grains and teas into little bags, arranging oranges in a bin or filling out order sheets, always with a notebook in my apron pocket on which I recorded prices, sources, recipes, whatever gems of information my mentor offered or that I could glean from the information on bills of lading, order sheets, and labels. While Mom fed my children lunch and sang them to sleep, I listened to conversations between staff and customers, recorded customer questions, studied the books that were in Earth Sign's well-stocked library and noted which books they offered for sale. Mine would soon be there, I thought. I was like a sponge, soaking up everything I could.

I began working my way through the ten steps listed in the SBA booklet. The first was to conduct market research, to gather information about potential customers and competitors. That wasn't too hard since there were no other natural food stores in Morgan Hill or any of the surrounding communities. Chamber of Commerce traffic study data enabled me to estimate the number of customers I could attract as a specialty store, and that provided a baseline from which to calculate how much stock I would need to put on my shelves and, therefore, how much money I would need to start.

Writing a business plan was fun. It was kind of like writing a magazine article, or a chapter in a book: "The Morgan Hill Trading Post will fill a need in the southern Santa Clara Valley for a source of natural foods and numerous other goods commonly desired by consumers of natural food products," I began.

After I figured out my customer base ("According to a survey … 80% of the customers in health food stores come from the upper-middle and middle-middle classes. … New Morgan Hill residents, according to … tend to be 25–40 years of age, college educated, with 2 or 3 children.") and wrote the business plan. My next task was to secure funding.

Having been turned down for a bank loan, I had to be creative. Several years earlier, when I worked for an insurance salesman, I had purchased a life insurance policy with a cash value. After some research, I learned that I could withdraw $5000 from that policy as a loan to myself without affecting the insurance and with a very manageable repayment plan. I submitted the forms to do that and brainstormed a list of people I would turn to next: my parents, John's parents, friends. Realistically, though, none of them could afford to help me.

Then I learned about Limited Partnerships. In a Limited Partnership, two or more partners jointly conduct a business in which the limited partners are liable only to the extent of the amount of money they have invested, while the general partner or partners bear the remainder of the liability. I needed some limited partners.

I hired a CPA to take my estimated numbers and create balance sheets and the related projected earnings and cash projections for each monthly period from January 1, 1977 through December 31, 1977. I drew a floor plan of the building I had secured, and created an inventory of products I wanted to have on my shelf on opening day. Pricing them was time-consuming, but my mentor at Earth Sign helped me locate sources and develop appropriate mark-ups for the various categories of product. I then compiled what I believed to be a professional-looking report, and sent it with letters to a dozen friends, former colleagues, and acquaintances, offering limited partnerships in my new venture. I raised another $5000 that way and, with that and my insurance loan, I had enough money to open the doors.

The next time I went to town, I noticed a 1943 Willy's Jeep parked on the Standard lot with a "For Sale" sign in the window. When I first saw it, I did a double take, made a U-turn, and came back to the station to inquire about its price. The Jeep was painted a sunny shade of yellow, and the interior had been customized with black leather and stainless-steel studs. There were no rear seats, and no heater or radio, but it had a large cargo capacity and 4-wheel drive. I fell instantly in love. In one of the least-considered decisions I ever made, I bought the Jeep for $1500.

When I finally told my parents my plans for the store, their immediate and enthusiastic support surprised me. This was an undertaking they could understand and appreciate. Dad offered to build shelving and signs, and brought home from work a station wagon full of used fence boards — each with 12 nails that needed to be removed. Mom offered to help in the store once it opened, and continued to take care of Doña and John while I worked to get it ready. She also removed about a hundred rusty nails from the boards that would soon be shelves and signage. Perhaps this venture would heal some of the wounds I had inflicted by — in their view — turning my back on the suburban middle-class existence my parents had made possible by coming to America.

The wife of the town veterinarian managed the rental of a small concrete block house on Fourth Street. We ran into one other downtown and, in catching up, I told her I had been looking for a commercial property to rent. It turned out that Gail's mother owned two blocks of downtown property. Gail showed me the house and said she had already decided to convert the house into commercial property — the mixed-use zoning would allow her to do that — but hadn't yet made needed structural and cosmetic changes. She offered me three months free rent while both of us worked on the house, and a generously low rent after that. I accepted gratefully.

Meanwhile, back at the homestead, John had ordered a water tank and several hundred feet of PVC pipe. One weekend, using a piece of equipment called a Ditch Witch, John and Pop dug a trench from the well up to the water tank and back down to the trailer. The ride-on trencher weighed 5000 pounds and scared me to death. I could imagine it turning over and taking one of the men with it. It cost $500 a day to rent, so Pop picked it up with his truck at 7:00 a.m. when the rental company opened, and they worked until dark, nearly twelve hours. It was hot, and they felt pressured to get the job done as fast as possible. I fed them on site and kept them supplied with water. Lillie Rist came back the next week to cut a level bed for the water tank, which was helicoptered into place. Once the water line went in, we had cold running water. Not much pressure, but I didn't complain.

One fall day, the children and I were "trapped" on the mountain without a car. I couldn't go downtown to work on the store, or take Doña to Heidi's, and, once I accepted that fact, we had an absolutely wonderful time. Doña wanted to play with Mr. Potato Head, and for that she needed a large potato. Once she was busy sticking eyes and ears and a mouth on her potato, I got the idea of taking some other potatoes and cutting designs into them, then making Christmas paper by printing the designs on computer paper with red tempera paint. That kept Doña busy for over an hour. I gave John his own potato and paper, and he went to town too.

On days like this, and remembering times in the past when we'd made puppets or clothespin dolls or baked together, I sorely regretted having enrolled Doña in nursery school. After we finished the paper printing, we dug up my tomato plants and planted bulbs. We transplanted herbs and tore out a huge clump of pennyroyal that was threatening to crawl into the trailer. We sprinkled garbage liberally over the old melon, squash and corn patch to start a compost pile. Then, while I weeded my flowerbeds, Doña warmed my heart by turning somersaults on our new lawn while BJ watched from the nearby sandbox. Book and Baby John notwithstanding, I decided that designing and building that fenced play yard had been my crowning achievement of the previous twelve months.

While I painted concrete walls, designed the interior of the store, and continued my correspondence with potential funders, Gail was supervising workers as they removed kitchen appliances and cabinets, repaired holes in walls, landscaped the front and back, and constructed a custodian's mop sink. Once Gail drew up papers and I had secured the lease for five years, I subscribed to Barbara Bermudez' Morgan Hill Newcomers service, providing her with literature promoting the store, projecting an opening date of January 15. Barbara was an inspiring entrepreneur who had started her business following the sudden death of her husband. She hadn't worked outside of the home for thirty years, but had quickly become a regular visitor to downtown businesses and a popular member of the Chamber of Commerce.

In October, I wrote letters to vendors — lots of them — requesting price sheets and photographs of products. In addition to food, I wanted to offer a variety of unusual food preparation tools and housewares, such as seed sprouters, cherry pitters, apple corer and peelers, yogurt makers, kerosene lamps, and hand-cranked ice cream freezers. I began attending auctions and estate sales and visiting second-hand stores looking for equipment I would need. I bought a manual cash register and western-style letters for signs from a department store remainder sale, a chest freezer from a second-hand store in the mountains along with an antique peanut butter maker and an amazing upright display freezer with oval windows. Installing the equipment and securing the permits, licenses, insurance, registrations, and inspections were the next steps, and they took most of November and December.

Meanwhile, *The Book of Whole Grains* had come out and my publicist was arranging radio interviews — one in Palo Alto, one in Los Angeles — a television appearance on *A.M. San Francisco,* and participation in the Palo Alto Junior League Holiday Book House. These events took me away from getting the store ready, but I knew they were important. Several friends also hosted autograph parties during this period, and the manager of Earth Sign invited me to sign books on a Saturday just before Christmas. Getting the permit and licensing approvals was taking longer than I had expected anyway, and it was looking like the store wouldn't open until February.

I reveled in the heady feeling common to new authors who think they've made the big time, and enjoyed the fuss … except when I felt terrified, such as when Jim Dunbar, a television personality, asked me to make tabouli on the air. My publicist had arranged for me to appear on *A.M. San Francisco*, a morning talk show on Channel 7 that I'd never even heard of, let alone watched. I was told to bring a cooking demonstration. As requested, I brought a bowl of prepared *tabouli*, and the ingredients necessary to make a fresh batch: cooked triticale, fresh tomatoes, cucumber, parsley, seasonings, a cutting board, a knife, and a bowl. I had to be at the studio super early. John and the children and I slept in a motel near the station, and I took a taxi to Channel 7. My high school friend, Barbara, had made a long blue dress for me to wear for the opening of my store, and I wore that. I had let my hair grow out again; I hoped I looked like a well-dressed hippie with my hair pulled back into my trademark red scarf and a pair of long dangly earrings.

Jim Dunbar was wonderful. He met with me ahead of time and told me everything that would be happening — which helped calm my nerves. After he interviewed me for a few minutes in front of the cameras about my store and the book — he clearly had read it — we moved to the kitchen set, and my anxiety returned. Watching me shake as I began to slice the tomato, Jim moved in to help — we made the triticale *tabouli* salad together as we exchanged pleasantries, which is some trick when you're scared to death. My friends and family said they couldn't even tell I was nervous. Jim was definitely a pro. I ran up $75 of expenses that day, but hopefully lots of people saw the show and immediately went out and bought my book.

I wanted The Morgan Hill Trading Post to be homey and welcoming to parents of young children. I designed the first room customers would see to look like a funky living room, with a wood burning stove and two rocking chairs, kerosene lamps on the walls, and a small child's table and chairs tucked against one wall. The cash register counter, rustically faced with fence boards, faced the front door, and narrow shelves behind me when I stood at the register contained vitamins, minerals, and food supplements — all out of reach of children's curious hands.

In one of the two back rooms, my father built a set of incrementally higher shelves for my grain containers, five-gallon food-grade plastic buckets I had purchased inexpensively from a supply house. He also built a shelving unit that held 25 glass jars of tea and herbs, and a worktable on which perched the antique peanut butter grinder and a grain mill. In the other back room, where the kitchen had been, Dad constructed child-sized bunk beds along the back wall by the door, and on two other walls he built wide counters with shelves beneath. He covered the counter with linoleum so I could use it to package food under the Morgan Hill Trading Post label and prepare meals for the children. These counters turned out to be useful for opening packages and inventorying their contents. The middle room, accessible from the front room through a door by the children's table, was slated for packaged foods. Here, Dad built shelving on all four walls, staggering the distances between shelves based on my instructions. These shelves would eventually be filled with bottles, jars, boxes, and bags of every manner of natural food I could procure — along with a small offering of organic vegetables. Samples of housewares on some of the shelves would break up the monotony of shelves lined with similar-looking containers.

As the opening of my store approached, Mom and Dad and I worked there almost every evening and weekend. Dad had figured out a way to fasten the fence boards together with 1" x 1" corregated metal strips underneath and use them as shelves. He constructed the exterior signs the same way and, when the Western style plastic letters were painted and glued in place, MORGAN HILL TRADING POST looked amazingly like a professionally-made sign. We hoisted it up in front of the store, anchored it on either end to the roof peak, and stood back. The old-fashioned paned windows seemed empty, and the strip of soil in the front called for more than the marguerite daisies the landscapers had planted. Dad made thin shelves across the inside of the windows, allowing me to place colored glass canisters and an interesting-looking grain mill on display. Mom and I planted two silver-dollar eucalyptus trees, one on either side of the front door. The man at the nursery had said they were fast growing. He was telling the truth; in two years the trees reached the sign.

The next event couldn't have been choreographed any better. In October, my publicist had sent a press release announcing the publication of *The Book of Whole Grains* to each of our three Morgan Hill newspapers and to the *San Jose Mercury News*. In December, a *Morgan Hill Times* reporter came by the store for an interview, and two weeks later a reporter from the *Valley World* did so also. In January 1977 Mary Phillips, Food Editor for the *San Jose Mercury News*, called and asked if she could bring a photographer when she came down for her interview. Mom and I were painting the walls that day, and I asked her to wait a few days, explaining my opening schedule.

Meanwhile, I had located an inexpensive source of 3-inch terra cotta plant pots, and had purchased a hundred of them as well as several flats of herb plants. Mom and I transplanted the herbs into the pots and arranged them just inside the front room along the far wall. These would be given to my first 100 customers.

With the help of my illustrator for *The Book of Whole Grains,* I had designed a logo from a sketch of an old-fashioned dry goods store, and used that as the basis of a quarter-page ad announcing my Grand Opening in each of the local newspapers. I then ordered business cards, stationery, labels to put on repackaged foods, and checks, all bearing the Morgan Hill Trading Post logo. The new Nob Hill supermarket chain had just had their trucks painted with colorful fruits and vegetables. I contacted them for the name of the artist, and hired her to paint my logo on the yellow vehicle. I had decided to use the Jeep as my regular car, so it became an effective traveling advertisement.

Mary and her photographer arrived a week before the Grand Opening, and found John and me sitting on the floor of the front room with the children, eating a picnic lunch. Mary was delighted to meet Doña and both Johns, and directed the photographer to take several photos of them, which he did. She and I talked for what seemed like very long time — about the store, the book, my family's immigration from England, and our homestead. She seemed to be interested in my life, and was a skillful interviewer. For a couple of hours, I forgot I had a deadline, and just enjoyed talking with her.

A few days before the Grand Opening, I invited several friends, the Chamber of Commerce, and the three local newspapers to attend a soft opening. They were all very kind as I learned how to use my new cash register, and seemed happy to mill around the store, make their own peanut butter, grind their own grain, and weigh their own purchases. Several times people remarked that this was a whole new kind of store for Morgan Hill, and complimented me for having the idea. I saved the potted herbs for the grand opening, but gave free granola bars to everyone who visited that day, and invited them to bring their friends on Saturday.

On the big day, John and I were at the store at 8:00 a.m. in heady expectation of the opening at 10:00 a.m. I hadn't slept much that week, and in my darkest moments I imagined that no one would come. I pushed that thought away. I had learned some things from the soft opening and had rearranged some products, priced the vitamins individually, and added instructions for the peanut butter grinder and grain mill. I'd also purchased a half dozen handled wicker baskets for customers to use to carry their purchases to the checkout counter. Today, I thought, should go smoothly, even if the turnout was small. Dorrie had stayed behind with John and Doña; she and Quincy would bring them down during the day to see how things were going, and keep them until we returned home that night.

The line began forming at 9:00 a.m. At 9:30, John went outside to talk to people, and when he came back inside he urged me to open the doors.

"There are already enough bodies out there to fill this little store," he said urgently. "We should let them in before they give up and leave."

I went to look. He was right. The line curled back from the front of the building around the side, where people had collected in groups, patiently and politely, to chat until the doors opened. I went to the front door and turned the sign around to OPEN, then opened it and welcomed my first actual customers.

"Our opening time is and will be 10:00," I explained, "but we're ready now, and you appear to be also. Come on in!"

I had put a kettle of water on the gas "wood-burning" stove (fire department regulations wouldn't let us have a real one) and made two cups of cinnamon-and-nutmeg-flavored tea for John and me to drink during that last half hour before opening. They sat forgotten on the stove beside the kettle, sending their sweet fragrance out to everyone who entered the room. Forty years later, when I asked friends for stories about this period of my life, several of them told me the fragrance of cinnamon spiced tea evoked memories of my little store to that very day.

By 10:00, the Morgan Hill Trading Post was packed with customers. They didn't stop coming until we closed at 6:00 p.m. John loved the attention my venture was getting and, while I stayed behind the counter talking to people and ringing up their purchases, he served as tour guide and assistant, helping customers make peanut butter — a real hit — and grind whole grains into flour. Several people who had attended the soft opening came back, and they helped newcomers settle their children at the children's table in the front room, introduced them to the three rooms of merchandise, and showed them how to weigh out ingredients and package them in the paper bags provided.

We were so busy, we didn't have time to wonder where all the people came from, but around midday an acquaintance from the Chamber of Commerce handed me a folded newspaper.

"You're famous!" She announced, smiling broadly. "Take a look at this."

I unfolded the paper, dated the previous Monday. It was the food section of the *San Jose Mercury News* and on the front was a full-page photograph of our son John surrounded by four of our wooden grain barrels on which had been placed a plate of cookies, a casserole dish of pilaf, and *The Book of Whole Grains*. I had provided the pilaf and the cookies, but the photo must have been staged while Mary and I had been talking. The headline read "Down to earth" and the caption under the photo went on to say "John Bumgarner, 14 months old, sampled the Peanut Butter Cookies, and is apt to dive into the Vegetable Pilaf next … his mother is a down-to-earth-cook."

Inside, a two-page photo spread told the story of our move to the land, my writing of *The Book of Whole Grains*, and the creation of the Morgan Hill Trading Post. Mary Phillips had given me a wonderful grand opening gift — an unbelievably successful opening day, and a far wider customer base than I could ever have hoped for. (She had also written that the store would be opening at 9:00 a.m. Saturday morning. Mystery solved.)

In mid-afternoon, John announced that we had run out of herb plants. Over one hundred customers had crossed our threshold and made a purchase. The final few customers were lingerers: they wanted to talk about what we were doing on our land, and if I would help them learn how to cook natural foods for their family. One final customer was the head of Morgan Hill Adult Education, where I had been teaching Children's Literature and Nutrition for Children classes. She asked me to add Natural Foods Cooking to my spring offerings. I went home that night light-headed and happy. My dream of opening a natural food store in Morgan Hill had come true, and my fear of having no customers had not. I would make a reasonable income from teaching three classes for Adult Ed and two for Gavilan College, and it looked like there might be an income from the store as well. That night I slept well for the first time in weeks. Our future looked good.

After our amazing Grand Opening, life settled into a routine. I set the opening hours at 10:00 – 6:00 Tuesday through Saturday in order to have time to do morning chores and take Doña to Heidi's each morning and get home to milk goats in the evening.

Business was brisk from the very beginning, but there were usually a few slow moments in the day when I could call in orders, shelve products that had arrived that morning, repackage teas and herbs, or snuggle with little John. I arranged to carpool with one of the other preschool parents, but sometimes I would have to close the store for 45 minutes to an hour while I drove to Gilroy to fetch Doña. I posted a permanent sign indicating that I might have to do that, and after a while my customers learned not to shop between 2:00 and 3:00. That became another time when I could manage the work of the store. Tuesday and Thursday, I drove to San Jose at 7:00 a.m. to buy raw milk, then pick up the carpool children and drive to Gilroy before I returned to open the store. After being late a couple of times, I changed the opening time to "*About* 10:00 a.m." Funky, but it worked, and no one seemed to mind.

Running the store suited me. I enjoyed the interaction with customers, talking about health and nutrition, and keeping the shop clean and well-stocked. On cold days, I ran the gas Franklin stove and kept a kettle of water on the top to make tea, which I offered to anyone who looked like they might have the time to sit in the rocking chair and drink it. Little John enjoyed playing with the other children who came into the store, and took his naps on the bottom bunk of the bed Dad had built in the stock room. It was close to the floor, so when he woke up, he just rolled off the bed and came toddling into the front room to find me. Every Thursday, as she had promised, my mother came from Belmont on the Greyhound bus. She often took John out to the park in his stroller. After he went to sleep, she would help me in the store.

A fascinating variety of people came through the doors. The law partners Rusconi, Foster and Thomas took a daily walk through town and frequently stopped in for a protein bar or bag of chips. Bob Foster and his wife Nancy became regular customers, purchasing four to six gallons of raw milk a week for their four children, and Ernie Rusconi brought his wife in to buy freshly ground peanut butter. A friend of John's from high school days, Jonine Cordell, shopped at the store and kept the accounts.

Mary Phillips, the food editor of the *San Jose Mercury News* who had publicized my grand opening so successfully, surprised me with a visit after the store had been open a few months. She asked if I would write a weekly natural foods column for the *Merc*. Of course, I said yes. After she left, I did a little jig. I felt giddy with success, and immediately began jotting down ideas for columns.

My cooking by this time had been heavily influenced by nutritionist Adelle Davis' book, *Let's Cook it Right*, and by Frances Moore Lappé's *Diet for a Small Planet*. I decided to draw from those sources to encourage readers and their families to eat a wide variety of natural foods, low in sugar, salt and fat, and without artificial flavors, seasonings or preservatives. Other topics I would cover, as Lappé did, were the health and ecological benefits of a plant-based diet.

Shortly after "Naturally Speaking" began appearing in the food section of the *San Jose Mercury News*, Sue Olson and her two young boys arrived one morning as I unloaded crates of milk from my Jeep. She had a list of questions, and began interrogating me as she helped carry in the milk. Why did she have moths in her whole wheat flour? Could she make a roux with arrowroot instead of white flour? How long could she keep the organic yogurt in her refrigerator?

Racing the clock to get Doña to Heidi's and get the store open on time, I asked her to come back another day. Recognizing the name of the

San Jose dairy on the milk crates, she offered to pick up the milk the following week in exchange for some of my time to answer her questions.

Thus began a partnership that eventually became a friendship. Sue would deliver the milk every Tuesday morning, and then stick around for several hours, nursing her youngest in the rocking chair and asking questions when I had a break in customers. I asked her to keep track of the questions so I could use them to create the curriculum in the natural foods cooking class the director of Adult Education had asked me to teach in the spring. I also used them to inspire me as I wrote my columns for the *San Jose Mercury News*.

I fastened an orange crate to one of the walls with masonry screws and turned it into a display case for La Leche League books and informational brochures. As the local La Leche League Leader, I frequently received calls from new mothers seeking help with breastfeeding or other care issues. I would invite them to our monthly meetings, but also encouraged them to come in to the store to talk with me if they could. Sue was also a member of La Leche League, and could be counted on to chip in with information if she was there.

One day, an older woman came into the store, looked briefly at the La Leche League display and then at the children's table nearby. John was sitting at the table, making words with magnetic letters on a cookie sheet, copying them from cards that had pictures of objects with simple names — such as cat, ant, pig, dog, and egg.

"Have you ever heard of Maria Montessori?" she asked. I had, and admitted that was where I had gotten the idea for John's activity. She accepted a cup of tea and sat in the rocking chair watching John with a benevolent smile for some time before stating the reason for her visit. Her name was Elmira Johnson, and she was about to open a Montessori preschool in Morgan Hill. The church next door to her building had agreed to allow parents to park in their lot, but the city required a variance hearing in order for her to obtain official approval for the arrangement. Someone had told her I would help. Would I?

I never found out who that "someone" was, but I attended the planning commission meeting with Elmira, she obtained her variance, and I gained a lifelong friend. When she opened her school in 1977, I transferred Doña there, and shortly afterwards John followed. My morning school drop-off and pick-up time had shrunk to 10 minutes.

Developing a line of credit with the major product distributors took six months. Until then, I had to pay for each delivery with a check. After purchasing all the fittings for the store and my initial inventory, I didn't have a very large bank account, so I ordered product two or three times a week, which was a nuisance. Once I obtained credit, I ordered once a week, which meant that I didn't run out of product as often, and customers were able to purchase more each time they came in. After a few months, the business became so brisk that there were fewer and fewer breaks when I could unpack boxes and shelve their contents, or even spend quality time with John and Doña. Much to my surprise, the Live Oak High School Emerald Regime came to my aid.

The Live Oak High School Marching Band and Color Guard was started in the summer of 1970 with 36 band members and 10 color guard members. Mike Rubino and Cricket Hathaway conducted band practice on the old Live Oak campus, a block away from the little house on Lindo Lane where we lived while I healed from my injuries. Every morning during first period — which started at 7:00 a.m. — the band would march down our street practicing their music and formations in preparation for home football games and local band reviews. I can't say I always loved the music, but after we moved back to the land, I realized I had developed a soft spot for the youngsters in the band.

The Live Oak band and color guard grew to 146 members in 1976 when, renamed the Emerald Regime, the band traveled to Whitewater, Wisconsin and captured the Marching Bands of America Grand National Championship. In order to pay for their travel, band members were encouraged to seek monetary support from local business owners, often in return for some kind of public service. Laurie Donaldson called me one day asking for a donation, suggesting that she might be able to help me in the store. Alas, Laurie was too young for a work permit, and therefore unable to use the cash register. Instead, I asked if she would come and play with my children a couple of afternoons a week. The children loved their new friend, and Laurie became a daily visitor, cooking meals for the children, making suggestions for more effective window displays or product purchases, and generally making herself indispensable. As soon as she turned 16, I hired her to work the front counter after school each day, and I returned to spending afternoons with my children.

About that time, a small group of boys showed up at my store, asking for work. They didn't play in the band, but I recognized them from when I had been student teaching at Morgan Hill School. Vandalism was becoming a problem in downtown, and I asked the boys to watch my store when it was closed and get the word out not to tag my building. I paid them a small wage for that and also to break down boxes and sweep the street in front of the store. They only stuck around for a few weeks, but whenever they appeared after that I offered free protein bars, and my store was never tagged.

By the end of the first year, I needed to hire another employee. Nina suggested Carol, a young mother who lived on the Anderson Egg Ranch, where I bought free-range eggs to sell in the store. Carol's older son attended the Montessori school with Doña, and Carol was delighted when I told her she could bring her younger child with her to the store. Having Carol there three mornings a week allowed me to attend meetings of the Chamber of Commerce and Downtown Business Association, which kept me appraised of bad checks or counterfeit bills being circulated, and to participate in decisions about opening and closing times, street fairs, and other community activities. Between these organizations and the Montessori school, I met new people and began to feel a sense of belonging to the community.

By then, I was teaching cooking classes in the well-equipped kitchens of Live Oak High School and the San Jose YMCA, as well as child nutrition and children's literature at Gavilan College. I felt appreciated and successful. I loved my town life, but I also really appreciated the peace and quiet of our farm on the hill, and savored the Sundays and Mondays when I could work in my garden, cook family meals, bake bread, make cheese and yoghurt, and watch the children play. I stopped worrying about when we would be able to build a house, and just enjoyed what we had.

24

VISITORS TO THE LAND

ONCE WE STARTED DEVELOPING OUR LAND, contractors and inspectors came up to the property on a fairly regular basis. One week, we had geologists, well inspectors, and the fire department roaming about the land. Curious to see what we were up to, neighbors started dropping in unannounced. Then deer season opened. Hugh Graves and his teenaged sons came up the road on their way to their own parcel further up Hawkins Lane. Mostly they hunted in the daytime, but sometimes the boys came up by themselves at night, directing a huge spotlight at the road ahead. They made me nervous.

It was a hot, hot day at the end of August 1976. Bill Carter had sold his trailer and adjacent land to Larry Orlando, and we had begun locking the gate at the bottom of Hawkins Lane. Hugh Graves had a key, as did everyone who lived on Hawkins Lane. We hadn't seen Carter for months. After milking the goats and feeding children and animals, I retired to the hammock with my book. While Doña and John played on the blanket beside me, I re-read a chapter in Jefferson's biography about the founding of The University of Virginia. Willie and Elsa were stretched out in the shade of the trees between which my hammock was suspended. I reached the end of a chapter and leaned back against the knotted ropes holding little John, who had crawled into my arms and fallen asleep. A cluster of chatty birds conversed in the branches above us. I can't tell one sparrow from another, and there are about 20 different varieties of them in California, but I'm pretty certain they were sparrows. I stretched my arms and legs, rearranged John so the feeling would return to my arm, and turned to the next chapter.

The birds heard the intruder first. Their sudden silence alerted the dogs, whose ears twitched, although they remained supine. When they heard the sound of an engine, they sat upright, their ears turning like periscopes. Now I could hear the vehicle also. It seemed to have stopped at our gate. The driver turned off the ignition. Silence.

My concentration was gone, and I listened for more sounds. Who had stopped at our gate? Was he or she walking up the road toward us? I wasn't expecting any packages or visitors, but I decided to return to the trailer with the dogs. I wanted a door between us and any uninvited guests. I heard the metallic sound of the gate being shaken, like someone trying to open it. The hair prickled on the back of my neck. Thinking to calm myself, I put a kettle on for tea, and opened the jalousie window over the sink in order to hear better.

The car didn't start up again, but no one walked up the road, either. The birds began to chatter, and the dogs returned to their naps. Then I heard a new sound, kind of a *"thunk."* It was repeated, once, twice, three times, then four, five, six. Could it be some kind of an animal making the noise? I put John into the Snugli carrier and hoisted him on to my back, took our .22 rifle down from the top cupboard in our bedroom, retrieved a box of bullets from the back of the kitchen cupboard, loaded the gun, and headed out the door, latching the screen and door quietly behind me. I cautioned the children to be very quiet so we didn't disturb our visitor, and walked slowly down the narrow pathway that ran down the hill from the trailer to the Quonset hut.

It was difficult to approach the gate on the road without being seen. I went instead through the tall weeds into the bushes by Bill

Carter's old horse paddock, now Bob and Jan's vegetable garden, and looked down the hill from the top of the rise. What I saw was a gaunt and disheveled Carter, several feet inside the locked gate, digging a hole in the side of the hill. Beside him was something wrapped in a pink blanket or cloth of some kind. It was all quite mysterious and spooky. I whispered to the children that we would leave the man to his task and go back home, which we did, through the bushes and weeds to the pathway, and up the hill to our little trailer, which felt cozy and safe. I called the sheriff's department on our new telephone and reported the incident, then made a cup of tea to await their arrival. After a while, I went down to unlock the gate.

When Deputy Hammelev arrived and knocked on my door, I greeted him warmly. We walked down to the gate together and he took a shovel from his car. Carter was nowhere to be seen. The grave was shallow, and in very short order the deputy had uncovered a pink shower curtain and was unwrapping it carefully. What he found was totally unexpected, and the sight of it filled me with sadness and remorse. A black dog, a brown leather jacket, and a bowl of dog food. Clearly a beloved pet. Was Carter merely a grieving owner with a desire to return his companion to the land over which he had once roamed? I apologized to the deputy. He was very kind, dug the grave more deeply, returned its contents to the earth, and piled rocks over the finished grave. He asked me to sign his report, shook my hand, and drove away.

Our nemesis appeared much diminished during this incident. I decided it was time to relegate him to the past. His daughter was right. He was a sad old man, possibly with some form of dementia. Surely there was no need to be afraid of him.

25

CHANGES AND CHALLENGES

1977

D UE TO ONE THING OR ANOTHER (raccoons and vagrant dogs mostly) our small flock of free-range chickens had been depleted. That spring, I bought more chicks from De Carlo's Feather Haven in San Martin. In addition to a half dozen Rhode Island Reds, which I thought would be good layers, Doña, nearly five, helped me pick out a variety of novelty poultry breeds — a Polish, several Araucanas, and a pair of bantams. We also bought ducklings and another pair of rabbits.

Those were ill-fated animals. We were still making beginner's mistakes. Over the next couple of months, most of the chicks drowned in dog water bowls and buckets that had filled up with rain water. Others were killed by owls, hawks, or cats. The first litter of rabbits from each doe were born dead, heartbreaking for all of us. Merv at the feed store had said it was normal, but it was still sad.

But the Banty rooster survived to terrorize Little John. One Saturday our little boy became so hysterical when the tiny rooster chased him around the clearing that Big John caught the offending bird and cut off its head. The rooster ran around headless for a good five minutes after that, with Little John in pursuit, giggling. Big John thought that was pretty funny.

Once we built a large fenced and roofed yard in which baby chicks could safely forage and grow, free from water hazards and predators, their life spans increased considerably. Soon adult chickens were again foraging under the children's watchful eyes, rabbits were multiplying like, well, like rabbits, and we began to get a regular supply of eggs.

I came home from the store one night to find Dorrie and Quincy and Nina all sitting around the outdoor picnic table beside the blue trailer. As the children and I walked up the path to find out what was going on, I saw the large red papers in Quincy's hand. Eviction notices from the Health Department had been taped to Nina's trailer and the Adams' schoolbus. Someone had turned them in for code violations — the septic tank issue again.

"Someone had to have tipped them off," Dorrie was saying. How the hell would they have known that we were up there at the top of the hill otherwise?"

We were all pretty sure it was Carter, but we had no proof.

The Adamses had been saving for a down payment, and this indignity convinced them it was time to start looking at houses.

Within a month, they put a deposit on a small house in Gilroy with some land. Dorrie's family drove north again and, as quickly as their farm had been installed on the top of the hill three years earlier, it was deconstructed and moved to Gilroy. They kept the parcel in case any of Dorrie's siblings wanted to live there.

For some months Nina had been living in San Francisco during the week while she worked toward a master's degree, returning to the land on weekends and holidays. She moved her possessions out of the trailer and we didn't see her again for a while After she finished her degree, she moved into a lovely redwood house on the property of her friends at the Anderson Egg Ranch. Only Bob and Jan, living in Bill Carter's old trailer adjacent to our land, and John and I and the children, were left on our little slice of paradise.

End of the Drought

It finally rained
After you left
I stood barefoot
Watching the chickens
Play soccer with an apple core
Straining in the silence
To hear your voice
I thought I heard a flute
Whistling wistful notes
But all was quiet

When I had first opened the Morgan Hill Trading Post, John would stop in on his way home to help me unpack boxes or restock shelves, but the novelty of those activities wore off quickly. He began leaving me to finish up while he took Doña and John to do the evening chores. He was a great bedtime parent, feeding and bathing the children, reading stories and putting them to bed. When I came home at night, exhausted, I had no desire to prepare a meal, or even carry on an intelligent conversation, but he greeted me cheerfully, sometimes with a Black Russian, my favorite cocktail.

I arose again at 5:00 a.m. to count the take from the previous day and prepare a bank deposit. As soon as it was light, I milked the goats, fed the animals, and raced to town with the children to start all over again. John was often still in bed when I left.

Keeping the shelves stocked was a major challenge. I now had credit with some suppliers, but I drove directly to others to save shipping costs. Once a month, my beloved Jeep took me to San Francisco to purchase teas, herbs, and spices in bulk. On the way I would stop at Guisto's Specialty Foods — a whole grain supplier and bakery in South San Francisco. Al Guisto had been helpful while I was writing *The Book of Whole Grains*, and he was always interested in new recipes to print on the back of his packages. I bought 25- and 50-pound sacks of grain from Al, and I enjoyed my visits with him and his brother Fred. They were, and still are, carrying on a business started by their parents before chemical-free foods and whole grains were popular. I made two weekly trips to a raw milk dairy in San Jose, and another to pick up fresh juice from an orchard in Watsonville.

I wanted my store to be unique. I went to gift shows and alternative lifestyle conventions where I purchased food- and lifestyle-related products to feature in the store. These happened on weekends, and John liked to go with me. Into my store came Aladdin oil lamps, hand-crank ice cream freezers, three-tier seed sprouters, apple corer and peelers, and portable food dryers. Once, in order for us to get it wholesale, John suggested I buy a couple of portable log splitters. They turned out to be quite popular, and I sold one nearly every month. From my artisan friends in Humboldt County, I purchased oil lamps with hand blown glass bases, earthenware tea pots and cups, and beeswax candles.

Soon after opening the store, I had begun to get requests to speak at nursery schools, women's groups, and La Leche League meetings. Once I began writing a weekly column for the *San Jose Mercury News*, I had columns to research, letters to answer, and more requests to speak. Food editors in other parts of the country asked to publish my column in their paper and invited me to speak locally. Morgan Hill Adult Education and the San Jose YMCA asked me to teach classes. A new publication for parents, called *Mothering*, commissioned one article a month on families and food. I didn't know whether to be flattered or overwhelmed. My plan of earning a living from running the store was successful beyond my wildest dreams, but I struggled to fit everything in. This wasn't how I had imagined running a store would be.

My garden was suffering, the animal pens needed attention, and the trailer always seemed to be in chaos. Each morning when I rushed the children out the door they were squabbling, and they were asleep by the time I got home. Here we were, living the dream on our land, but I never seemed to be there.

In his long evenings without me, John turned to writing. His first article was published in a popular computer magazine. He also completed the thick application for the NASA Space Shuttle program and felt the sting of rejection when he became one of about 8000 people who were turned down that year. He began to imagine a future for himself as a consultant. He had letterhead printed with the business name of Ancon — which meant ancillary, or connective bracket. He was doing the same kind of work he had at ESL, but with more emphasis on hardware. The highlight of his work year was installing an image processing computer system in Las Vegas. He didn't gamble, but he loved the desert and he enjoyed the chance to visit it again.

Feeling nervous about being alone, especially at nights, I had continued to lock the gate at the bottom of the road, but shortly after the shower curtain and the dog incident, we received a letter from Carter's attorney saying that Bill could only access his 40 acres through our land, and we were "not to interfere in any manner whatsoever with Mr. Carter's right of free and unobstructed passage through the gate and onto his property." I hadn't known that Bill still owned any land near us. In fact, I wondered if he had just told the lawyer that in order to get the letter. Obediently, however, I unlocked the gate.

John began staying home with the children on Saturdays while I worked at the store. He used the time to start on some construction projects. By fall, he had built a porch the length of the trailer and made it watertight and warm by Christmas Day. That was a wonderful gift to all of us. Although it had been great to upgrade from the 16-foot trailer to a 40-foot mobile home — five hundred square feet just was not working with two active children, their toys, and the over-abundance of books, magazines, and papers that supported our writing projects. The enclosed porch allowed John and Doña and their friends to spread out their games and toys, and to ride wheeled toys from one end to the other. As the end of the year approached, we installed a small wood-burning stove in the corner of the new porch and set up the Christmas tree just outside the trailer door leading into the living room.

Doña had turned five years old in 1977, John Rowland became two, and I entered my third decade. Doña was learning how to read. Little John was learning how to talk in complex run-on sentences, and loved the sound of his own voice. John and I were doing our best to get by on less sleep, fewer meals together, and always having small people between us. This was also the year of our tenth wedding anniversary. At Christmas, we invited Nina and Dorrie and Quincy to join us on the hill for a land potluck. We had sold the piano, but Quincy and Dorrie brought their guitars, and Bob played the harmonica. For a few hours, it was just like old times.

But our happiness was tinged with sadness. 1977 had also been the year we learned that Pop had pancreatic cancer ... The year we sat with him at San Jose Hospital and shared with one another our feelings of fear and loss ... and the year we watched our beloved Pop, John Charles Bumgarner, leave this life.

∗ ∗ ∗

The Christmas season brought bountiful profits to the Morgan Hill Trading Post and, after inventory and sales tax season, I felt flush enough to suggest we take a short vacation. Between Carol, Laurie, and my teenaged security staff, the store would be in good hands, and I looked forward to returning to work refreshed and renewed as we prepared for spring. I was recovering from a virus, and we were mired in mud up at the property. The vision of hot showers and warm rooms had been with me for weeks. John had been sad and uncommunicative since his father had passed away, and I hoped some time alone would provide us with opportunities to talk and help him work through his feelings.

After convincing my parents to take both children for a few days, I booked the bridal suite at the West Wind Lodge in Monterey. We had spent the final night of our backpacking honeymoon there in 1967, and I thought it would be fun to go back. The room had a fireplace and a Jacuzzi; we hadn't had that kind of luxury in a very long time.

Entering the foyer of the West Wind Lodge was *deja vu* all over the place — the curving stairs to the mezzanine, the long front desk with four clerks ready to serve us, the plush carpet — it was all the same. I was only 19 when we had been there before, and it seemed very glamorous at the time. This time, through more mature eyes, the foyer looked rather shabby. Still, our room was large and clean, the Jacuzzi worked, and we settled in for three days of indolence.

A full night's sleep without interruptions from either child or my own coughing (as I was still recovering from the flu) was glorious. I awoke refreshed. I'd promised John "no work," but when he went off for a swim, I wrote a column while he was gone. After that, breakfast, a nap, and a walk around town. We made good use of the sauna by the pool, walked a lot, ate lunch at cute little restaurants, and talked, and talked, and talked. We hadn't done that in such a long time. On our last night in Monterey, we went to a Lillian Hellman film, had dinner in a German restaurant, and then went for a final swim and a sauna before returning to our room. This was heaven.

On the dresser was a bottle of wine and a vase of flowers, courtesy of the hotel. I ran the Jacuzzi and John poured the wine. Once we were settled in the tub with our glasses, John dropped his bombshell.

"I think you should sell the store."

I thought I'd heard him wrong at first, and asked him to repeat what he had said. He did, and then he explained.

He had realized this week how much we had been missing. We hadn't been sharing meals together, walking or working on the land, talking. This week, he said, had been like it was when we were first together.

There were holes in his argument, and I pointed them out. When we were first together, we didn't have two children. When we were first together, we both worked in technology and could share experiences. We both were home for dinner every night. After we moved to the land, he worked late most nights, and frequently traveled out of state. The children drove him crazy when he tried to work at home. He wasn't interested in hearing about the store, and rarely talked about his own work.

He said the real problem was that I spent all my time at the store.

I pointed out that the Morgan Hill Trading Post gave me a purpose, filled the gaps in my week when he was working, not to mention an income. John argued that it was the store that was keeping us apart. It would be different. He would come home at night and stay on the land on weekends. I had never been good at debate, and I couldn't refute his argument that the time I spent running the store was taking away from our personal time. It was touching that he wanted to spend more time together, but I doubted he would change his habits, even if I were home all the time. We finished the wine and continued our conversation in bed.

"I need to bring in an income, John," I told him. "I'm afraid we'll never be able to build a house on the land. It's been over three years, and we don't even have a building permit. "

"If you weren't running the store, you could keep ahead of whoever keeps turning us in for code violations. You could monitor our permit applications, make sure we're complying with requirements, and keep us on track to complete the land division."

"Besides," he said, and this was the clincher. "You are a writer at heart, not a shopkeeper." He had hit a nerve. I *was* a writer. "I want to see you working on another book," he continued, "not ordering whole grains and hardware."

Against all my instincts, I agreed to sell.

The following week, I contacted my lawyer, my insurance agent, and our landlord, the three business professionals I trusted most in Morgan Hill. Each of them recommended the same realtor: a woman who specialized in bulk sales of business properties. With a heavy heart, I signed a listing agreement.

In February, I contracted pneumonia again. One night, trying to finish the weekly supply order from our distributor, I developed a high fever and struggled to stay on task. I didn't trust myself to drive. Carol took the children home when we closed the store and called Dorrie to ask her to drive up to the property and feed my animals. I called John at work to tell him where the children were. He wasn't in his office. I left a message asking him to help me finish the order and drive me home. He hadn't called or arrived by the time I finished the order. I lay down on a cot I kept in the back room, fell into a deep sleep and spent the night there. John never came home that night, or the next.

Dorrie found me the next morning. Eight months pregnant, she had milked and fed our animals the night before, and stopped at the store to check on me on her way to work. I felt bad to be leaning on her, but she waved away my concerns. She drove me home, wrapped me in a quilt, gave me aspirin for my fever, then headed back out to fetch John and Doña.

John, meanwhile, had flown to Los Angeles for an emergency meeting with a colleague. Quincy, Jan, and Bob all knew that he had gone, but didn't realize he hadn't told me. By the time he came home, I was too sick to ask where he had been, but I was still hurt that he hadn't at least telephoned. He apologized, but, seeing that Nina and Dorrie were taking good care of me, he went back to work as usual.

I only remember vignettes from the following weeks; most of them are fuzzy. There was a trip to Emergency, antibiotics, and lots of time spent on the couch while the children played on the floor beside me. Nina stayed with me part of the time, and Dorrie too. At one point I remember being alone with the children. After a long morning playing with her brother, Doña decided to clean out the refrigerator. She stood on the table that sat between the fridge and the couch and methodically took everything out, one shelf at a time, and carefully wiped the shelf with a washcloth and put everything back.

By the time I felt well enough to make a decision, several potential buyers for the store had emerged. After interviewing them, I agreed to sell to an older man who seemed knowledgeable about nutrition and health, and enthusiastic about running a little shop. He was personable and friendly. I could imagine him behind the counter greeting customers and, after talking with him for an hour, I believed he would carry on my vision. He was retiring from a long career with a newspaper, and would be receiving a sizable cash settlement, enough to double the inventory. He readily agreed to my price, which was sufficient to repay each of my limited partners their investment plus interest, pay off the Jeep, and provide me with a few months income while I figured out what to do next. We signed the papers, and I ordered an inventory and a final accounting report.

Jacob Michael Adams was born at the Adams' new home in Gilroy on March 24, 1977. Quincy and Dorrie had found a cute little bungalow with an acre of land just outside Gilroy. I began driving to Gilroy after dropping John and Doña at school and spending time with Dorrie and the baby. She had done so much for me; it seemed that the least I could do was hike up her back 40 and feed the chickens, help her with the laundry and the dishes while she rocked her son and sang to him. Being in the house with her, talking for hours about our husbands and our babies and our chickens, helped to bring me some perspective. Once again. I found myself thinking about moving to a house in town. I still wanted to build a house on our land, but I didn't see how that could happen. An older couple had recently bought a piece of land along Chesbro Lake Drive and built a barn. They were living in the barn while they built a house. A big one. They had sold their home in the valley. They had lived in that house for 35 years — it was probably worth nearly a million dollars. They had enough money to pay all the permit and inspection fees, money to hire contractors, money to buy lumber. That's what we were missing. Money.

The couple I had been visiting in Oakland had fallen in love with our land. They talked about selling their 4-unit apartment building and buying a parcel adjacent to ours. John floated the idea of starting a business together and homeschooling our six children. The bubble burst when Richard and Ginger visited the county offices and determined, as we had, that chasing down inspections and permits was so time-consuming that one of them would have to devote full time to the endeavor.

Another friend asked John if we would board her Welsh Pony. John thought it would be good for Doña to have a pony to ride and groom and feed. Popcorn came to live with us, but we couldn't afford riding lessons, and so all Doña was ever able to do was ride him while someone else held his lead rope. In the end, he became one more chore.

While the sale of my store was still in escrow, John invited me to dinner. I assumed we were celebrating the sale of the store and the start of our new life together. I bought a new dress, and had my hair done. Dorrie agreed to do our evening chores. Nina invited the children to spend the night with her. They thought that was a treat and I helped them pack their overnight bags. As I drove to Sunnyvale, I felt my excitement building. I looked forward to our new start. We could bring out John's plans for the dome again and figure out where we wanted to build it. We needed an accurate plot plan for the building permit.

John had asked me to meet him at a French restaurant on El Camino Real. From 1967 to 1972, I had worked in Mountain View in the aerospace industry, first as a typist, then a technical editor, and, finally, as a technical writer. Part of that time we lived in Mountain View. Dinner in a nice restaurant in those years was a common experience. But now, I felt out of place, a country bumpkin. I thought about getting back into my car and driving back to Morgan Hill. Then the *escargot* arrived, and I got caught up in the fussiness of remembering how to eat a snail.

As I sucked the garlic out of little pieces of French bread and sipped my wine, John told me his latest news. He had been flying to Los Angeles fairly often the last couple of months. I had assumed he was supporting software for whichever startup he was working for.

He said no, that he had actually been working in Manhattan Beach, a coastal city near Los Angeles. He had been collaborating with Charles Moore, who developed the computer language known as FORTH. The waiter came with our food then, and we both turned our attention to eating. After the dishes had been cleared away, John poured wine into each of our glasses.

"Moore is working to standardize the language so that it will be more widely accepted and used," John explained, his voice animated.

Then the bombshell. Moore had asked John to move to Manhattan Beach and work with him to complete the process. John would live in a garage apartment at Moore's house, work with him during the week, and fly home on weekends.

John was flattered. He admitted that his self-esteem had been battered from working alongside Quincy at ESL, who he called The Human Dynamo, or sometimes the Energizer Bunny. He really wanted to accept Moore's invitation. I kept a straight face, but I felt like he had just punched me in the stomach. How could he ask me to give up my store and then, before the ink was even dry on the transfer papers, move to Los Angeles? And why hadn't he ever mentioned that he was having problems working with Quincy?

I flashed back to early in our marriage, when John had precipitously dropped all his classes at San Jose State midyear and moved us to San Diego. Then, after graduation, when we had both applied for and been awarded master's degree fellowships, he talked me into giving up my studies to move to New Mexico so he could enter a doctoral program in astronomy. Two years later, he walked away from his doctoral program over a spat with his advisor — just days after I had been accepted into a doctoral program in Educational Psychology.

These weren't coincidences. This was a pattern.

I felt myself pulling into myself. It was too late to back out of the sale of my store, but clearly I needed to start thinking differently about my future and that of my children. John was correct that I wanted to write, but I would have been perfectly happy continuing as I had been, writing my columns and articles while running the Trading Post. Now that he had taken that away from me, I would have to ramp up and start selling articles to better-paid markets.

John took the job in Manhattan Beach, and for a year he flew home on weekends. We visited him for a week at Easter. Our regular babysitter Betty came with us and took the children to the beach while I looked for places to live. But John liked his weekends in the country and made it clear he didn't want us to move south, even if I could have brought myself to do so. Unfortunately for our marriage, by the time John left FORTH, Inc. a year later, the children and I had learned to get along without him.

26

ALONE ON THE HILL

1978

WHILE THE MORGAN HILL TRADING POST TRANSFER was mired in escrow, I was emotionally in a limbo of my own. I had come to think of myself as a businesswoman — the proprietor of a successful business and a participant in city affairs. When I passed people on the street, or took my daily deposit to the bank, they recognized and acknowledged me. I felt like I mattered.

Without the store, I didn't know who I would be.

I couldn't fret over that for long. The process of selling the store was nearly as complicated as starting it had been. I was responsible for arranging and paying for a professional inventory; sending written notifications to the Board of Equalization, Health, and Fire Departments; ordering final inspections; terminating insurance policies, business license, and fictitious business name; changing my name on bank accounts, etc. Each task cost me emotionally. I felt like I was dismantling a carefully-built Lego castle, and each brick I removed took me further away from a time and a place that I had loved, but, like Brigadoon, would never be again.

About to lose the store as a platform, I started a mail-order business called Country Girl Trading Company, to facilitate selling my books and other items. I applied for a new business license and fictitious business name and began identifying activities where I could sell books, schedule speaking engagements, or otherwise bring in income. Since I would soon be handing over the store, I also needed a new place to work.

Gail Richter, whose mother owned the Trading Post building, also managed several blocks of downtown property. I rented a storefront three blocks away from the store on a month-to-month basis and furnished it with a desk and some work tables from the Salvation Army. I brought in pillows, blankets and toys for the children, a small bookcase and their table and chairs from the store. I rented an IBM Selectric Memory Typewriter from an office supply store that had opened on Monterey Highway. It wasn't quite a computer, but it was a vast improvement on old typewriters, and I had learned to use one when I had been a technical writer in San Diego. The magnetic storage capability meant I no longer needed to type certain passages twice, or to manually set the margins or tabs.

From March until June, I worked mornings at the store. Carol and Laurie ran things in the afternoons while I spent time in my new office. I slowly worked my way through the list of tasks required to transfer ownership of the store. In May, I was still making phone calls and writing letters to my bookkeeper, accountant, the Board of Equalization, and attorney trying to get final tax return and profit/loss statements.

During that time, I also carried on an active correspondence with St. Martin's Press, trying to stimulate the marketing of my book. The publicist who had set up my initial interviews and book signings had left the company, along with my editor, Paul de Angelis. My book was orphaned, delegated to a junior staff member with no personal connection to me, the book, or its success. I wrote to my new publicist complaining that even though the food editor of the *San Diego Union* had received a sample book from the publisher, there were no copies in local bookstores — a fact we discovered after she interviewed me, wrote up the interview, and then heard from her readers. I arranged a visit to Washington D.C. in conjunction with a Child Development conference in April, and tried to get the publisher to help me coordinate speaking engagements there and in New York with little success. I did manage to arrange a meeting with the editor-in-chief of *Mother's Manual*, who had published several of my articles and poems, and with Paul, who was supportive, even though he no longer worked for St. Martin's Press. While in the D.C. area, I personally placed copies of my book at ten natural food stores, and a friend who had driven me around to those stores offered to place twenty more copies after I left.

Finally, in July, the transfer of my store to the new owner was complete. I took Laurie and Carol to Digger Dan's for dinner and gave them bonus checks as a thank-you for their loyal service to the store, to the children, and to me. My heart was aching. This was a miserable business. I felt I had let them down, abandoned my loyal customers. I thoroughly regretted having agreed to John's request.

It was a tearful farewell, during which we recalled happy memories and exchanged photographs and forwarding addresses. Carol stayed on at the store for a while, working for the new owner, but she also applied to a graduate program at UC Santa Cruz. A few months later, she moved over the Santa Cruz mountains to begin her studies. Laurie continued to travel with the Emerald Regime, which won many regional and national championships in 1978. She earned her required financial contribution to the band by staying with my children while I taught, typing columns from notes I made while nursing John, and helping me keep up with my increasing correspondence.

I had become a letter-writing machine, sending queries to stores to carry my book, to preschools to hire me as a speaker, to magazines to publish my stories. I answered letters from readers, wrote letters to venders and manufacturers to research topics for my newspaper columns. After the children went to sleep, I wrote letters to friends around the world to assuage the loneliness I felt. My daily visit to the post office box felt like Christmas, and each response gave me the encouragement I needed to keep going.

While I grieved the loss of my store and my identity, a poet named Ellen Bass came into my life. I met her at a local authors' night at the Morgan Hill Public Library. We were both speaking that night and sharing our writing. I carried a flyer home that advertised her poetry class, which she called *Writing About Our Lives*.

I soon began driving over the Santa Cruz Mountains once a week to attend Ellen's evening sessions. The drive over the mountains was scary at first, but invigorating. The tall trees along Hecker Pass Highway, the manzanita and piñon, all produced a heady fragrance that I pulled into my car by leaving the windows open, even when it was raining. I found Ellen's poetry moving, and her teaching inspiring. Hearing other people's lives in short story or poetry form was a new experience for me, and as I began to share my own poems I found understanding and support. Ellen encouraged us to use our lives as a palette from which we would paint our poetry. It was an interesting analogy that built on what I had heard during consciousness raising groups in D.C. before Doña was born. I began to see my life as bigger than just the trailer, bigger than just the land, bigger even than Morgan Hill Trading Post or *The Book of Whole Grains*.

I met all kinds of women at Ellen's sessions, and was introduced to new ideas about how to live my life. More than just poetry, Ellen taught me how to look inside myself to find my confidence and strength. Here was one of my first attempts to do that:

Trees

He's coming home
He says
Not this week
Or even next
But sometime soon
His work is nearly finished there
He says
And he can come home
Last time he came home, he put plastic windows
In the porch walls
So I could see the trees
While I fold his clothes

The light through the vinyl is thin
Thin and tight
I light the fire
Using an old Sears catalog to start the flame
Feeding it with a chopped up Presto log
We have five acres of oak trees
But no firewood cut for the winter
He was away all summer
And I was folding clothes
And reading picture books
And helping a junior mechanic
Build an airplane with tinker toys
So he could fly to Los Angeles
To see his Daddy
She doesn't answer
when I tell her Daddy says
he's coming home
She snuggles closer to my side
And turns the page
My eyes wander from the book
To the pile of Presto logs
Beside the stove
I think I will sharpen the axe tonight
and cut some wood.

I could only attend one eight-week session of Ellen's weekly classes. With Nina and the Adamses gone from the land, I found it difficult to get anyone to stay with the children at night. I would have to limit myself to an occasional weekend retreat.

John had worked at ESL for five years, longer than he had ever worked anywhere. He used his retirement account to pay off our credit cards, buy lumber for the front porch, and acquire a second-hand redwood hot tub, which he nestled under a tree just behind our trailer. The latter was John's response to my love of Sue's hot tub. He planned to heat the water in the tub using the windmill he was still working on. I tried to act appreciative, but couldn't quite bring it off.

FOUR

EMBRACING THE FUTURE

1979

- Dan Bricklin develops VisiCalc, the first spreadsheet program for personal computers
- Kevin MacKenzie invents symbols such as :-), or "emoticons," to mimic the cues of face-to-face communication

1980

- The Arpanet has 430,000 users, who exchange almost 100 million email messages a year
- Seagate Technology introduces the first hard-disk drive for personal computers
- Sony introduces the double-sided, double-density 3.5" floppy disk that holds 875 kilobytes
- Onyx launches the first microcomputer running the Unix operating system

1981

- The IBM PC is launched, running an operating system developed by Bill Gates' Microsoft
- The Xerox 8010 Star Information System is the first commercial computer that uses a mouse

1982

- Apple's employee founds Electronic Arts to create home computer games
- John Walker founds Autodesk to sell computer-aided design software

27

STARTING OVER

JOHN'S INCONSISTENT EMPLOYMENT since leaving ESL had left our finances in shambles. Charles Moore paid him a small salary plus room and board, but some months there was barely enough money to make our land payment. I had been paying for animal feed and groceries out of my draw from the store. If I wanted to keep the animals, I would have to support them.

I'd also learned from my unsuccessful correspondence with St. Martin's Press that, if I wanted my book to continue to sell, I would have to become my own publicist. I developed a brochure that could be used as an order form for *The Book of Whole Grains*, and that also promoted my classes and availability to speak to parent groups about natural foods. Laurie had discovered a treasure trove of telephone directories at the public library and she researched the addresses of bookstores, preschools and childcare centers for a 100-mile radius. Painstakingly, she addressed envelopes and mailed my brochure to each of them.

I already had several part-time income streams and, once I finished the paperwork for the store transfer, I used the time in my new office to build more. I wrote my weekly column for the *San Jose Mercury News* a month ahead of time and pitched related ideas to magazines; I developed the curriculum for four new classes teaching specific elements of natural food cooking: yogurt and cheese making, sausage making, sprouting seeds and legumes, and dehydrating fruits and vegetables. I marketed the classes to adult education programs in several different school districts. At our local Fotomat, Laurie printed colored flyers promoting the child development classes I was scheduled to teach at Gavilan, and we personally delivered them to every preschool in Morgan Hill, San Martin, and Gilroy to make sure the classes didn't get cancelled due to low enrollment. Using a similar approach, I offered my services as a speaker to schools, churches, bookstores, and La Leche League groups all over the Bay Area. The previous fall I had returned to my pursuit of a master's degree in child development, and expected to finish my coursework in June. I would need to collect data from area preschools for my thesis, so I kept in touch with each director who contacted me.

Soon I was earning enough money to support us and put a little away in my personal account each month. I didn't like being gone from the children at night, but the trade-off was to be gone all day, which I liked even less. I scheduled my classes at the YMCA in the mornings while the children were in school. Bookstore appearances were usually in the late afternoons, and my classes at the community college and adult education were after the children had gone to bed. Speaking engagements at preschools were always in the early evening. Sometimes I took the children with me to those, and Doña gradually took on the role of assistant, setting out books for sale on a table, collecting checks, and entertaining John while I lectured about cooking natural foods for families. Betty and Barbara, my fearless babysitters, were another year older, and enjoyed the money I paid them. They also recruited their friend Julie to help me on nights they weren't available. My evening child care challenges were over for a while.

The days and evenings were hectic, but I strove to be calm and cheerful and loving during the limited time that the children and I had together. I managed to hold it together most of the time, but sometimes, after I had read the last book, carried in the last glass of water, tucked in the last child, I would collapse into my rocking chair and sob with discouragement and exhaustion. I slept the sleep of the dead most nights, and sometimes awakened to a sodden pillow. My husband was so intensely involved in his work with Charles Moore that he rarely called, never wrote. I would call his garage apartment sometimes after the children were in bed, but he was never there. I knew his work habits — he and Charles probably worked until midnight, and would be sleeping in the morning when I awakened the children and got them out the door. I wrote to him once or twice a week, giving him news of the land and the children. When he did come home, he said he enjoyed the letters, but he never answered them.

In May, I attended my first intensive poetry workshop with Ellen Bass. John came home from L.A. that weekend, and while he took care of the children, I spent three days in Santa Cruz writing and sharing with women who had been strangers on Friday morning, but were *compadres* by Sunday. That weekend changed my life; by writing in the company of others, and sharing my work openly, I discovered that many of the challenges I faced as a writer, mother, and wife were known to others — even the money worries. I drove back over the mountains on Sunday afternoon feeling less alone, and hopeful that I would be able to figure out a way through what had seemed impossible just a few days earlier.

Toilet Training

I awaken in the hallway
on my way to your room.
How many nights have I made this pilgrimage?
Doña will be six next month
and I know that
many times I awakened this way
in the middle of my dreams
to rescue her.
She was drowning, she'd say

but it was only her bed
soaked through with the urine she had held
until three a.m.
when she would release it,
calling me.
Now I am rescuing you
and I awaken halfway there
not even sure you called.
You awaken to pee
never liking soggy sheets
but you like to have company
for your walk down this hallway
to the bathroom.
We tried putting a potty in your room
but it was too low.
You peed on the wall above it
in your half sleep
or sat down and went back to sleep
without getting up.
Now we have a trail
of nightlights for you to follow.
I brush past the paintings on the wall,
flowers from Mount Hamilton
pressed by John's mother long ago,
faded reminders of a distant time.
I reach for the light switch
then stop without touching it
Seeing you in the moonlight
bravely
walking toward me.

A small cadre of friends' teenaged daughters — including Laurie, Betty, Barbara, and Julie — provided the child care and clerical assistance I needed for my way of life to work. I felt grateful for their courage, and that of their parents, allowing them to drive up our dirt road and spend so many evenings alone in the trailer with my children.

It helped that we had a telephone now, and that two of the girls lived in a house at the top of a hill across Chesbro reservoir; their mother could see a light in my trailer window and developed a code that they used to reassure one another that everything was ok. We also had not seen Bill Carter in over a year.

My mother continued to ride the Greyhound Bus to my downtown office each Thursday. In the morning, she helped me put address labels and stamps on flyers; in the afternoon, she would take the children to the park (or, I later discovered, the ice cream parlor). At first my parents were hurt that I had sold the store so soon after we had worked so hard to create it. Once they understood my conflict between keeping the store and saving my marriage, and the sadness I felt, they had become my staunch supporters.

One Thursday, while pushing little John toward the park in an umbrella-style stroller, my mother was accosted at knife-point by a teenaged girl. The attacker demanded Mom's purse, but she didn't know who she was dealing with — Mom had lived through World War II bombings and blackouts unscathed and wasn't about to give up her money, or her grandchild. She shoved the stroller away, lifted her purse up to use as a shield, grabbed the girl's arm, and screamed at the top of her lungs. I could hear her a block away, and so did several other people. By the time I got there, two men were chasing the girl down the street, two women were comforting mom, and a third was retrieving John, unhurt, from the gutter. Mom wasn't upset; she was furious. I made her a cup of tea and, after we retrieved Doña from school, I drove her home to Belmont. The girl, it turned out, was trying to get enough money to buy tickets to a concert that her father had refused to bankroll. Mom was ok, thankfully, and I attempted to convince my father that this was a really unusual event in our sleepy little town. Just the same, he forbade Mom to travel down on the bus anymore. A few months later, they went to the hearing and Mom spoke in favor of the girl doing community service instead of being incarcerated in juvenile hall, which I thought was awfully kind. I didn't see my mother in Morgan Hill again for a very long time.

In early June, Gail told me that in the fall she would be leasing the space I had been using as an office to someone who planned to open a restaurant. Mom couldn't come down to help me any more anyway; Laurie was leaving on a road trip with some friends. I decided it was time to move my endeavors back to the land.

By the end of the summer, the children and I had settled into our new routine. With no one else to help with the chores, I scheduled my day around them. I usually rose before Little John and Doña, and wrote for an hour or two. After that, I would prepare breakfast and wake the children so they could walk up the hill with me. They happily played in the trees and bushes or in the little blue trailer while I milked the goats and fed the animals. After chores, we would trek back down to our trailer to eat. If it was a school day, I dressed the children; if not, they might stay in their pajamas or underpants all day. Elmira's Montessori preschool and kindergarten was open and, although tuition was expensive, having Doña and John there bought me time to write and teach. Doña had grown into a quiet, thoughtful child, with one or two close friends. The structured curriculum suited her very well. John was very active and talkative, just the opposite of Doña, but the structured curriculum worked well for him too. Since they were both happy there, I kept the children in school even through the summer.

That summer I taught natural food cooking for children at the YWCA in south San Jose, then drove north to teach two more classes in the Almaden Valley — one to adults and one to children. On Thursdays, I taught three classes at the Mount Madonna YMCA in Morgan Hill. After I picked up the children from school, I worked in the garden and completed household and animal chores. They quickly learned to entertain themselves in the sandbox, on the lawn, or in the vegetable garden.

I built several bookshelves in the blue trailer, moved in my books and papers and typewriter, and began to use it as a writing studio. When I needed to type, I powered the rented Selectric via a very long extension cord strung through the trees from Bob Fabini's trailer. I wrote after the children went to school in the morning, researched topics for the newspaper column and magazine articles at the library on days when it was too hot to go home, then returned to the trailer in the evenings to do the chores, answer correspondence and send out book promotion material. The children napped on the bed at the back of the trailer, or played beside me with puzzles or coloring books. As my feelings about John's career decisions began to fester, I began to sleep in my studio when he came home from L.A. on weekends.

It had broken my heart to see Dorrie and Quincy leave the property. I turned to my own little family, my garden, and our animals for solace. I tried to visit the Adamses as often as I could, stopping on the way to Gavilan College before teaching my two classes.

In August 1978, Sue Olson, who had traded milk delivery for information about natural foods when I first opened the store, came to work in the trailer for several weeks with her two young boys. Her husband had been laid off from work and they had sold their house in San Jose. They were staying in a campground, but she needed somewhere where she could prepare and mail out his resume. This she did skillfully, and eventually he was offered a job in Ramona, just north of San Diego. Sue helped me with clerical work while she was on the hill — compared to my high school-aged staff, she was Superwoman. She cut through my correspondence and mailings in no time. Taking advantage of her willingness to milk my goats and feed my livestock, I took a week off to drive to Vancouver Island with my mom and the children to see the parcels of land Mom and Dad had purchased. They had decided to retire there.

The drive north in our aging VW bus was memorable, both because of the long conversations mom and I had along the way, and because every time we stopped at a rest stop it seemed some part of the vehicle fell off and had to be wired back together. We drove up the Olympic Peninsula, a gorgeous place, and spent the night in Port Angeles to await the morning ferry. I put the children and Mom to bed and went downstairs to the hotel bar, where I listened to music, nursed a drink, and imagined what it would be like to be single again. My mind had been going there more and more lately. I didn't want to leave John, but recently it felt like he had already left me. Could our marriage survive this separation?

During the three days we stayed on Vancouver Island, the children and I went clamming and learned how to make delicious chowder, watched a wood carver work, visited three craft fairs, and picked buckets of blackberries. Mom and Dad had purchased a building site in paradise. Mom had also bought two lots in a more rural community, one each for my brother and me. She offered one to me while we were looking at them. I demurred, but she said the offer would stand in case I ever needed a place to go. Driving home, I thought about all the things John and I had done before we bought the land, all the places we'd seen. Sometimes I felt trapped on our land. Living in solitude was nothing at all like living in community. I missed Dorrie, Quincy, and Nina. I missed the Adams' dogs, the sounds of their animals. I even missed Quincy's radio.

I kept writing my weekly column and pitching ideas to magazines. In September, I wrote a lengthy article reviewing hand-operated and electric grain mills for the Canadian publication, *Harrowsmith*, and was invited to write an article on dehydrators. In October, two of my poems were published in *Matrix* magazine in Santa Cruz. My writing career was established, and I felt confident about that part of the future.

Sue and I had gotten along well while she was on the land, and so did our children. I missed them when they moved into their new home in Ramona, about 20 minutes north of San Diego. I began driving to Ramona whenever we had a school holiday. I hired a local 4H-er or one of our cadre of babysitters to milk the goats and feed the animals, and the time away was good for all of us. Sue's spacious log house had several large tables where I could set up my work and write while the children played together. Sue had a hot tub with a gorgeous view of the high desert. I always felt refreshed when I headed back up Highway 101 to home. I began to yearn for a house of my own. It didn't look like we'd ever build one on our land.

One weekend, sitting in the hot tub with glasses of wine, Sue and I came up with the idea of taking the many letters I had received from my readers and using them and my columns as the framework for a new book. As if that wasn't enough to do, we also decided to publish a quarterly alternative lifestyle newsletter that we titled *Natural Living Newsline*. We would mail out the first issue to the 800-name mailing list I had compiled from customers at my store and readers of my column who had written to me. I began thinking of writers I could tap for the first issue, which we decided would be published in January.

As 1978 wound down, I concentrated on making a normal life for the children and me — as normal as I could under the circumstances. Doña was nearly 6; John was nearly 3. Our Halloween tradition had been to join some friends who lived in a subdivision near the elementary school both children would be attending, and we did that again. I took apart my pink brocade Junior Prom dress to make a Little Bo Peep outfit for Doña. An outgrown crib sheet became a ghost costume for John. In an effort to control his hyperactivity, I'd put him on the new Feingold Diet, and it appeared to be helping. One of its key elements was avoiding artificial coloring in food. After they finished Trick-or-Treating, the four children negotiated and bartered for the rest of the evening as John attempted to offload his most brightly colored candy for the slightly more acceptable chocolate.

We all missed John, but of the three of us, Doña seemed to feel her father's absence the most. She began wetting the bed during the week, but never on the weekends when he came home, which were now about every other week. Mornings were difficult; most days she refused to go to Elmira's Montessori kindergarten, and I finally succumbed to keeping her home on the days I didn't teach. Long after I had read the children their bedtime stories and turned out the light, I would hear her tossing and turning, sometimes sobbing into her pillow. I tried holding her, talking to her, encouraging her to write to John, but nothing would alleviate her sadness except having him home.

It seemed important to insert some fun in her life. I invited several of her classmates up to the property for her birthday at the end of November. The next day, we drove to Belmont to celebrate Thanksgiving with my parents. In early December, the children and I took the train from Morgan Hill north and saw a memorable performance of *The Nutcracker* at the San Jose Center for the Performing Arts. The excellent Orchestra seats were the gift of Dorrie and Quincy. As souvenirs, I bought two Nutcracker finger puppets, the least expensive items in the gift shop. Doña suggested putting a hook through them and hanging them on our tree on the front porch. I still hang them on my tree every year.

The following week, Mom and Dad and I took the children to the Dickens Faire at the Cow Palace in San Francisco; Mom and I entered plum puddings in a contest to get free entry ($8.95). Neither of us won any prizes, even though our English puds were authentic and tasty. After looking at the winners, we agreed we would have to improve the way we displayed our puddings if we participated again the next year. Not bothered by our disappointment, the children enjoyed the Dickensian Era entertainment and games and, for a short while, all of us were happy.

Little John was still nursing, but I had told him that Big Boys drank their milk from a cup. On his third birthday in early December, I poured warm goat milk into a brand-new Spider-Man cup and prepared to read him a story when he awakened.

Rather precocious and very verbal, John emerged from bed looking thoughtful and prepared with an alternative plan. "Mommy, could we wait until I'm four before I get a Spider-Man cup?"

Laughing, I said no, and handed him the new cup. And just like that, he was weaned.

Little John's third birthday was celebrated at Farrell's Ice Cream Parlor, and my very elderly English Aunt Rose joined Mom and Dad in making him the center of attention for the night.

Big John didn't join us for any of these events, but he did come home for a week at Christmas. I made a new dress for Doña, along with a pinafore, like Holly Hobbie, her newest doll, thinking it would be perfect for school pictures. He repaired a water pipe that had cracked when the temperature dropped below freezing. I watched him so I would know what to do if it happened again. We hadn't used the heater in the trailer yet, but it had been very cold in the mornings and I had pleaded with him for money to pay for fuel. Now he agreed and ordered 357 gallons of propane, which cost $180.

The wall heater was similar to one we had had in San Diego, although the weather was so warm there that we hardly ever used it. It was at the back end of the trailer, between our bedroom and the bathroom, facing one of the doors of the trailer that opened out to the porch. John and I cleaned the grill, and he replaced the filter and showed me how to light the pilot light. After the first of the year, John returned to L.A., and the children and I went back to our busy schedule, facing rain, muddy animal pens, and slippery roads for the fourth year in a row. At least the trailer would be warm.

28

ORGANIC COOKING
FOR (NOT-SO-ORGANIC) MOTHERS

L A LECHE LEAGUE INTERNATIONAL was approaching the 25th
anniversary of the breastfeeding and support organization. Their
leaders were gearing up for a national celebration in 1981. I had met
Edwina Froelich, one of the founders of the organization, at a
conference where I spoke and promoted *The Book of Whole Grains*.
She liked my book, and told me that La Leche League International
planned to commission a book of natural food recipes attractive to
young families for the occasion. I told her about my new book idea
and she suggested that I pitch it to the board of directors. If they chose
it, they would pay for the publication and printing.

I asked Maryanna Kingman, who had illustrated my first book, to
sketch some ideas for the new one. Sue and I envisioned a
spiral-bound publication that would be organized by meal type:
breakfast, lunch, dinner, snacks, and desserts. I asked Maryanna to

base her illustrations on my two children and our rural life. Bob Fabini's teenage friends, Dean and Lance, reminded me that their mother was also an artist, so I asked her to propose some illustrations as well. I told both artists that this was a pitch, and that it may or may not result in a contract. I wrote several sample chapters, selected some illustrations from each woman, and sent them off to Edwina.

My contract with St. Martin's Press stipulated that they had "right of first refusal" on my next book. I had learned that St. Martin's did not play well with others. Bookstores, natural food stores, and mail-order catalogs had reported that my book was not available through the typical distribution chains, and that it was not discounted sufficiently by the publisher to motivate them to carry it. A plan for sister publisher Macmillan to produce a British edition had been abandoned by St. Martin's after several months of transcontinental communication and proofreading. Ditto an effort to secure Australian rights and market the book there. This, combined with the total cessation of marketing efforts on the book domestically, in spite of my letter-writing campaign requesting targeted promotion combined with speaking engagements that I would pay for myself, had turned me against the publisher.

Feeling confident that I would write more books and that I would be able to get them published elsewhere, I decided to utilize the right of refusal clause to free myself from my contract. I pitched the new book to St. Martin's in April, when I went to Washington D.C. and New York to attend a writing conference and visit friends. When St. Martin's Press sent me a rejection letter, I resolved to publish what we were now calling *Organic Cooking for (not-so-organic) Mothers* even if La Leche League did not do so.

In late September, Edwina had written "Go ahead with the new book. The LLL Board loves it." I gave the go-ahead to both Maryanna and Dean and Lance's mother; I would use illustrations from both of them. After getting out the first edition of *The Natural Living Newsletter,* I wrote to Tine Thevenin, author of *The Family Bed,* and asked her how she had produced her book, which was self-published. Tine responded with very specific details about typewriters, word processing systems, and the benefits of self-publishing. Susan Gibbs

Mallett, a publicist based in Santa Cruz, had read my poems and an advertisement for my book and newsletter in *Matrix* magazine. She subscribed to the newsletter, but also suggested we meet to talk about a marketing plan for my work. She wrote the cover copy for the new book and suggested several markets for publishing it, should the La Leche League offer be withdrawn.

That October, I once again began attending weekly writing workshops with Ellen Bass — this time during the day. Ellen provided prompts and feedback on our writing. It was wonderful. I could steep myself in poetry, yet be back over the mountains in time to pick up the children from afterschool care. For ten weeks, my mind soared with new possibilities for my life as a woman and my development as a writer. Most of the participants, like me, had written many poems, but had received no training or feedback. In this group we wrote to prompts, shared our work, and helped one another find the right words or tone to communicate the thoughts and feelings we were trying to express. Ellen was a gentle teacher. She shared her own work with us, as well as her successes and her disappointments. Those ten weeks validated my feelings of discontent and unfairness, and gave me courage to change our life.

Once Sue settled into their new home, she began transcribing my columns, which I had originally written on an manual typewriter with a cloth ribbon. Using a carbon ribbon on a new IBM Selectric she was able to produce camera-ready copy for La Leche League. Working together, in the end we crafted a 165-page typed and illustrated manuscript that could make its debut at the La Leche League 25th Anniversary Conference in Chicago. I sent a prototype to Edwina and awaited her response.

Meanwhile, I began learning the WordStar word processing language and producing our newsletter on a borrowed PET computer in Oakland. I had been a technical writer in the early years of our marriage, and I enjoyed the challenge of learning WordStar. However, technology moved quickly in the 1970s. Over the next year and a half, we struggled with emerging technology, incompatible platforms, dot matrix printers, and clumpy 300-baud modems as we tried to send files between Bum Flats and Ramona.

29

SHATTERED HOPES

1979

WHILE I WAS MILKING GOATS IN THE DARK and the mud through January and February of 1979, John's college friend Glen had been consulting with various Silicon Valley firms from Santa Rosa, north of San Francisco. Glen and John had met at San Diego State in 1970 and had collaborated on several projects in the years since. Glen was working on something he called a Ham radio repeater detector, a microprocessor-controlled system to locate Ham radio frequencies while on the road. He invited John to be a partner in a start-up company he was calling Parsec and write the necessary software.

John flew home from Los Angeles that weekend and we drove 70 miles from the San Francisco airport to Santa Rosa to discuss the possibilities. While the men talked shop, the children and I explored the area. That night, John proposed that we move there together, and asked me to look for a piece of property with room for animals and a second unit where his mother could live. She had offered to fund the down payment. He had already talked to Bea and invited her to join us the next weekend we drove up. John was moving awfully fast, but I felt tempted. It could be a new start for all of us. I would finally have a house, and I wouldn't have to leave John to get it.

The previous summer, Bea had put a camper on Pop's pickup and driven his ashes to their hometown in Illinois. She had taken two months to drive across country, stopping to see old friends, relatives, and sights that they had visited together. Then she continued on to West Virginia and Pennsylvania to visit shirttail relatives John and I had discovered while living in the D.C. area. She had kept a journal of her travels and seemed to find the adventure satisfying. Upon her return, she had found a lump in her breast and was soon scheduled for surgery.

Visiting her in San Jose Hospital, where Pop had died, John was gripped by a profound sadness and wanted to leave. We waited for the down elevator. The up elevator stopped on our floor and the doors opened. Bill Carter was standing at the front. His eyes were sunk into his head, and appeared to be circled in mascara. I immediately backed away. The hair on the back of my neck prickled, and I prepared for some kind of insult or threat. None came. Carter was thin, very thin, and his hair was scraggly. He looked at me without recognition. As I stared at him, I realized that the man was much diminished, certainly no longer a person to fear. The elevator doors closed, and he was gone. That was the last time we ever saw Bill Carter.

Now living alone in her little camping trailer in Redwood City, twenty miles south of San Francisco, Bea was at loose ends and lonely. She was delighted at the idea of trading life alone in a trailer for joining our family in a rural community. I felt I could handle having Bea nearby, so long as we weren't sharing a kitchen. But I was finally growing wary of John's sudden changes of plan. One day, after a morning spent viewing houses and property, Bea and I ate lunch in a cute little tearoom in Forestville, a small community near Santa Rosa. I told her my concern that John wanted to move our family north before he and Glen had even figured out what their business relationship would be, and what kinds of contracts they would pursue. I wanted him to slow down, wait a few months before Bea invested her money and I uprooted the children. Bea didn't agree. She argued that having his family nearby would be the steadying influence John needed to make this work.

Earlier that day, we had toured a cute red barn-styled house in Forestville on 2-1/2 acres with a matching red granny cottage. It already had animal pens and an actual barn, with lots of room for storage. Bea loved the place and, in spite of my misgivings, she put a deposit on the property that afternoon. Doña had also fallen in love with the red barn house and, when we got home, she drew three pictures of it. She put one on our refrigerator and asked me to mail one to Grandma and the other to the two ladies who owned the house. She told all her friends that we were going to move into a barn. Realizing that the house purchase was a *fait accompli*, I enrolled in my last six units of master's coursework, and planned to move at the end of the school year.

About that time, Doña's cat Pandora birthed a litter of six colorful kittens — no two alike. Doña stayed up all night with me as the kittens appeared one at a time in their little "space ships" (as she called their amniotic sacs), and she could talk of nothing else the next day.

A week later, on a cold and rainy morning, I propped the screen door open when I took the children to school so that Pandora could go outside and re-enter the trailer to tend her babies. When I returned, all but one of the kittens were strewn around the living room, bloody and dead. Pandora was licking them frantically, trying to bring them back to life. It was shocking, of course, but I'd seen enough dead animals that I wasn't so much upset for myself as I worried about the children. Who or what had killed the kittens? How would I explain it to Doña and John? How would they take it? I called Elmira at the Montessori school and asked her what to do. By the time I got through my story, I was sobbing. Elmira scolded me for giving my children so little credit for being able to cope with real life. She told me to clean up the mess and put the babies in a shoe box, then take the children out to lunch before returning home and explain calmly what had happened.

"Doña's a real scientist," Elmira warned me. "She might want to see the kittens. Don't show them to her unless she asks, and probably best not to show little John. He probably won't notice they're gone anyway."

I did as Elmira suggested, and events went pretty much as she said they would. Doña was sad, but not devastated, curious, but not overly so. We buried the five dead kittens in the vegetable garden. One more reminder of how fragile life is. And how resilient children can be.

I'd seen Willie running around loose that day. He frequently managed to push their trailer door open. I assumed it was Willie who slipped through the small opening I had left for Pandora. That it was Willie who killed the kittens. I marched down to Bob's trailer that night and demanded he be more vigilant about keeping Willie in the trailer when they were away. He and Jan were shocked and hurt that I would even think it could have been their gentle Willie, and hurt that I would talk to them in such a way. Our relationship was strained after that. Months later, I read a book about cats and realized it could just as easily have been the tomcat who killed the babies — or Pandora herself. We would never know. By then, Bob and Jan were on their way to Alaska, and I had never apologized for my hasty assumption.

In mid-March, we received a letter from Glen saying how excited he was about the new venture, and inviting us to a May Day party to celebrate John joining Parsec. John gave notice at FORTH, Inc., in L.A., Bea made the down payment on the red barn house, and I started to pack. At John's urging, I called a realtor and listed our land for sale.

The response was immediate. Several people toured the property in early April, and two couples returned for a second look. In very short order, a young couple from Colorado put a deposit on the land and began to search for financing to build a house.

Meanwhile, I had another emergency. Lying in bed one morning, snuggling with the children and trying to convince myself to get up and get started making breakfast, I heard a great *Whoosh!* coming from the hallway. I jumped out of bed and ran to the bedroom door, which was open so the cats and dogs and children could come and go during the night. Flames were shooting up through the grating of the heater. I grabbed a towel from the bathroom and removed the grating to could see the controls better, then turned off the gas. Flames continued to burn at the top of the heater. It wasn't a huge fire, but it looked like the insulation in the wall was burning. Afraid that the fire would spread inside the wall, I threw a pan of water on the flames, then opened the door to the porch so I could get John and Doña out of the trailer. I wrapped them in blankets and carried them out, one at a time, and set them down in the middle of the lawn several feet away from the trailer. On the way back, I turned on the water and dragged the hose from the garden. While I tried to keep a clear head, I sprayed the fire with water, then called 911 and gave them our address. Then I went back to spraying the fire with water from the hose. My hands were shaking, but I was feeling like I had the fire under control.

The fire was just smoldering by the time that the smallest fire engine I've ever seen came racing up our road. The two firefighters soaked the heater and the wall and ceiling all around it. Then one man pulled out the insulation, and along with it a mouse nest and several very fried mice.

"Yup," the other firefighter said. "Figured as much. You gotta keep an eye on critters when you live in a place like this."

"Good thing you were awake when it happened," the first man commented, folding up his hose. "You could have ended up looking like those mice."

"Thanks a lot," I said, rock solid until then, but now beginning to shake. "That's all I needed to hear."

As the firefighters packed up to go, I commented on how quickly they had found our place, considering how tucked away in the hills we were.

"Remember that plot plan you had to file to get your fire clearance? And the water tank you were required to install?" the first man asked. "We've got a file on you in the rural fire station office, and when you gave us your address, we went straight to it."

"Keep that water tank full," said the other as they got on the truck and began turning around. "It's the only way we can fight fires up here, and my guess is this won't be the last one."

And on that cheery note they were off. John and Doña and I were soon perched in the kitchen wrapped in blankets, eating Cheerios and talking about our morning.

"Mommy, can I use the fire for Sharing this morning?" asked Doña.

"I didn't think Mrs. Johnson had Sharing in her school."

"She will today, I think. Everyone loved the story about the dead kittens, and now I can tell them about the dead mice."

I groaned. I couldn't think of a response. What must Elmira think of me and my parenting?

"Time to get dressed, you two!"

My fears about Parsec had been well-grounded. John and Glen's partnership lasted less than six weeks. I knew they were in trouble when Glen called me one morning about 9:00 a.m., growling, "Where the hell is John?"

The board of directors was meeting that day, and John wasn't there. I could have told Glen that scheduling a meeting at 9:00 a.m. would always be a bad idea, but I kept my mouth shut. As it turned out, John was still in bed at his mother's trailer in Redwood City, waiting for the rush hour traffic to clear before driving north.

Fortunately, I convinced the couple who had put the deposit on our land to search elsewhere for their building site. I returned their deposit check and, before I parted company with the prospective buyers, we agreed to work together on a children's book. Bea hired an attorney to help her get some of the down payment back, and there was no more talk of moving off the land that year. Soon after the debacle with Glen and the board of directors, John returned to the land, chagrined, but excited to be free from the constraints of working with and for other people. He wanted to build a prototype for a briefcase computer and was confident he could find funding to market it. After that, he would consult from home and restart his plans to build a geodesic dome. We argued a lot during those first few weeks that he was home, I wanted him to get another job; my small savings account would not last long without him drawing a salary.

He said that working towards someone else's goals had been killing him. He had so many ideas, so many dreams. The technology was changing at a rapid pace, and could do so much. He wanted to learn more, build more computers and write more software. But he wanted to do it on his own terms.

I threatened to leave and take the children if he didn't get a real job and put some money in the bank first. That got his attention. He said that our leaving would be the end of him. He needed his family around to feel whole. We were what fed his imagination. He broke my heart; he was so intense, and so very unhappy. He didn't understand why I always seemed so focused on money. I tried to explain that I found it difficult to understand his desire to pursue his dreams when we were living so close to the edge. I worked so hard to earn money for our everyday necessities, and he just let me. I desperately wanted — needed — to feel that our children's lives were secure.

The truth is I had never known a creative person — not up close. I judged John against my limited experience of husbands and fathers who went to work each morning with a lunchbox. I knew at some level that this wasn't fair. John was brilliant, and he was a natural inventor. What he needed was a business manager. I didn't have the maturity or the insight to realize that, however, and so I stayed with my insistence that he get a job with another technology firm and start bringing home a regular paycheck.

One more time, I made an intentional choice to stay with him, to hitch my hopes and dreams to this man who tilted with windmills. During these difficult conversations, my daffodils were blooming on either side of the pathway between our two trailers and on the way down to Bob's trailer and our communal garden. It cheered me to see their sunny faces when I walked those paths, and their steadfastness helped me to remember my dreams of a thriving homestead, and to stay the course.

John didn't attend church, but he did enjoy celebrating Easter. As that holiday approached, we were all feeling the absence of Dorrie, Quincy, and Nina — and especially of Nina's delicious Austrian pastries. On April 14, Easter Saturday, John and I hiked to the top of the hill beyond Dorrie and Quincy's old homestead. We were accompanied by our children, and by Bob and his teenaged weekend companions, Dean and Lance. And, of course, Willie and Elsa. After circling around like puppy dogs to find the best and most level spots, we climbed into our sleeping bags to watch the stars. Bob lit his Primus stove and made hot chocolate for everyone — with marshmallows — and eventually we all slept.

In the morning, I awakened with little John snuggled inside my frost-covered sleeping bag and Doña and Elsa tucked cozily between John and me. While Willie snuffled about looking for interesting smells, we watched the sunrise from our leafy beds and enjoyed the fragrance of fireplace smoke wafting up from the valley.

I may have been the only one who felt sunrise to be a spiritual experience, but the joy that came from Bob's coffee pot and the Easter baskets in John's knapsack was shared by everyone. As we sat together that morning, nibbling on chocolate bunnies, watching our collective breath appear in the cold air, and enjoying the view, I thought about all the adventures John and I had had together. As furious as I often was with him, I still loved this man, and that morning I vowed one more time to keep our marriage and our homestead together.

When we went down the hill, I took out a cookbook, adapted a recipe for Easter Egg bread to use whole wheat flour and the spicy orange peel and cardamom Nina used in her pastries, and set it to rise while I made our breakfast. I ate mine outside, watching John and Doña playing in the crisp spring sunshine. Later, the children and I tied onion skins on a dozen eggs and hard-boiled them. I had read about this in Carla Emory's *Old-Fashioned Cookbook*. This resulted in a lovely, almost tie-dyed look in several shades of brown.

With four eyes watching, I then braided the bread and inserted six of the eggs into the openings where the strands crossed over one another. I showed the children, and Dean and Lance, how to encircle each of the other eggs with bread dough to create individual loaves. One more rising and the bread was ready to bake. That Easter we had fresh Easter Egg bread for lunch, served with our own home-made butter and jam. Thus began a family tradition that continues today.

✳   ✳   ✳

Some months after Nina and the Adamses received their eviction notices and moved into town, Nina asked if she could come up sometimes to write in our little trailer. She was now working on her doctoral dissertation, and found our land a peaceful place to work. I liked the idea. During the week I still worked in the store, and John was usually at work or traveling. I didn't like there being no one on the land in the daytime to keep an eye on things, and I was angry with whoever had turned my friends in and happy to flaunt the rules. I agreed.

Nina began coming several times a month, sometimes on Sundays when she knew I would be there too. Sometimes we would drink tea and chat, or one of us would make lunch. It was a comfort to have her there.

We had found a new home for Diamond, Elsa's pup, because she had been caught killing chickens at Walt and Fran Peters' place further down Chesbro Lake Drive. The Peters had two big dogs that barked a lot, and they had raided our farm and that of the Adams' on two occasions. Tensions were building between us and the Peters. We had started keeping Elsa inside a fence when we were away, and I had asked Bob to keep Willie in his trailer. But Willie had a way of getting the trailer door open. He would waddle up the hill to visit Nina and she usually let him into the little blue trailer where he happily slept while she worked. Nina thought Willie was the "funniest little sausage" and had wondered out loud, "How the hell does he make it up the hill with those short little legs?"

Willie had a sweetness about him that appealed to Nina. Having grown up in Austria, she had never warmed to German Shepherds, which were used by the *Polizei* as fierce guard dogs. She and Elsa and had a polite "truce," but Willie and she had a "big sister, little brother" kind of relationship. She told me she felt protective of him, and when she lived on the land had often fed him when Bob was late coming home.

One day when Nina drove up the hill in expectation of a quiet afternoon of writing, she heard a commotion down the hill. Elsa was barking fiercely, and other dogs were also.

"I ran down the hill to the Bumgarner trailer," she told us later. "No one was home, but in the yard was an awful scene: there were three large dogs — two strange ones and Elsa — all jumping fiercely on a small little animal in their middle. And my heart sank when I saw it was Willie they were about to tear apart. They had already bitten him, and he was screaming."

I don't know how Nina found the strength and courage to confront those three big dogs that were all in a blood frenzy, or how she managed to avoid serious injury, but her love for Willie prevailed.

"I picked up a stick," she explained, "and drove them off. I managed to carry the bleeding Willie down to Bob's trailer and take care of him and then call Bob. Willie survived, but my trust with Elsa was broken forever."

I always had trouble with Nina's description of events. How could Elsa possibly have attacked her own pup? Surely, she was trying to protect him. But that's what Nina said she saw, and she was certain that is what happened. What is not in doubt is the fact that she saved Willie's life, for which we were all very grateful. Especially Bob.

At the end of April, I received a letter from Sam Lieberman, the owner of Marianne's Ice Cream in Santa Cruz. He wanted to put a copy of my column titled "Sugar is Sugar is Sugar" under glass on the counter of his store. While his request wasn't going to pay the bills, it did cheer me up and increase my hopes of a better future.

I resolutely double-dug our little garden and planted vegetable seeds, worked on my thesis proposal, and taught my classes.

In May, John traveled to Amsterdam to attend the FORTH International Team Standards meeting, something he had agreed to do for Charles Moore when he was still working for FORTH Inc. He brought back a picture book for the children, *Barbapapa*, by French authors Annette Tison and Talus Taylor. They kept that book for many years, and we read it so often the pages fell out.

When school ended in June, I decided not to send the children to summer school. We couldn't afford the tuition, and I wanted to spend more time with them. Doña was an avid reader, and John liked to play in the fenced yard we had built for them, or with the goats and the chickens. We often invited his preschool friends Danny and Thys up to play; Thys brought his older brother and Danny brought his brother and sister. The older children got Doña out of her books and into the outdoors; having friends for the children to play with freed me to write.

John and Doña were now old enough to go to my classes and evening speaking engagements and entertain themselves, leaving John free to work at home. I did sign them up for two weeks of nature camp, which was held at a rural one-room schoolhouse near a creek. I hoped that would be a good experience for them.

In June, Bob and Jan left their jobs at ESL, packed his VW bus, made a cozy space in it for Willie, and drove to Alaska, a trek they'd been planning all spring. While sorry to see them go, John and I finally had what we originally had said we wanted — we were totally alone on our land.

I remember that summer with mixed feelings. Even with our differences, having John around all the time made life much easier. He helped with the milking and feeding the animals, and driving the children to camp and back. I went back to making cheese, yogurt, and butter, baking bread, and consciously managing the breeding of our rabbits and goats. I had become fairly skilled at killing and cleaning chickens, and, although I never got comfortable butchering a rabbit, I could if needed. Now that he was home all the time, John usually butchered the animals, and I skinned them and prepared them for the freezer or table. We rented a meat locker in town, and through the summer stocked up sufficient meat for the following year.

We had running water now, and I had help to dig in the fertilizer provided by our animals. Our garden flourished. I experimented for the first time with a drip system for the root vegetables and lettuce, and planted some new varieties — loofa sponges and yard-long beans. I bought several dozen pint and quart jars, and canned beans, carrots, corn, and tomatoes. John built a set of shelves in one of our sheds and I filled them with our colorful bounty.

John had consulted for the Monterey Institute for Research in Astronomy (MIRA) before he left for Los Angeles, hoping to build a relationship with the astronomers that would lead to a future partnership. With the proceeds from that job, he had purchased enough lumber to build the frame of a small geodesic dome. The wood was still piled up at the building site.

He began to work on the dome on weekends, when I could help fetch and carry and hold things as he drilled holes and screwed in the bolts at each hub. The sound of the power saw and his mallet against the wood and the metal bolts was music to my ears. Perhaps we would have a completed frame by the end of the year. This tiny structure was not our long-dreamed-about home, but would serve as a study, and possibly a swing space where we could live while we moved the 40-foot trailer off the land to begin the construction of the actual house. All this was dreaming, of course. We still didn't have a building permit.

That fall, we enrolled Doña in public school. To my dismay, although she had loved Mrs. Johnson's Montessori school, she hated the new school. She suddenly found herself sitting in a circle with 30 other wiggly children in an acoustically bright portable building, being instructed on the date, the time, and the classroom rules. She said she was "bored" (a word that hadn't previously been in her vocabulary) during the 15-minute circle time as well as during the Language Arts lessons, during which she was not allowed to read, but had to participate even though she already knew all her sounds and letters. I liked her teacher, and recognized that her open classroom environment and short, focused lessons created a good learning experience for most children. But Doña was sensitive and shy and liked to watch for a while before joining any activity. The teacher and parent assistants encouraged her to participate, but she didn't often do so.

Doña also disliked the bus ride that took her to this alien place every morning. She said it was loud and the children didn't obey the driver; she was afraid of getting hurt, or of the driver losing control of the bus. She began wetting her bed at night again, refusing to eat breakfast, refusing to get dressed. She would cry all the way to the bus stop, and cling to me when the driver arrived. In desperation, one day I took her to the bus in her nightgown. I regretted it immediately and took her home for the rest of the day.

I began volunteering in the classroom once a week, and became sympathetic to Doña's situation. This classroom reminded me of the sixth grade in which I had done my student teaching. Mrs. Craig did not attempt to control the noise level in the room, which she believed reflected the children's natural exuberance and love for learning. Group sizes for free choice activities were small, which was helpful, but looking at it through the eyes of a 6-year-old Montessori-trained child, I could see how the lack of structure and procedure in the classroom upset her. She didn't know where to put books or other materials after she was finished with them, and explained that children just left everything lying around until Clean Up Time, which was heralded by a song. During the song, the children tossed cars, blocks, dolls, etc., into bins and boxes, and she couldn't figure out what went where.

I had been following the work of educator John Holt for many years. His 1960s landmark books, *How Children Learn* and *How Children Fail* had shaped my understanding of the mismatch between some children and traditional American public school — something that had occurred during my husband's schooling, causing him to leave high school without graduating. Holt based his explanation for the failure of many children in kindergarten and first grade on three factors: fear, boredom, and confusion. Also, for fear of disappointing what Holt calls, "anxious adults," children worried about falling below adults' high expectations.

I saw these three elements at play within Doña, and it worried me. She had always loved to "play school" and had looked forward to going to the "Big Girl" kindergarten after completing the preschool and kindergarten curriculum at the Montessori school. I didn't want her to hate it.

John Holt had begun publishing a newsletter in 1977, titled *Growing Without Schooling* (GWS). GWS was the first magazine published about homeschooling, unschooling, and how learning works outside of school. I subscribed to it at the outset, and within its pages I found support for pulling Doña out of kindergarten.

One of the most powerful passages I remembered from Holt's writing came from the first issue of GWS: "In all the schools I have taught in, visited, or know anything about, the social life of the children is mean spirited, competitive, exclusive, status seeking, full of talk about who went to whose birthday party and who got what Christmas presents and who got how many Valentine cards and who is talking to so and so and who is not. Even in the first grade, classes soon divide up into leaders, energetic, and (often deservedly) popular kids, their bands of followers, and other outsiders who are pointedly excluded from those groups."[2]

---

[2] Holt, J., *Growing Without Schooling*, August 1977, page 3

That had certainly been my experience in school, and I didn't particularly want Doña, until then a kind and thoughtful child, to face that kind of dynamic until she was older and surer of herself. Kindergarten was not mandatory in our state, so no one would come after us for taking her out of school. And as soon as I did so, two friends asked if I would help them set up an informal educational experience for their own children. Thus began Country Living Day School. I had become pretty good at filing Fictitious Business Name Forms, so I did so again, and I registered with the State School Superintendent's office as a private school.

Our new "school" consisted of a series of visits to our farm to collect and count eggs, measure out feed and feed the animals, plant vegetables, and other life-based educational experiences. Each parent was responsible for setting up an additional activity a week, which could take place anywhere and teach anything. Glen and John's friend Liza Loop, founder of the online education Loop Center (Learning Options*Open Portal — LO*OP) had donated her family's Welsh pony to our farm, so pony rides, pony care, and Logo programming (her suggestion) also became part of the curriculum. After a flurry of activity that carried us through the winter, we relaxed into meeting just once a week together, and mostly planning activities for our children in our own homes. Doña read the entire Laura Ingalls Wilder series of books that semester, and together we got a United States map and plotted the Wilder family's ramblings on it. Privately, I decided that we would simply have to take a trip one day to follow the route and learn more about the Wilder family.

In order to keep Doña at home, I needed to limit some of my writing and speaking efforts, but I did continue to write the weekly column for the *San Jose Mercury News* and bimonthly features for *Mothering* magazine. I taught my classes at Gavilan College and for the YMCA and Adult Education, and put a little money in my personal bank account each time I received a paycheck. Although John and I had settled into a comfortable routine, we had not resolved the big issue of money and how — if ever — we would build an actual house. I wanted to make our life and our marriage work, but I was also keeping my options open.

30

THE BIRTH OF CHESBRO PRESS

1980

B ILL SHURTLEFF, AUTHOR *of Book of Tofu, Book of Miso* and *Book of Tempeh*, had agreed to write for my newsletter, as had Carol Flinders, co-author of *Laurel's Kitchen* and *Laurel's Kitchen Breadbook*. Getting to know each of them — rock stars in their niches — was eye-opening. I learned that both lived very simple lives, on very little money. In June, I visited Carol at the Blue Mountain Center for Meditation.

She was very supportive of my writing, teaching, and raising my children at home and urged me to keep trying to make it work. "So many women give up their dreams for their families, and spend the rest of their lives regretting it," she warned me. "Don't do it."

Several other writers agreed to provide articles, and two local writers wrote original material for a gardening column and book reviews. I typed the address labels and newsletter copy on Cottage Computing's PET computer, which meant a visit to my friends in

Oakland every two months. The glorious thing about this was that once I entered the address information into the computer memory, I could print labels as often as I wanted without having to retype the information. It was the same with the newsletter copy. I could go back and make modifications without having to retype a whole page. It seemed like magic.

A typesetter in Palo Alto produced the galleys from the digital files and sent them to Sue. She pasted the illustrations onto the galleys and had the newsletters printed near her home. She and her children folded the finished product and stuck labels and stamps on them. We published six issues in 1979 and planned to publish the same number in 1980. Our success at this venture — which had 100 paid subscribers — and talking to Carol and Bill, had given me the confidence to contact Lendon Smith, the author of *Feed Your Kids Right*. Another celebrity author, Smith was a highly sought-after speaker who promoted healthy diets for children free from sugar, fat, salt, and artificial coloring. I asked him if he would read *Organic Cooking for (not-so-organic) Mothers* and consider writing a foreword. He agreed and I sent him a typewritten copy at once.

I started 1980 by writing a rather nervy letter to Elisabeth Alston at *Redbook* magazine regarding a Yorkshire Parkin recipe that had been plagiarized from the *The Book of Whole Grains*. I told her that ironically, I enjoyed seeing it in the magazine because I'd been unsuccessful so far in all my queries to *Redbook*. She responded with an apology. The author of the article couldn't remember where she had found the recipe. Elizabeth had done her own research and admitted that she had not been able to find the recipe anywhere else but in my book. She didn't pick up on my comment or offer me a commission, however.

I had more success with *New Mexico Magazine*, which accepted my query regarding writing a biographical piece about Clyde Tombaugh, John's mentor at New Mexico State, and the man who located the "planet" Pluto after hundreds of hours looking for it with a blink photometer. Rodale Press agreed to read sample chapters from my proposed book about home schooling, so I prepared a proposal for that. They also paid me to review several books.

John completed the prototype for his briefcase computer, using the smallest television he could find for a screen, and a keyboard salvaged from a damaged Pet computer. He began negotiating with an attorney and funders for a first run of 250 units. He sent out several proposals, and was hopeful that he would obtain some contract work very soon. Otherwise he wasn't working. During one of our arguments during that period I asked a scathing question that has come back to haunt me: "Why in the world would anyone want to take a computer home?"

In February, Peggy McMahon asked me to be a Contributing Editor to her new enterprise: *Mothering* magazine. She and her husband John had been running it and, when they purchased it, they put Peggy in charge of editorial. The position would involve writing a regular feature, *Home Cookin,'* being on the Board of Advisors, and getting a free display ad for my books in each issue. I liked the idea very much. I also agreed to review a few books each month. Fifty dollars and five copies of the magazine per article was not much remuneration, but I felt the exposure would be good.

About this time, I heard back from Edwina Froelich. La Leche League had decided they could not afford to publish my book. Instead, they would update *Mothers in the Kitchen* for the Anniversary. I had known all along that this was a possibility, but just the same, her announcement hurt. Crestfallen, I began searching for print shops that could produce the book, and asked them to submit bids. They ranged from $2000 to $3000 to produce a batch of 500 spiral-bound volumes from typewritten copy. Those were impossible amounts of money. I couldn't possibly produce my own book if it cost that much.

Then I received a telephone call. My new marketing consultant said she had lined up three new speaking engagements in May. I decided to postpone the book project for a while. John offered to ask around at the next meeting of the Homebrew Computer Club and, at the upcoming West Coast Computer Faire, to see if new technologies could make the publication process less expensive. I thanked him, but didn't expect anything to come of it.

On one of my weekend getaways to Sue's house in Ramona, a little hot tub therapy produced an idea. What if we did all the paste-up ourselves, then after the pages were printed, we collated them ourselves? How much could we save? We started to do some research. Meanwhile, John had learned something very important that saved us thousands of dollars over the next few years.

In the intervening months since I had sent the prototype to Edwina, a new technology *had* emerged — a photo typesetting machine. It could interface with the PET computer to produce traditionally typeset print. John had found a typesetter in Palo Alto who had purchased one, and we decided to take advantage of it. Over the next few months, the children and I traveled to Oakland almost every weekend so I could use our friends' PET computer to transcribe the typed manuscript Sue had produced into WordStar and save it on magnetic disk. It could be read and output in TrueType, ready for paste-up, for a mere $500. I filed a new Fictitious Business Name application, this time for Chesbro Press.

In March, we learned that John's requests for funding his briefcase computer had been rejected. His response was to fall into despair once again, walking for hours on the land, lying in the hammock and reading science fiction, sometimes sleeping all day. My response was to print a stack of resumes and send them out to local public schools. If I could land a full-time teaching position, I could pay all our bills and put us into the black and John could take care of the children. But 1980 was not the year to find a teaching position in Santa Clara County. Due to statewide budget cuts, teachers were being laid off and were using their seniority to bump younger teachers. There were literally no openings. I did obtain a part-time position as a reader in the English department, and home support teacher for the Morgan Hill School District — positions I held for many years, and enjoyed, although they never resulted in more than about 10 hours a month of paid work.

It had worked for me before, so I cobbled together several part-time income streams instead. Apple computers were starting to appear in schools and homes, and parents were floundering as they tried to use this new technology. John and I had attended the West Coast Computer Faire in 1978 and 1979, and I had attended workshops there that taught me to write simple BASIC programs for the new Apple II. I set up a computer workshop for parents and their children at the Learning Lab, a special educational resource center run by a colleague, where families could pay a flat rate to learn how to program and I would help them troubleshoot problems. I taught a natural foods cooking class in Belmont, hosted by my mother's church. I had developed a survey for parents of preschool-aged children for my master's project. I spent some time connecting with newcomer's groups and preschools themselves getting the survey into parents' hands. Perhaps some of those connections would turn into job opportunities.

For some time, I had been receiving requests from different parts of the country to speak at preschools and health food stores, and had been keeping those requests in a file. One day it occurred to me: Why not go on the road with the new book and sell it as I traveled? Carla Emory, the author of *Old- Fashioned Cook Book*, had done just that with her 700-page tome. I remembered reading about her. I rifled through all my copies of *Mother Earth News* until I found the article. Carla had published her book in serial form, taking out ads in the back of *Organic Gardening* magazine and offering the book as it came out, one chapter at a time, for $3.50. She mimeographed the book and, at first, she mailed out the chapters. The costs of mailing and advertising quickly ate into her profits and she came up with the idea of going to craft fairs. She loaded her children into the car, filled the trunk full of books and went from one craft fair to another for a whole summer, selling books and visiting major sights in the country at the same time. It sounded lucrative, and it sounded like fun. I sent off a letter to my store helper Laurie, in Alaska, asking if she would like to travel around the country with the children and me.

June, July, and August were super-busy. Once again, I taught cooking classes in San Jose for the YMCA, and wrote several query letters — this time mostly for book ideas rather than magazine articles. I had realized that my rate of return for articles was low, but had high hopes for a couple of book ideas that Rodale and alternative presses had seemed interested in: one about the rise in homeschooling, and the other about working from home using a portable computer. An agent I met through California Press Women was lining up speaking engagements for me in the fall. I still made weekend trips to Oakland to transcribe *Organic Cooking* onto magnetic disk.

In late August, I finally finished that task. With my latest YMCA paycheck, I took the disks to Abracadabra Typesetting in Palo Alto, where they transformed the digital files into type on an Itek Quadritek machine, programmed in FORTH, the language John had helped to standardize. While I waited for the work to be done, I prepared course outlines for my upcoming fall semester classes, paid the mortgage and telephone bill, bought a little more feed for the animals, and took care of a couple of fence repairs. My summer classes had ended, and I wanted to get down to Sue's and finish the book before starting the new semester.

I went over all the animal chores with John, and he assured me he could handle them. He expected to hear about two projects that week and receive good faith money when he signed the contracts. I hoped that was true, because our checking account was nearly bottomed out. I reminded him that Seventeen needed to go back to the vet to have the bandage on her infected hoof changed, and I left the Jeep behind for that errand. Dorrie had offered to help; he had only to call.

I loaded John and Doña into the VW bus and drove to Ramona. We were in high spirits, singing "On the Road Again" along with Willie Nelson as I drove down Hawkins Lane. As soon as we arrived, Sue and I began pasting the illustrations provided by Maryanna Kingman and Jean McManis into the galley proofs from the typesetters. After two weeks of long days and breaking backs, we took them to A-D Graphics in Poway to print 500 copies of the book. I decided then that we deserved a vacation. We all went to the San Diego Wild Animal Park together, stayed late one night and attended a concert by the Limelighters.

I wanted to stay in Ramona until the pages were ready to collate on Sue's table. Since that would make us miss the first day of school, Sue and I set up a little "home school" for Doña and Sue's son Chris in one of her bedrooms. I wasn't even sure I was going to take Doña to first grade when we returned; she seemed quite happy learning on her own. When they were ready, we picked up the boxes of printed pages and began the tedious process of building books. We took all of Sue's long dining room table — and most of the hallway floor — to lay out the pages. We pushed through to completion as fast as we could, but it took several weeks.

31

WELCOME HOME

I DROVE STRAIGHT HOME FROM RAMONA on a hot September day and pulled in beside the trailer, grateful to be home at last. Sue's boys had been boisterous and loud and I was looking forward to some peace and quiet. John wasn't there. Opening the trailer door, I nearly passed out. The trailer smelled like a kennel. My houseplants were dead, and the red plaid carpet was several-layers thick with the outside dirt that had been brought in. The refrigerator was bare. As I stood in shock, John sauntered down from the hill above, apologized for "the mess," explained that he'd run out of animal food, and climbed into his car. He was meeting an old Air Force buddy at the Air Races in Reno, he said as he waved to the children. He'd be back in a few days. I hadn't said a word — I hadn't been able to speak.

I got the children out of the car and fed them, then began to take stock of our little farm. The chickens and ducks had been let loose to forage; from the look of the place, they'd been out for some time. The doughboy pool I had bought for the children earlier in the summer reeked with the feces of the ducks that had been swimming in it, and the chickens had gotten into my garden and eaten many of the plants. By the time the children finished eating, they had been bitten several times by the fleas that now infested the couch, the carpet and, I later discovered, all of our beds. Clearly John had let the dog sleep in the trailer wherever she wanted. A quick call to our bank told me our account was overdrawn. In a fog, I walked up to the goat pen.

The gate was wide open, and the hay, which I had stacked outside the pen before leaving, was no longer in bales. It looked like a nursery rhyme haystack — only not so neat. Wattles was grazing nearby, her udder distended. I took pity on her and milked her where she stood. Her milk was stringy and lumpy. I hoped desperately that she had not developed mastitis.

I didn't see Seventeen anywhere, but the dome skin had been finished, and the shingles were in place. It looked to me like they'd been put on by professionals. That must have cost a lot. I wondered where John got the money. I'd ordered the glaziers to put windows in the dome earlier in the month, and it was good to see that work had been done, but the builder's rubble, including hundreds of glass shards, was still there, inside and outside the dome, waiting for someone to clean it up.

The phone was ringing as I walked back down the hill. It was my parents. They had been in Monterey for the day and called to see if I had come back from southern California. I told them what had happened, tears streaming down my cheeks, and they agreed to come up and help. They hadn't been to Morgan Hill since Mom's incident with the girl and the knife, but they said they'd pick up groceries and be there in an hour. Doña called to me as I hung up the phone. Looking through the window above my desk, she had spotted something at the bottom of the hill. She thought it was Seventeen.

I ran down the hill to the goat, who was lying against a tree in the shade, breathing hard. She smelled ripe, and I saw that her bandages were soaked yellow and green and were grimy and torn. Clearly, John had not taken her back to the vet. This of all things brought me to my knees. The John I knew would save a baby bird that dropped from its nest; he would carry an orphaned fawn for miles to his mother's home;

he would stop on the road in the middle of the night to rescue a dozen possum babies — *that* John would never leave a goat to die alone. Who *was* this man? What had happened to him? Looking back over the years, it is pretty clear to me now that he was suffering from depression. But at the time I was clueless. We both were.

I couldn't move Seventeen by myself, but I brought down some water for her. She licked it disinterestedly, then looked at me for a long time with her big brown eyes. I felt awful for leaving her, and for not asking Dorrie to help John take her to the vet.

Mom and Dad were great. Convinced that this was the last straw for me, they brought groceries, helped me move Seventeen, and then bury her when she died a few hours later. They caught all the chickens and ducks and put them back in their pens. Dad took me to the feed store to buy supplies. Meanwhile Mom cleaned the trailer, cooked dinner, and put Doña and John to bed. Not one word of disapproval from either of them. They had already said everything about John they needed to say. His actions justified their scorn.

The fury I felt that day, building as I watched Seventeen die from simple neglect, carried me through the next difficult weeks. I filled out so many job application forms on Monday and Tuesday, my eyes began to hurt. Dragging the children along with me, I applied for teaching jobs in high school and elementary school at each school district within 20 miles north and south, put my name on the substitute teaching list in Morgan Hill, and, holding back tears, drove to the county welfare office to apply for food stamps and medical assistance. I felt demoralized and ashamed. I justified my actions by telling myself the children would have to go to school so I could work, and they would need physical exams.

Back on the land, I sent the children out to locate eggs. The chickens had been loose for some time and had been laying wherever they felt like it. I milked Wattles several times a day, and soon her lovely white milk returned. No mastitis. I felt immensely relieved. After the children were in bed, I attacked the two boxes of mail that had arrived in my absence. I realized as I did so that I had stopped thinking of John as my husband. He was still the father of my children, however, and I wracked my brain to think of how I could be supportive of their relationship without continuing the destructive path he and I were on.

Tuesday night, which seemed like a month after I had driven home Sunday, would be the first meeting of my Fall Child Health and Nutrition class at Gavilan College. I loved being a college instructor, and I didn't want to blow it. Betty came over to stay with Doña and John.

My class was well-attended. I hadn't adequately prepared to lecture on the topic, but somehow I got through the night. We had been assigned a huge lecture hall for my class of 25, complete with stage and grand piano. I called the office, which began a comedy of errors that had us trekking from one side of the college to the other in search of a room, which, like Goldilocks and the three bears' furniture, was "just right." Fortunately, it took so long to process Late Admits and find an appropriate vacant room, that our discussion of the course outline and class expectations used up the remaining time. I would have another week to get my act together.

While I struggled with my first class session, John returned from Reno, packed his suitcase, and left for Los Angeles. He left me with no money, no childcare, and a farm that looked like the Beverly Hillbillies had come to stay. Thirty-some chickens and ten ducks, three goats, five cats, and several dogs had all roamed loose on the land during my absence, and there was debris all over our land. Droppings everywhere; plants chewed to the ground, mulch and compost scratched through and spread around; alfalfa hay scattered to the winds.

Was John gone for good? I had no idea.

Wednesday, I received notification from *Who's Who of American Women* that they wanted to include me in the 1981 edition. Thursday, *Contemporary Authors* announced that they wanted me in their book. Thursday night my new Writing for Publication class met, and I had thirteen registrants, compared to the usual 5 or 6. "Thirty-five dollars times thirteen," I found myself thinking during class. Friday, I received a call from the television station I was scheduled to appear on the next week for final details of the program.

By the end of the week, my ego had begun to heal. I began to rehearse what I would say to John when he returned. I would tell him

I understood he was still grieving. That we needed to go to counseling. I knew a program in town that would help us. They charged a sliding scale. If John wasn't willing to go with me, I would take the children and strike out on my own.

John returned late Saturday night. On Sunday, before I had a chance to deliver my speech, we lost another goat.

*   *   *

Snowball had been born the previous May during a full moon on a cloudless night. I had prepared the birthing pen with a layer of fresh straw and, when it became obvious that Seventeen had gone into labor, I bundled Doña, Little John, and myself into warm jackets and sleeping bags and prepared to spend the night bedded down with her.

Seventeen rested for a while, then milled around the pen, mooing softly to herself. After several hours, she lay down in the rain shelter and delivered two babies, one after another, into the waiting arms of my children. They were so amazed by the miracle taking place in front of them that they completely ignored the yucky parts of the birth. Seventeen washed her babies awake, then nuzzled them to her distended udder. While we watched them butting her and one another in their attempt to get milk from their mother's long teats, the children named the babies — one each: Doña pointed out that there really was no better name for the fuzzy white baby but Snowball; John named his litter-mate Lucy, after a favorite teacher at nursery school.

Snowball and Lucy grew rapidly. When she had driven up to see them, Dorrie reminded me to take them away from their mother after three days, but they continued to thrive on her milk, which we fed them from bottles. Doña fed the kids before breakfast, holding both bottles at the same time. It was great. For that short time in her life, I didn't have any trouble getting Doña up and dressed in the morning. It thrilled her to have the babies come to her and lick her hands. They would climb into her lap and butt the bottles until she could get the nipples into their mouths. At first John wanted to help, but he lost interest after the kids became bigger and more active. Soon they were almost as big as he was and could easily knock him over. We fed the babies around the clock for several weeks until they were able to eat grain and hay on their own.

I sold Lucy to some friends as a milker. I couldn't use any more milk than Seventeen and her mother Wattles provided, even making butter and cheese every few weeks, and using milk in practically everything I baked. When Snowball was seven weeks old, we paid a local rancher to castrate him. Gully, as the rancher was called, made the circuit of small farms to help them with horseshoeing, castrating, and slaughtering. Snowball was destined to be our winter meat, along with a dozen rabbits and chickens that would die as they were needed, and we would ask Gully back in the fall to help us with that task.

During the summer, Snowball grazed happily in a small fenced field beside my vegetable garden, and followed the children around like a pet dog when they came home from school and preschool. Doña liked to dress him up, and I never knew what to expect when it was feeding time. Sometimes Snowball was wearing a ski hat; sometimes a dress with an apron tied behind his back.

✳   ✳   ✳

While John was in Los Angeles, I had received a "Welcome to Mothering" check from Peggy McMahon at *Mothering* magazine and used it to bolster our checking account. The day after he returned home, I went into town to buy supplies. While I was gone, John decided Snowball would make a good weed-eater. During the spring and summer, the weeds had grown everywhere we didn't drive or walk, and now they were turning brown. I worried about fire and hidden rattlesnakes, and we'd talked about using our goats to get the hillside behind our trailer under control. Unfortunately, instead of tethering Snowball by an ankle, or enclosing him with temporary fencing, John had slipped a dog choke chain around his neck, then fastened the tether to that and to a stake in the ground. Munching happily on the hill slippery with dry grass, Snowball lost his footing, perhaps tripped on the chain, and fell.

I knew when I drove around the last curve to the trailer that something was wrong. John was standing beside the road, his watch cap pulled low over his forehead, his hands in his coat pockets. He looked like a ten-year-old boy who'd just broken a window. Snowball was lying on a blue tarp beside the trailer. Feeling a wave of nausea and a sense of *déjà vu*, I told the children to stay where they were and jumped out of the Jeep to see what was going on. Just like Dreyfus, Snowball didn't appear to be dead at first. His fur was soft to the touch, and his body wasn't stiff.

I waited to feel sad, but all I could feel was anger. As John stammered an explanation and an apology, I stood over Snowball, my fists clenched. How could he have been so stupid? Angry words formed in my throat, but, as usual, I stopped them.

Looking back, I realize this was the beginning of the end. It was the proverbial "last straw." I don't think I realized it yet, and I did know this wasn't the time to think about either blame or regret. We had a problem to solve. I covered Snowball's body with another tarp and told John to go to town in my Jeep and buy some ice, then cover him with it until I fed the children and got them to bed. They had lots of questions and, as usual, Doña wanted to see the dead body. We made one pilgrimage to say goodbye to Snowball and then we went inside and cried.

Once the children were asleep, I turned to our homestead library. A recent issue of *Country Women* described slaughtering and butchering goats, and I refreshed my memory with that. The night we skinned and butchered Dreyfus was still etched in my memory, but the details were fuzzy. Snowball was much smaller than Dreyfus had been. By the time I emerged from the trailer, John had rigged up a hook on the sturdy frame he had built at our garden's entrance, and he had tied Snowball's feet to a 2 x 4, and then hung the carcass from the hook. He'd already cut off the goat's head and bled him, but that was all he could manage. He took the head off to bury in the valley behind our trailer, and didn't come home until after dark.

I skinned and dressed the carcass, using a flashlight and the magazine article set on a TV tray next to me. I had wanted to become self-sufficient, but this was ridiculous. It was nearly midnight before I finished that part. The next day, John took the children down to play with friends in town. They played in the pool most of the day and enjoyed watching the boys' dad barbecue steaks for dinner. Then all four of the children fell asleep on the floor in front of the TV watching a movie. John spent the night on their couch.

While they were gone, I cut the carcass into pieces, sometimes random pieces, but something we could cook. I wrapped them in Doña's art paper, taped them closed with masking tape, and put them in our three ice chests, covered with the rest of the ice John had bought. Friends from San Martin came up that afternoon to help butcher rabbits in exchange for some of the meat. They offered to take what was left of Snowball to the locker in town. By the time they drove off, I'd seen all the fresh meat I wanted to for a while.

*   *   *

I had been homeschooling Doña for two years, since I'd taken her out of public-school kindergarten in Fall 1979. After returning from Ramona, I enrolled her at Machado School, a rural two-room schoolhouse not far from the bottom of our road. She liked that I could take her to school each morning, instead of her having to ride in a bus, and she enjoyed the country setting. She also liked her first-grade teacher, and so did I. Mrs. Balestrieri's first-second combination was a quiet, orderly classroom, which she controlled by whispering. After a week, she moved Doña to 2nd grade, and began sending her next door to 3rd grade for reading.

John began taking the bus to Paradise Valley School, where he entered the first kindergarten class at the new school. Doña's nemesis, Mrs. Craig, was his teacher. He loved kindergarten, he loved the lively school bus, and he loved Mrs. Craig. Now John and I could both concentrate on earning money and healing our marriage.

I had lots to look forward to. I'd been asked to teach Children's Literature at Gavilan College again in the spring. Author John Holt was scheduled to speak at several venues in April, and the staff of *Growing Without Schooling* had asked me to meet him at the airport and arrange housing during his stay. My mom and dad had agreed to host him in their home, and *Mothering* magazine had commissioned an interview. I would schedule that on one of the afternoons before a lecture. Each morning when I dropped the children at school, I came home to our land with a list of things to do, and every Thursday night through the winter John and I met with a therapist.

After Snowball, John had agreed to attend marriage counseling and to interview for jobs. He applied at three companies and was accepted for a management position in Sunnyvale. He lasted six weeks. He tried again with another company, and lasted three months. He couldn't handle the working hours, he explained — the structure, the deadlines. Most of the year he was unemployed, but he did pick up a few contracts and managed to make the land payments.

Dorrie and Quincy's second child, Jancilyn, was born that spring. While Dorrie was home on maternity leave, we met often for play dates, and cemented a friendship that would last until her death in 2014. We knew that our time on the land had been something special. The experience had changed us both in ways that we wouldn't understand for many years. It had also made us strong.

I went ahead with my plans to travel around the country the following summer to promote my books. While the children and I were away, I reasoned, John could immerse himself in the new technology and find a role to play in it. He needed success, and he needed solitude and time to deal with the loss of his father. I may have been ready to leave him and start fresh somewhere else, but I wasn't ready — yet — to take the children away from him.

With that in mind, I began to reflect on the time we had spent on the land. What had we accomplished? What had I learned? I knew that I loved the daily routine involved in raising animals. It was satisfying to produce our own eggs, milk and meat, and to harvest food from a garden that was fertilized by our own animals. The taste of fresh eggs and spinach and tomatoes for breakfast had forever spoiled me for supermarket produce. The purity and rich flavor of our farm-raised poultry and meat would lead me to seek out pasture-raised meat, free of hormones or antibiotics, for the rest of my life.

I had learned to live in community, to build things with others and to work together to accomplish tasks that would be impossible alone. I enjoyed sharing meals and music with my friends and being surrounded by people who loved the land as much as I did. But I could also stand on my own two feet. I could do difficult things. I had even learned to treasure time alone and the long winter nights no longer frightened me.

Our children had also thrived in the country. They loved the animals and our garden. They knew where our food came from — they helped themselves to fresh peas, tomatoes, mint, foraging their way through the garden to the hose when asked to water. They understood that water was precious, and how to conserve it. They completed their chores without complaining. Our simple life had shaped them into capable, contributing members of a community.

32

ON THE ROAD AGAIN

O N JUNE 16, 1981, THE CHILDREN AND I SET OUT on our Great Trek. I had leased a 1978 EZ Ryder motor home and purchased a utility trailer, which was filled with 1000 copies of *Organic Cooking with (not-so-organic) Mothers*. Using telephone directories, my Christmas card list, and a roster of La Leche League chapters around the country, Laurie had organized a detailed itinerary. She had made arrangements for me to speak to preschools, bookstores, natural food stores and Le Leche League groups in over 30 states. On weekends, we would visit friends, and I would meet my parents on Vancouver Island by Labor Day. I would call John every Sunday and report on our progress. Laurie was waiting for us in Los Angeles, so that's where we were headed first.

Sue and her husband had separated. She moved into our little blue trailer to take care of our animals — and hers, who she trucked up from Ramona — for the months I would be gone. My wonderful high school helpers had agreed to help fulfill book orders and answer correspondence.

I didn't know what would happen when we returned, but I was no longer afraid of the future. I had grown up during these years on the land, and so had the children. Doña was eight and a half now; Little John was five. We would be fine.

Sue and Big John stood by the dome, waving, as I slowly maneuvered the EZ Ryder down Hawkins Lane. Doña already had her nose buried in a book. Little John, riding shotgun, expertly pressed a cassette into the player and pressed PLAY. As we passed through the gate at the bottom of our land and turned onto Chesbro Lake Drive, you could hear us singing *On the Road Again* with Willie Nelson.

POSTLOGUE

"WAIT. YOU CAN'T STOP THERE, GRANDMA."
Stella and I were snuggling on the couch. I had just read the last chapter to her. It had been two years since she had spied my first pair of work gloves hanging above the bench.

"Why not?"

"Because I want to know what happens next, and what happens after that, and what happens when you come home, and what happens to all the people."

"What people?"

"Quincy and Dorrie, and Nina, and Bob and Jan. Those people."

I cast my mind back over the last forty years. How could I summarize so many lives?

"Well," I began slowly, "Quincy and Dorrie had Jacob and Jancilyn. They moved to a big house in Gilroy where they could keep animals and grow vegetables. Eventually they got divorced and Quincy married Melissa. I camp with them every year at the Strawberry Music Festival."

"How about Dorrie?"

"Dorrie married Patrick and they had two sons. When the children grew up, Dorrie and Patrick moved to the Weiss family farm in San Luis Obispo. Dorrie died there a few years ago. Her whole family was with her when she died, even Quincy."

We were quiet for a while, then I continued.

"When Bob and Jan came back from Alaska, they got married. Jan went back to ESL while Bob finished college and began to teach high school math and science. They had three children, Richard, Doug and Ellen. You know them. Jan stayed home when the children were little, then worked as a substitute teacher. Now Bob has retired, and he spends lots of time playing music and fly fishing.

"Nina taught literature and writing at San Francisco State, then moved to a tiny town in the mountains. She flies to Austria every few years to spend time with her nieces and nephews."

"What about John?"

"After I came back from my trip, John and I decided we couldn't be happy living together, so your mom and Uncle John and I moved to a house in town. Their dad stayed on the land. Many years later, you were born and he became your wonderful Baba."

"And then he died."

"Yes, he did. He died of cancer. But you remember him. And your Noni still owns the land. The dome is still there, too."

"Of course. But I think that's a very sad story."

"I like to remember the happy parts. There were lots of happy parts."

"Ok. I'll remember the happy parts too. The end. Now it's finished."

She sighed, and snuggled closer.

AFTERWORD

WHEN THE CHILDREN AND I RETURNED from our 7,500-mile adventure, John had removed his wedding ring and was ready to start life apart. Sue and I moved our animals and our children to a farm just north of Morgan Hill. Sue worked as a freelance technical writer in Silicon Valley while I wrote copy for some of her clients and homeschooled our children. I missed Bum Flats terribly, and I missed John. My sadness felt like an ache, deep in my heart, but I believed it was best for the children if they had more security in their lives. It didn't take long for Sue to realize she hated commuting and move to Sunnyvale. The kids and I were on our own.

There were no teaching jobs to be found that year — state funding for K-12 was down and teachers were receiving pink slips. I renewed my conract as a substitute teacher, but didn't earn enough to pay our rent. Sadly, I sold the animals and rented a condo in town. I finally found work writing technical manuals at IBM and for two years I commuted to San Jose and then to Sunnyvale. I met my second husband during this time. John and Doña were now joined by two-year-old Jamie and then by a baby sister, Deborah. Meanwhile I was awarded a master's in Early Childhood Education. In 1985 I was offered a coveted tenure-track position teaching child development at Gavilan College. After a challenging and satisfying career, I retired in 2011 to help Doña take care of her new baby, my first granddaughter, Stella.

After we left Bum Flats, John joined Jef Raskin, the father of the Macintosh computer, at his startup company, Information Appliance.

309

Jef went on to develop the Canon Cat computer and John became an Apple evangelist. He forged a career out of consulting and working for startups, living in the tiny dome. He never did get a building permit, although he held several patents. While he was being treated for cancer, which he lived with for many years, John came up with the idea of creating a timeline on Google Docs — "For the children," he said. He and I worked together on that timeline virtually during his chemo infusions, and it became the outline for this book. He died in 2016. I never stopped loving him, and I miss him very much.

Rural life had taught me the importance of community, and my students, colleagues, friends and family now became mine. I had also learned that I needed to feel the rhythm of the earth. I grew vegetables and daffodils wherever we lived, and we cared for a wide variety of animals: hamsters, guinea pigs, dogs, cats, pet rats, lab rats, a lop-eared rabbit and an iguana named Rico Suave. I still raise vegetables, and buy most of my food from a farmer's market. I eat with the seasons. My eggs come from Doña, who raises chickens in her back yard. Each year when my daffodils begin to bloom, I think of the ones we planted along the path in 1975.

I can be found online at *marlenebumgarner.com.* I hope you will drop by and chat.

Marlene

ABOUT THE AUTHOR

After teaching at Gavilan Community College in Gilroy for 30 years, Marlene Anne Bumgarner moved to the California coast when her first grandchild was born. There she volunteers in the Young Writers program in local schools, leads writing workshops, and enjoys walking along the coast with her border collie, Kismet. The author of *The Book of Whole Grains, Organic Cooking for (not-so-organic) Mothers,* and *Working with School Age Children,* she is now writing a historical novel set in 19th century industrial England. Find out more about Marlene's family life, cooking, and gardening at *marlenebumgarner.com.*

Made in the USA
Columbia, SC
09 November 2020